WHO IS THE CITY FOR?

WHO IS THE CITY FOR?

ARCHITECTURE, EQUITY,
AND THE PUBLIC REALM
IN CHICAGO

BLAIR KAMIN

WITH PHOTOGRAPHS BY
Lee Bey

The University of Chicago Press
Chicago and London

The University of Chicago Press, Chicago 60637
The University of Chicago Press, Ltd., London
© 2022 by The University of Chicago
Photographs © 2022 by Lee Bey unless otherwise specified

Published 2022
Printed in the United States of America

31 30 29 28 27 26 25 24 23 22   1 2 3 4 5

ISBN-13: 978-0-226-82273-0 (cloth)
ISBN-13: 978-0-226-82287-7 (e-book)
DOI: https://doi.org/10.7208/chicago/9780226822877.001.0001

This publication is made possible through support from the
Richard H. Driehaus Foundation and the Graham Foundation
for Advanced Studies in the Fine Arts.

Library of Congress Cataloging-in-Publication Data

Names: Kamin, Blair, author. | Bey, Lee, 1965– photographer.
Title: Who is the city for? : architecture, equity, and the public
realm in Chicago / Blair Kamin ; with photographs by Lee Bey.
Description: Chicago : University of Chicago Press, 2022. |
Includes index.
Identifiers: LCCN 2022014543 | ISBN 9780226822730 (cloth) |
ISBN 9780226822877 (ebook)
Subjects: LCSH: Architecture—Illinois—Chicago. | City
planning—Illinois—Chicago. | City planning—Social
aspects—Illinois—Chicago. | Chicago (Ill.)—Buildings,
structures, etc.
Classification: LCC NA735.C4 K357 2022 | DDC 720.9773/11—dc23/
eng/20220509
LC record available at https://lccn.loc.gov/2022014543

♾ This paper meets the requirements of ANSI/NISO Z39.48-1992
(Permanence of Paper).

To Barbara, Will, and Teddy,
and in memory of my parents

CONTENTS

Part Two
Urban Design: Boom Times for Cities, but Who Benefits?

Part Three
Architecture: Are Buildings
Good Citizens? 97

INTRODUCTION

Looking back on nearly thirty years of architecture criticism at the *Chicago Tribune*, I realize that I have borne witness to a dramatic transformation of Chicago, from a declining industrial colossus to a dynamic yet deeply troubled postindustrial powerhouse, whose favored emblem is a jellybean-shaped sculpture of highly polished steel. The mirrorlike surface of that sculpture, officially titled *Cloud Gate* but widely known as "the Bean," reflects the striking skyline of the city's ever-growing downtown, now home to $10 million condominiums, Michelin-starred restaurants, and an elegant promenade that rims the once badly polluted Chicago River. But the Bean does not reflect the reality of a very different Chicago. That Chicago, though not without distinguished buildings and untapped economic potential, is also a place of weed-strewn vacant lots, empty storefronts, and unceasing gun violence. Indeed, *Cloud Gate* may be the ultimate shiny, distracting object. While the 2020 census revealed that Chicago's population grew by nearly 2 percent during the previous decade, to 2.7 million, the dramatic disconnect between the two Chicagos prompts the question: Is this a good city, a just city? Absolutely not. Which prompts a second query: Can those responsible for building the city advance the fortunes of neighborhoods devastated by decades of discrimination, disinvestment, and deindustrialization? On that crucial matter, the jury is still out.

Cloud Gate sculpture in Millennium Park: Is the new icon of Chicago also the ultimate shiny, distracting object? Photo by Lee Bey.

This book, my third collection of *Tribune* columns published by the University of Chicago Press, is loosely framed around a central issue of our time: equity. What can architecture, traditionally the province of the rich and powerful, do to make cities like Chicago more equitable, serving poor, working-, and middle-class people, not just the 1 percent? A related question can be asked of the fields of transportation and urban planning, which in the wrong hands have led to such notorious projects as freeways that divide Black neighborhoods from white ones or sever one part of an impoverished neighborhood from another. The question applies, too, to the field of historic preservation. Whose history gets remembered and whose history is erased, either by bulldozers or by willful ignorance?

In short, who is the city for?

Let me start by clarifying that I take *equity* to mean fairness or justice in the way people are treated rather than the term's economic meanings—a share of stock or the value of a piece of property after debts are subtracted. This emphasis on fairness has significant implications for architecture and the built environment. One side of town shouldn't have bigger, more amenity-packed parks than the other just because it's inhabited by the wealthy. If anything, the poor parts of a city should have the prime parks, because their residents live in far worse conditions than the rich.

That was among the essential points of my 1998 series of articles examining the problems and promise of Chicago's greatest public space, its nearly thirty miles of beaches, harbors, and parkland along Lake Michigan. The series, "Reinventing the Lakefront," documented a shameful disparity in acreage, access, and amenities between shoreline parks bordered by mostly white, affluent neighborhoods on the city's North Side and those lined by largely Black, poor neighborhoods on the South Side. Since then, city agencies and the Chicago Park District have spent hundreds of millions of dollars on the south lakefront, including architecturally ambitious pedestrian bridges and a harbor and marina that welcome parkgoers as well as boats. But any discussion of equity, I argue, should not be limited to apportioning resources fairly or controlling soaring rents.

A wiser alternative, in my view, is to expand and enrich the social meaning of "equity" by borrowing from its economic counterpart, so that, when we use the word, we're talking about the physical environ-ment that we *share*. Shared spaces encompass all aspects of the public realm, from sidewalks and streets to transit stations, to public librar-ies and public housing. Private buildings, be they skyscrapers, flagship stores, or museums, do just as much as, if not more than, public ones to shape the public realm. At best, the public realm can serve as an equalizing force, a democratizing force. It can spread life's pleasures and confer dignity, irrespective of a person's race, income, creed, or gender. Shared space suggests shared destiny. Or, to put matters in terms of hard-nosed self-interest rather than empathetic generosity, the recognition that cities are shared ventures—and that the fate of one section of the city is inseparable from another—represents a far more viable long-term strategy than its opposite: containment of the poor, whether in ghettos, public-housing projects, or dysfunctional neighborhoods.

The shootings and thefts that have spread from Chicago's South and West Sides to the downtown and affluent North Side neighbor-hoods like Lincoln Park make clear the costs of failing to address the root causes of long-festering problems associated with high concen-trations of poverty. No neighborhood is an island, as the shattered glass of North Michigan Avenue storefronts hit by smash-and-grab thieves and the fatal May 2022 shooting of a teenager in Millennium Park near "the Bean" reveal.

To be sure, the notion that Americans can share *anything* may seem incredibly naive in light of the nation's deep political and cultural di-vides, or the way metropolitan areas like Chicago are fractured by chasms of race and class. Indeed, as the columns collected here re-veal, the on-the-ground reality in Chicago often falls painfully short of my ideal of urban equity. But the columns also show the power of architecture and urban design to aid the prospects of both communi-ties and individuals.

Revered as the birthplace of modern architecture and for its sin-gular role in the development of modern city planning, Chicago pres-ents a still-relevant stage for analyzing the human impact of the ur-ban drama. Its litany of influential projects spans centuries and has shaped design throughout the world, from the pathbreaking skyscrap-ers of the 1880s to the triumphant, albeit belated, 2004 opening of Mil-lennium Park. The city's architecture and urban-design pratfalls, like the demolished public-housing high-rises of the Robert Taylor Homes and Cabrini-Green, are as notorious as its exemplary buildings are glorious. As I wrote in my first collection, quoting the urban historian Perry Duis, Chicago is "the great American exaggeration," expressing at larger scale—and often in excruciating contrast—design trends evident in smaller cities. It gives us the best of the best and the worst of the worst of American urban life, a role it has reprised of late— heroically, with bold new skyscrapers like Jeanne Gang's St. Regis Chicago tower, the world's tallest building designed by a woman, and, tragically, with more than eight hundred homicides in 2021, its highest total in decades. By comparison, New York and Los Angeles, the nation's two largest cities, had a combined total of about 980 killings in the same year.

Like my first two collections—*Why Architecture Matters: Lessons from Chicago* (2001) and *Terror and Wonder: Architecture in a Tumultuous Age* (2010)—this one covers a roughly ten-year span. It, too, was tumultuous, though there was no repeat of the September 11, 2001, terrorist attacks, carried out by Islamic extremists, that made the World Trade Center's twin towers collapse in a heap of smoke and ash. In this case, the terrorism came from within—the January 6, 2021, assault on the temple of democracy, the US Capitol, by pro–Donald Trump insurrectionists trying to overturn Joe Biden's election. The nation was further jolted by a pandemic that lasted more than two years and disrupted nearly every aspect of life; the racial reckoning that followed the police murder of George Floyd; life- and property-destroying storms and other consequences of worsening climate change; and rising income inequality. All had an impact on architecture and urban design.

The columns collected here were originally published in the *Tribune* between 2011 and 2021, when I left the newspaper after twenty-eight years as its architecture critic. I have tweaked and sharpened the columns and, where relevant, added postscripts to bring the stories up to date. The powerful photography of *Chicago Sun-Times* editorial writer and architecture critic Lee Bey illustrates and illuminates the columns. (Images by other photographers also appear.) While Lee's new monthly column on architecture is an important addition to the civic conversation, it's telling that, as of this writing, neither the *Tribune* nor the *Sun-Times* has a full-time, on-staff architecture critic. As the book's epilogue makes clear, the digitalization of the media landscape and the weakening of once-mighty metropolitan newspapers like the *Tribune* have dealt a major blow to architecture criticism. That is the story behind the story.

The book's five parts are organized thematically, beginning with the era's two central political figures, Trump and Barack Obama—the former a hard-right, wildly impulsive Republican; the latter a left-leaning, coolly professorial Democrat. These diametrical opposites, it turned out, had something in common: a controversial Chicago design project. Obama's was his planned presidential center in historic Jackson Park; Trump's, the grotesquely gigantic sign that the future president (in 2014 still a developer and reality TV star) slapped on his mostly handsome riverfront skyscraper across from the downtown Riverwalk. The book's first part critiques those projects, exploring the conflict between the substantial egos of these two powerful men and their impact on the public realm. Echoing the overarching theme, I ask, in effect: Who is the riverfront for? Who is the park for? The first part also examines Trump's sycophantic, vitriolic relationship with architecture critics and his ill-considered, authoritarian plan to mandate that federal buildings be designed in classical and traditional styles.

In the second part, I investigate the question "Who is the city for?" in greater depth, beginning in the smog-filled air of China, where several Chicago architects exported their skyscraper expertise to survive the lean years of the Great Recession. Training a critical eye on Shanghai and other Chinese boomtowns, I ask whether cities in our rapidly urbanizing world are becoming livable as well as dense. Subsequent columns return to Chicago, exploring successful efforts to ensure that new transportation infrastructure is evenly distributed, so that people of all races and income levels can easily (and even pleasurably) get around the city. Echoing an essential theme of the 1998 lakefront series, I also examine whether all sides of Chicago have parks that provide a respite from the stresses of urban life.

That series grew from my philosophy of "activist criticism," which I defined this way in *Why Architecture Matters*: "Activist criticism is based on the idea that architecture affects everyone and therefore should be understandable to everyone. It . . . [places] buildings in the context of the politics, the economics, and the cultural forces that shape them. Activist criticism invites readers to be more than consumers who passively accept the buildings that are handed to them. It bids them, instead, to become citizens who take a leading role in shaping their surroundings."

I still believe that today, even if my thinking, like my hair, has more shades of gray. Citizen participation is no guarantee of design excellence, as the innovation-deadening influence of the not-in-my-backyard (NIMBY) movement has shown. In addition, as I learned from my repeated attempts to stop the Klingon-meets-Parthenon fiasco that is Chicago's renovated Soldier Field, critics can set the agenda of the public conversation, but they do not have the power to enact that agenda. Nor should they. The purpose of criticism is to open people's eyes to architecture and to raise their expectations for it, not to impose the critic's tastes and values on the cityscape. In that sense, every column, not just an impactful series of articles, is a work of activist criticism. By framing our understanding of a completed building, the critic can affect the contours of the next one.

In the book's third part, I highlight an essential tool of the critic's trade: the yardstick for measuring whether buildings are the architectural equivalent of good citizens. Does that eye-popping new skyscraper enliven the street as well as the skyline? What, if anything, do new or proposed flagship stores, museums, and public buildings contribute to the public realm? Yet today, good architectural citizenship is no longer confined to whether a building responds sensitively to its urban context. With global warming contributing to vast wildfires, intense hurricanes, and rising seas—and with buildings and their construction accounting for a significant share of annual energy-related carbon-dioxide emissions—good citizenship means addressing the global context of climate change as well as the local context of a building's environs. So it's important to take the measure of a building's ecological impact, as I do in my review of the new McDonald's flagship restaurant in Chicago. Broadening the critic's lens to assess architecture's social impact, the book's third part also explores innovative neighborhood housing that strives, with mixed success, to integrate poor and low-income residents into city life.

One of the decade's defining characteristics, such examples reveal, was the growing attention that architects and architecture critics alike paid to social and environmental matters that the field's tastemakers, with their relentless focus on aesthetics, once deemed marginal. The first Chicago Architecture Biennial, held in 2015, was a signal event, confirming a break from the visually hyperactive, digitally enabled "starchitecture" that dominated the field before the Great Recession. Though sprawling and sometimes unwieldy, the international exhibition nevertheless succeeded in showcasing the socially relevant buildings and visions of a new generation of architects. As the exhibition's introductory wall text at the Chicago Cultural Center aptly stated, in reference to such pressing issues as housing shortages, climate change, and ever-expanding income inequality, "None of these are spatial questions alone, but none can be effectively addressed without design." The new generation was asserting, in effect, that architects have a significant role to play on these fronts—that they have "agency," to use the fashionable term.

Which is not to say that architects, landscape architects, and urban planners were always on the side of the angels in these years. All too often, as seen in my assessments of new residential high-rises in Chicago, they were capitalists' tools, draping profitable square footage in ordinary dress. Or they did the progressive thing, and negative, unanticipated consequences followed. Chicago's 606 trail, the city's answer to New York's High Line, brought much-needed open space to the city's park-poor Northwest Side, but it also encouraged a wave of new luxury housing that displaced some of the very longtime residents the trail was meant to serve. Such outcomes demonstrated that, without careful planning, attempts to correct inequities in one aspect of city life could lead to inequities in another.

In the book's fourth part, I turn from the fraught urban present to the equally contested architectural past. Or should I say "pasts"? There's the recent past (buildings less than fifty or sixty years old) and the distant past (those that have reached a more venerable age). As the demolition of Bertrand Goldberg's Brutalist old Prentice Women's Hospital revealed, architecture critics face an uphill battle in making the case that recent buildings should be saved. Yet these years also featured sparkling rebirths of significant structures from the distant past, from Frank Lloyd Wright's Robie House to the once-threatened old Cook County Hospital. At the same time, reflecting shifting attitudes in the broader culture, a new emphasis was placed on safe-guarding Black and Latino historical sites such as the former home of Emmett Till. Yet, following the troubled pattern of the 606, the outcomes were anything but simple. Fearing additional displacement, residents in the Near Southwest Side neighborhood of Pilsen banded together to foil the city's seemingly benign attempt to create Chicago's first Latino landmark district.

The fifth and final part returns to the core issue "Who is the city for?" and the question, as the *Washington Post* recently put it, of whether revitalization is possible without gentrification. Resentment of aldermanic corruption and a widespread recognition that Chicago wasn't working for all its people led voters in 2019 to back a significant left turn: from the pragmatic centrism of Mayors Richard M. Daley and Rahm Emanuel to the progressivism of Lori Lightfoot, the city's second Black mayor and first openly gay mayor. Under Lightfoot's chief planner, Maurice Cox, the drive for equity became systematic rather than sporadic, as it had been under Daley and Emanuel. Cox instituted policies and plans that sought to bring new vitality to ten beleaguered South and West Side business districts. The cornerstone project, the $750 million Invest South/West initiative, wisely didn't try to turn the clock back to the massive urban-renewal programs of Lyndon Johnson's Great Society or the public works of Franklin D. Roosevelt's New Deal. Nor did it rely on the free-market-capitalism policies that had gained favor in the Reagan era. Rather, Invest South/West drew on the Chicago tradition of the public-private partnership, attracting about $1.4 billion in investment to some of the city's poorest neighborhoods. Whoever Chicago's next mayor is—the next election is in 2023—the effort deserves to be seen through to completion and, if it succeeds in sparking revitalization, dramatically expanded.

For all its long-term promise, however, Invest South/West confronts daunting short-term realities: heightened gun violence, carjackings, expressway shootings, and the two rounds of looting that followed Floyd's death. These troubles raise vexing questions: How much of a difference can architecture and urban design make in reviving a city's fortunes? Without urban order, is urban revival possible? Is it more important to rebuild the structures of broken families and communities than to focus on the structures worthy of an architecture critic's attention? In the end, both kinds of structures matter. But far too little attention is typically devoted to what architecture can do to build more livable, more equitable cities.

Which brings us to the future and what we might expect from the post-pandemic city. For the foreseeable future, we're likely to see a continuation of hybrid work arrangements, which means high office-vacancy rates that will slow the recovery of downtowns. But in the long run, who knows? Predictions invariably miss the mark; the pandemic's ever-shifting scourge has consistently defied the forecasts of experts. Ultimately, it's more important to explore possibilities than to venture predictions; the most pressing task is to respond to the dramatic inequalities that the pandemic has exposed and deepened, particularly the shortage of affordable housing and the need to improve transit and, with it, access to jobs. While the columns in this book assess myriad attempts to address that lack of equity, they are as concerned with processes as they are with outcomes. To achieve equity, architects and urban planners need to design with their ears as well as their eyes, even if that slows the path to winning approval from public bodies and breaking ground. As Jane Jacobs wrote in *The Death and Life of Great American Cities*, "Cities have the capability of providing something for everybody, only because, and only when, they are created by everybody."

Who is the city for? Ideally, for everyone, as Jacobs asserts, even if the realities of our polarized present insistently suggest otherwise. Architects and the architects of public policy need to broaden the spectrum of people who can afford to partake of urban life. They should seek not only to express social diversity; they should find new ways to encourage the diversity of uses that Jacobs so persuasively championed as a vibrant alternative to orderly monotony. They should reimagine and revive pandemic-battered downtowns as well as downtrodden neighborhoods. None of that will be easy amid the clashing priorities that invariably pit one side of town against another. But the city ultimately can be a shared enterprise, its built environment a commonweal that can enrich countless lives, a glue that binds together an ever-more-fractured society. That's the inclusive, equity-driven direction we must take as we reconsider and rebuild one of humankind's great achievements—the city.

Part One

PRESIDENTS AND THEIR LEGACY PROJECTS

SELF-AGGRANDIZING OR CIVIC-MINDED?

The ten-year span that began in 2011 revolved around two polarizing US presidents—each, it turns out, the driving force behind a high-profile Chicago design: the huge sign that Donald Trump, then a developer and reality TV star, plastered on his riverfront skyscraper; and the high-rise presidential center that former president Barack Obama sought to insert in verdant Jackson Park.

The projects revealed that these polar opposites actually shared something: a substantial ego (Trump's bigger and more brittle). Trump and Obama also had in common a desire to imprint their images at large scale on the cityscape. Given the projects' sensitive settings—Trump's, across from the downtown Riverwalk; Obama's, in a South Side park designed by Frederick Law Olmsted and Calvert Vaux—the designs raised fundamental issues about cities' ability to balance the competing interests of private development and public space.

Trump's reaction to the controversy sparked by his sign foreshadowed his vitriolic treatment of the news media during his presidency. At the end of his term, his executive order mandating classical styles for federal buildings exemplified his authoritarian impulses. As for the Obama Center, as the *Wall Street Journal* observed, its long slog from proposal to approval gave the former community organizer a bitter dose of the power of community organizing.

The Trump sign: a blatant display of ego that blights public space. Photo by Lee Bey.

TRUMP TAKES AIM AT DESIGN AND THE DESIGN PRESS

The Trump Sign, a Poke in the Eye, Mars the Riverfront

JUNE 5, 2014

When I informed Donald Trump that I would not be writing a rave review of the ginormous sign workers are installing on his Chicago skyscraper, he had a ready reply.

"As time passes, it'll be like the Hollywood sign," he said, referring to the beloved symbol of the US movie industry. In fact, Trump added, the skeptics who at first expressed revulsion at the idea of the 20-foot-6-inch-high stainless-steel letters spelling out his last name are coming around.

"People were saying, 'Don't put a sign up,'" Trump said. "Now, they saying, 'We love the sign.'"

My emails suggest that opinion is not universally shared. In an unsolicited note, the chief designer of Chicago's Trump International Hotel & Tower, architect Adrian Smith, wrote: "Just for the record, I had nothing to do with this sign!"

Reader Ted Naron called the sign "graffiti." He beseeched me to "use your pulpit to stop the vandalism of our cityscape currently in progress."

I've been typing sentences like that for years now, but that hasn't stopped these warts from pockmarking Chicago's renowned skyline.

It's a sign-plastered world out there, and nothing, not even Wrigley Field, is safe or sacred. When Cubs owner Tom Ricketts floated a plan last month to rim the outfield of the once-pristine ballpark with two video boards and five other signs, hardly anyone raised a red flag. Signs are so pervasive that we've become numb to them and their impact on our psyches and surroundings. Complaints are routinely dismissed as rants from the taste police.

It is hard, however, to miss Donald Trump's sign or to dismiss the anger it's provoked in some quarters. When finished, the sign will measure slightly more than 141 feet long—nearly half the length of a football field.

Not surprisingly, the developer and reality TV star, a man of no small ego, wanted the sign to be even bigger. He originally proposed that it cover 3,600 square feet, according to Peter Strazzabosco, a spokesman for the city's Department of Planning and Development. City officials cut that by roughly 20 percent, to 2,891 square feet.

As conceived by Catt Lyon Design + Wayfinding, which has a Chicago office, with details by the Poblocki Sign Company, of Milwaukee, the sign is an on-steroids version of Trump's ubiquitous logo and its bold serif typeface. Workers were recently installing the "M" after spending weeks painstakingly getting the "T," "R," and "U" in place more than 200 feet above street level.

At night, Trump told me, the letters will be backlit with LED fixtures. That will be "much more subtle," he said, than conventional lighting.

Subtle? This thing? As subtle as Godzilla.

Let's come back to that.

Despite its enormous girth and subpar spire, Trump's ninety-eight-story hotel and condominium tower is a plus for the skyline. Architect Smith and his former firm, the Chicago office of Skidmore, Owings & Merrill, endowed the tower with stainless-steel fins that catch the light beautifully. From certain angles, like the one on Wabash Avenue looking north, it dazzles. No one expected refinement like this from the Prince of Glitz. People formed a kinship with the skyscraper—which helps explain why they now feel betrayed.

"I almost hate to walk down Wabash Avenue anymore, just to avoid seeing those giant Trump letters desecrating the building's once-proud presence," wrote one reader, who requested anonymity because he works for the City of Chicago.

The developer's bait and switch also grates. No renderings of the sign were evident a dozen years ago when the tower needed approval from the aesthetically fastidious Mayor Richard M. Daley. In 2012, after I criticized the proliferation of skyline commercialism in a piece prompted by a new sign atop the elegant green-glass skyscraper at 333 West Wacker Drive, Trump said he had no plans for a sign, though he coyly added: "You may force me to do it."

Now, he insisted in our interview: "It was always my intention to put it up."

It's bad enough, as readers are lamenting, that the sign's grotesquely overscale letters mar the surface of an otherwise handsome skyscraper that is Chicago's second-tallest after the Willis Tower. It's worse that the sign is utterly out of character with its surroundings.

The big letters loom over the Beaux-Arts DuSable (originally Michigan Avenue) Bridge and the great skyscrapers, from the wedding cake of the Wrigley Building to the corncobs of Marina City, that are visible from the span. To be sure, the nearby Tribune Tower has a prominently displayed sign, but it's on an attached structure, not the neo-Gothic skyscraper itself. The Trump sign, by comparison, is a poke in the eye.

The big letters also spoil the view from the Chicago Riverwalk, which Mayor Rahm Emanuel is spending millions to extend. Docents on the architectural tour boats that ply the river should tell visitors to avert their eyes.

Who greenlighted this thing? Strazzabosco, the planning-department spokesman, explained in an email that large-scale signs like Trump's require support from the local alderman, plus approval by the full City Council. Ald. Brendan Reilly, in whose Forty-Second Ward the skyscraper is located, declined to return a phone call.

But the culprit isn't Reilly. It's a lack of sophisticated design guidelines as well as the teeth to enforce them. Trump's sign isn't the only offender—it's just the most egregious—in a city where skyline branding has run amok.

Postscript: To prevent a repeat of the visual carnage inflicted by the Trump sign, the City Council in 2014 approved an ordinance that regulates the size, placement, and materials of high-rise signs along the downtown riverfront. Because Trump had followed the previous set of rules, however, the city allowed his sign to remain. Yet far from becoming beloved, as Trump had predicted, his sign formed a perfect, camera-ready backdrop for protestors against him and his policies once he was elected president.

Trump's Sycophantic, Vitriolic Treatment of Architecture Critics

OCTOBER 7, 2016

Donald Trump doesn't just aim his nasty, middle-of-the-night tweets at beauty queens he thinks have gained too much weight. He also targets architecture critics, me included, who've gotten under his prosciutto-thin skin.

At 3:12 a.m. on June 22, 2014, Trump directed his wrath at two of us: "I loved the day Paul Goldberger got fired (or left) as New York Times architecture critic and has since faded into irrelevance," he wrote. "Kamin next!"

The tweet came amid the war of words that ensued after I zinged Trump for the humongous, hideous sign he'd stuck on his mostly handsome Chicago skyscraper. I bring up the tweet ahead of the second presidential debate because Trump's character and temperament have become major issues in the campaign, and I can speak to both based on more than a decade of experience.

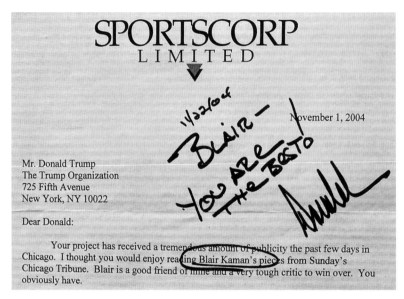

A cheery note from Trump: his glad-handing didn't last. Collection of Blair Kamin.

Over the years, Trump has courted me, comforted me, criticized me, and sent me a handful of sometimes-fawning letters and notes. I saved the correspondence. Wouldn't you?

It's fun to run your fingers over gold, raised-print letters that say "TRUMP." And the missives are telling. Combined with other things he's said and written, they show that candidate Trump isn't all that different from developer Trump. He remains a master media manipulator who can be charming, mercurial, and vengeful. Only now he wants to be the most powerful man on Earth.

In one of the notes, dated November 22, 2004, Trump responded to a letter from a Chicago sports consultant notifying him that I'd praised the latest design for his then forthcoming Chicago skyscraper. It was, I wrote, a major improvement over the original design, which would have foisted a squat, bloated hulk on the riverfront.

Trump mailed the letter back to me with this message: "Blair—You are the best!" (No self-respecting critic would want to hear such words from a man whose idea of good taste includes gaudy golden chairs that resemble thrones. But I digress.)

Ten years later, after Mayor Rahm Emanuel called Trump's sign "tasteless" and the national media jumped on the strange saga of two powerful men squabbling over aesthetics, Trump said on the *Today* show: "This was started by a third-rate architectural critic from the *Chicago Tribune* who I thought got fired."

Uh, no. I was actually on a journalism fellowship at Harvard during the 2012–13 academic year. Goldberger, who once labeled Trump a symbol of 1980s glitz, wasn't fired, either. He left the *Times* for the *New Yorker* and now writes for *Vanity Fair*. Trump clearly has a thing for critics who challenge his self-promoting narratives. He can't dispatch us into oblivion, so he does the next best thing—insinuating that we're gone when, in fact, we're still breathing, typing and assessing whether his projects live up to his P. T. Barnum hype.

On Twitter, people called out his flip-flop about me. One wrote to him: "What's funny is how U were very complimentary of @BlairKamin in the past. You can't keep your stories (or hair) straight."

While the sign battle brought out the classic Mean Trump, I feel compelled to point out that there is also a Nice Trump, at least when being nice suits his ego and long-term business interests. Consider the letter Trump wrote on May 21, 2004, after I'd told him that I was about to have a medical procedure to correct an irregular heartbeat.

"Don't worry—you will be 100% perfect after the procedure. As I told you, I know at least ten people who have been through the same problem and all are now in great shape." He underlined his closing words in black: "Take care of yourself."

It was hard not to be touched by that. On the other hand, I kept in mind the old Chicago journalism adage: "If your mother says she loves you, check it out." (The procedure, by the way, was a complete success.)

By 2009, the Donald and I arrived at the moment of truth: my review of his ninety-eight-story condo and hotel tower, which was chiefly designed by architect Adrian Smith of Skidmore, Owings & Merrill. (Smith has since established his own firm.) At the end of a short interview before the review appeared, Trump asked for my assessment.

"It's a good building," I said, praising the tower's glistening exterior but faulting its uninspired spire and riverfront bulk.

There was a pause.

"'Good'?" Trump said, sounding shocked. He had "sucked up" to me for all these years, he said, "and all I get is 'good'?"

The gloves came off in 2014 when he blighted his skyscraper with the sign that looms over the Chicago River—five stainless-steel letters, twenty feet high and nearly as long as half a football field. As I pointed out at the time, they constitute a wildly inappropriate commercial incursion on the civic grandeur of the DuSable (originally Michigan Avenue) Bridge and the 1920s skyscrapers around it, not to mention the downtown Riverwalk. I called the sign "as subtle as Godzilla" and "a poke in the eye."

Now, in Trump's eyes, I was no longer "the best!"

I was "dopey" and "a lightweight," two of his stock epithets.

Addressing architect Smith's remarks about the offensive sign— Smith emailed me to say he had nothing to do with it—Trump made this preposterous claim to the *Wall Street Journal*: "I had more to do with the design of that building than Adrian Smith did." Sure, Donald, sure, and I designed the Tribune Tower.

In a biting *Daily Show* segment about the sign feud, Jon Stewart mocked Trump's need to take on every critic: "What the (bleep) is wrong with you? Do you have to answer everybody?"

As revealed by his self-destructive Twitter attacks on the former Miss Universe, Alicia Machado, and his widely panned first debate performance, Trump hasn't taken that advice.

Will he in the second debate?

Would he if he were elected president?

In governance, as in architecture, it is essential to keep things in proper proportion. And in governance, the stakes are immeasurably higher.

Postscript: I hoped this column would make a splash, but it was completely overshadowed by the *Washington Post*'s virtually simultaneous publication of the notorious *Access Hollywood* video, in which Trump bragged in graphic terms about his ability to seduce women. The column, however, did foreshadow two defining characteristics of Trump's presidency—his deliberate distortion of inconvenient facts and his verbal assaults on journalists, whom he infamously deemed "enemies of the people." And the stakes of governing did turn out to be immeasurably higher than those of architecture, as the soaring death toll resulting from Trump's mismanagement of the coronavirus pandemic made clear.

How Should Trump Make Federal Architecture Great?
By Ignoring the Ideologues Who Speak
for Modernism and Classicism

FEBRUARY 11, 2020

Casting a critical eye at banks that resembled Roman temples, the great Chicago architect Louis Sullivan famously wrote nearly 120 years ago that their bankers should wear togas and sandals, and conduct business in Latin.

To Sullivan, Roman Revival banks were architectural fakes, their columns and pediments mere drapery that had nothing to do with their underlying construction.

Yet today, it's hard to stroll down Chicago's LaSalle Street financial canyon without admiring the banking temples along the street. They may be stage-set architecture, but they're stage sets for the ages—their proportions, materials, and details powerfully communicating a message of financial stability.

I bring up Sullivan and the LaSalle Street banks because the debate over a profoundly misguided Trump-administration proposal, which would establish classical architecture as the preferred style for many federal buildings, already is devolving into a superficial style war—a new front in the culture wars roiling Trump's America.

Predictably, left-leaning opponents of the plan are portraying classicism as reactionary, arguing, as a recent *Chicago Sun-Times* editorial did, that the plan would take us "back into a bygone era when women wore bonnets, men wore tricorn hats and the only acceptable design for a federal building was a knockoff of a classical Greek or Roman structure."

The view from the right is equally warped. Writing on the *City Journal* website, the critic Catesby Leigh opined that modernist federal buildings fail to "speak to the aspirations of ordinary citizens."

How does he know?

Chicagoans rightly admire the modernist design of Ludwig Mies van der Rohe's Federal Center, but Leigh puts down its handsomely proportioned, elegantly detailed high-rises as "boxy," trashes its transparent low-rise post office as "squat," and deems the entire complex, including the vibrant plaza highlighted by Alexander Calder's bright red *Flamingo* sculpture, as "not exactly a tour de force."

Wintrust Bank building, 231 South LaSalle Street: stirring, stage-set classicism. Photo by Lee Bey.

The people who live here know better.

Here's the point: style wars invariably fail to address the underlying characteristics—function, security, sustainability, accessibility, and compatibility with site, climate, and culture—that render architecture and urban design worthy or not. No style, classical or modernist, has a monopoly on quality. The problem with the proposal in question isn't classicism. It's the *imposition* of classicism and other traditional styles from a single central authority, a move that would undercut the very democratic ideals that classicism is supposed to represent.

True, the federal government once set aesthetic standards for federal buildings, opting for a graceful, streamlined Art Moderne during the Depression. Yet the nation has changed markedly since then, and our expectations for federal buildings should change with it.

As the Chicago-based Society of Architectural Historians and other organizations just wrote in a letter to Trump, joining opponents of the plan such as the American Institute of Architects and the National Trust for Historic Preservation, "The dictation of style—any style—is not the path to excellence in civic architecture."

The controversial plan, a draft executive order circulating in the Trump White House and first revealed by *Architectural Record*, would overturn guiding principles for federal courthouses, agency headquarters, and the like that have been in place since 1962. The forward-thinking principles have been a touchstone for the General Services Administration, the agency that commissions federal buildings. In 1994, it created a Design Excellence program that has tapped the talents of such Chicago architects as Carol Ross Barney, designer of the Oklahoma City federal building that replaced the one that a truck bomb destroyed in 1995, killing 168 people.

Written by future New York senator Daniel Patrick Moynihan, the principles, critically, are neutral on the question of style. Federal buildings "must provide visual testimony to the dignity, enterprise, vigor, and stability of the American Government," the principles say. But they add, pointedly, that "the development of an official style must be avoided. Design must flow from the architectural profession to the Government, and not vice versa."

Official styles were for the totalitarian governments America was fighting during the Cold War era of the 1960s. Moynihan's principles, in contrast, equated democratic freedom with architectural pluralism: federal buildings should reflect regional architectural traditions and, by implication, the diverse character of the American people.

That is very different from the stereotype of one-size-fits-all, steel-and-glass modernism.

The organization spearheading the draft executive order is a tiny

Washington, DC–based nonprofit, the National Civic Art Society. In 2012, *Philanthropy* magazine reported that its chief funder was Chicago investor Richard H. Driehaus, sponsor of the Driehaus Prize for traditional and classical architecture.

Anne Lazar, executive director of the Richard H. Driehaus Foundation, confirmed that personal contributions from Driehaus to the group are ongoing. But she declined to answer what Driehaus thinks of the draft executive order, whose title, "Making Federal Buildings Beautiful Again," grovelingly echoes Trump's slogan to "Make America Great Again."

The National Civic Art Society's position, however, is quite clear: modernism is a plague on our collective house, a rupture with the evolving classical tradition that began with the Greeks and Romans, flowered during the Renaissance via such masters as Italy's Andrea Palladio, and informed the Founding Fathers, especially the architect-president Thomas Jefferson.

"The public finds [modern architecture] ugly, strange, and off-putting," the group's website claims. "It has created a built environment that is degraded and dehumanizing."

Wiser classicists know better: modernism, now well over a century old, is, like it or not, a part of history. Its impact cannot be wished away. And while modernism's glassy, transparent volumes boldly departed from the solid masses of classically inspired buildings, its masters, like Mies, simultaneously learned from that tradition and enlivened it by placing their buildings and urban spaces in vivid counterpoint to it. A sterling Chicago example, chiefly designed by Jacques Brownson, is the Richard J. Daley Center, the muscular courts high-rise whose bridge-like beams relate directly in scale to the monumental Corinthian columns of the City-County Building across Clark Street.

There are few better examples of what the Yale architectural historian Vincent Scully called "a continuing dialogue between the generations which creates an environment developing across time."

Both sides in the federal-buildings debate need to take off their ideological blinders. There is nothing inherently regressive about a classical federal building, just as there is nothing inherently progressive about a modernist one.

The spectrum of classical design ranges from the transcendent excellence of the Parthenon to the megalomaniacal vision for post–World War II Berlin drawn up by Hitler's architect, Albert Speer. So, too, with modernism, which spans the gamut from the rigor and refinement of the Mies-designed Federal Center to the coarse concrete of the Brutalist FBI headquarters on Washington's Pennsylvania Avenue, by Chicago architects C. F. Murphy Associates.

I am not alarmed, as the *New York Times* was in a recent editorial, at the move to construct more federal buildings in a classical style. If local communities and their leaders choose in coordination with the federal government to build in that style, and it serves functional needs in a reasonably economical way, those communities and leaders have every right to do so.

The US is more diverse, not just demographically but architecturally, than it was in the Greek Revival era of the nation's founding or the streamlined Moderne days of the Depression. Pluralism reigns, just as our national motto (*E pluribus unum*, Latin for "Out of many, one") suggests it should.

Our buildings should reflect that diversity, not mask it.

Postscript: In December 2020, Trump signed an executive order mandating classical architecture as the preferred style for federal public buildings in Washington, DC. The order stopped short, however, of requiring that federal buildings nationwide be built in a classical style. Soon after taking office, President Joe Biden revoked the order.

THE OBAMA PRESIDENTIAL CENTER: NO WALK IN THE PARK

As president, Barack Obama didn't shy from pressing for major change, the foremost example being his signature health-care legislation, "Obamacare." As the client of a Chicago presidential center dedicated to inspiring a new generation of leaders, Obama proved no less ambitious. He reportedly told his architects that one of their early plans was "too quiet," then unveiled a multibuilding proposal that called for erecting a slant-walled museum tower in the pastoral landscape of Jackson Park and shutting down part of a major road used by thousands of commuters. So much for the quick, easy approval the

First museum-tower design for Obama Presidential Center: too heavy, too funereal, too pharaonic. Image credit: Tod Williams Billie Tsien Architects / Obama Foundation.

popular ex-president might have expected in his adopted hometown. Fears that the center would accelerate gentrification in surrounding neighborhoods and lawsuits against the project compounded the delays. While the jury is still out on the planned museum tower, the center as a whole is likely to benefit the long-underserved South Side and become a symbol of African American ascendance.

Obama Center Design:
Promising, Populist, not Yet Persuasive

MAY 4, 2017

"I wanted to be an architect when I was a kid," Barack Obama cracked as he gave the world a first look at the conceptual plans for his presidential center. "Somehow, I took a wrong turn."

The former president was in fine form, mixing comedic riffs with a vision of his center that was as populist as it was presidential: a campus-like cluster surrounded by dramatically sculpted parkland

Revised museum-tower design for the Obama Presidential Center: much improved, but the jury is still out. Image credit: Tod Williams Billie Tsien Architects / Obama Foundation.

and assorted urban delights—a sledding hill, children's play areas, community gardens, barbecue grills, and food trucks serving tacos.

"We will have basketball," Obama joked, drawing appreciative laughter from a crowd of about three hundred invited guests at the South Shore Cultural Center.

What are we to make of this? My take, which is as preliminary as the plan itself, is that Obama's team of designers has made a good start on urban planning, but the architecture isn't yet persuasive. That's fine because, as Obama said: "This is just the beginning of a process, not the end."

Led by New York architects Tod Williams and Billie Tsien, along with Brooklyn-based landscape architect Michael Van Valkenburgh, the design team has started to strike a compelling balance between Obama's desire for a strong architectural statement and the need to respect the historic landscape of Jackson Park, which was designed by Frederick Law Olmsted and Calvert Vaux and is listed on the National Register of Historic Places.

Williams and Tsien push their trio of buildings to the park's far northwest corner, a short walk from the Museum of Science and Industry. That's smart. The science museum, a Beaux-Arts legacy of Chicago's celebrated 1893 World's Fair, is a well-known landmark. Luring potential visitors to the center, especially those who wrongly think the entire South Side is plagued by violence, will be easier if they can hopscotch to the center from a familiar destination.

The most prominent of the three buildings, a stone-sheathed museum tower with splaying walls, would rise as high as 180 feet, forming a vertical marker that would announce the center from afar. To its south would be a pair of one-story structures whose low-slung profile and rooftop greenery would defer to the landscape of Jackson Park—a "forum" containing an auditorium, and another building that could house a Chicago Public Library branch.

The three structures would frame an outdoor plaza along Stony Island Avenue, another good stroke, because it would enliven the urban west side of the center (as opposed to the verdant east side). Williams and Tsien are known for breaking potentially large buildings into smaller, human-scaled ensembles that encourage people to interact. That's what they're striving for here, though their plaza feels a little bare.

Obama himself championed the plan's boldest stroke, which calls for shutting down Cornell Drive, the six-lane road that cuts through Jackson Park, to create a South Side version of the sylvan Museum Campus that unites the Field Museum, the Shedd Aquarium, and the Adler Planetarium.

Cornell Drive slices Jackson Park into dull patches of green, the former president correctly said. Eliminate it and you'll replace roughly five acres of ugly asphalt with glorious green space.

Talk about audacity!

Thousands of drivers who use Cornell as they rumble between South Lake Shore Drive and the Chicago Skyway are sure to complain that closing Cornell will lengthen their commutes. But if alternative routes and effective traffic-control strategies can be found—admittedly, a big "if"—the proposed closure isn't just a bold move, it's the right move.

Do it and the center could fulfill Obama's dream of a teeming civic hub. Without it, the center would be a lonely island of green, strangled by traffic.

So far, so good, but there's a disappointing disconnect between the plan's signature architectural flourish—that slant-walled museum tower—and Obama's stated desire to avoid the syndrome of presidential libraries that are "see what I did" monuments to the past. He wants a forward-looking building, one that will symbolize the center's mission to train future leaders who will make a difference in their communities, countries, and the world.

Nice rhetoric, but it's not yet supported by the architectural reality.

In its current form, the tower suggests an expanded version of a truncated obelisk. It's too heavy, too funereal, too pharaonic, too pyramid-like. The I. M. Pei–designed John F. Kennedy Library in Boston, with its signature geometric shapes of concrete, steel, and glass, creates a more fitting version of monumentality, combining bracing modernity with a traditional sense of permanence.

Many other aspects of the design remain unresolved: for example, what will activate the center's library building in light of the surprise announcement that Obama's archives will be digitized and the physical records themselves will go to another, yet-to-be-determined site?

Even so, this is a promising beginning. It's worlds better than the recently defeated plan for the Lucas Museum of Narrative Art—not a screaming "look at me" object plunked down in the park, as that design promised to be, but a series of structures that seek to engage the landscape, each other, and the community around them.

Postscript: Responding to criticism that the original museum-tower design was squat and forbidding, Williams and Tsien unveiled revisions in 2018 and 2019 that made the tower taller and more transparent, with lighter-colored stone, more windows, and a more gracefully sculpted profile. Screenlike walls will display excerpts from Obama's "You are America" speech marking the fiftieth anniversary of the Selma to Montgomery, Alabama, march for voting rights. Before those changes were introduced, however, the former president's remark that the freshly unveiled design was "just the beginning of a process" proved all too prescient. A series of controversies beset the center, including the contention that it would do lasting damage to the Olmsted-designed landscape of Jackson Park.

Obama Center's Plans Won't Destroy Olmsted's Park—They Should Be Improved, not Rejected

JANUARY 22, 2018

As debate heats up over the wisdom of putting the Obama Presidential Center in historic Jackson Park, opponents are painting the project as a land grab whose slant-walled 235-foot museum tower would blight a park codesigned by the great nineteenth-century landscape architect Frederick Law Olmsted.

"There is no need to destroy one significant cultural legacy in order to celebrate another," Charles A. Birnbaum, president of the Cultural Landscape Foundation, a nonprofit located in Washington, DC, wrote in the online publication *Dezeen*.

Destroy Olmsted's legacy?

Please.

Birnbaum and other opponents of the Jackson Park site, including a group of University of Chicago professors who signed a letter condemning the location, are ignoring how the Obama plans would improve a scruffy landscape that is poorly maintained, brutally interrupted by a wide road, and seriously underutilized as a result. They also fail to recognize, as Olmsted did, that parks need to evolve with changing circumstances rather than remain rigidly fixed.

At worst, the opponents are imposing a narrow aesthetic perspective on plans that promise to be an economic boon—and an enormous source of pride—for African Americans who have long suffered from racial discrimination and the underinvestment that accompanied it.

"As far as the tallest building, I see it as a beacon of hope, a beacon of change," Russell Pike, of the Jackson Park Highlands Association, which represents a historic district to the park's south, said at a recent public meeting. "We need something like this to help us with the development of our community."

Granted, the revised plan for the museum tower still needs to become less bulky and more elegant. But that's no reason to ditch a privately funded project that backers predict will create nearly five thousand jobs during construction, attract as many as 760,000 annual visitors, and have an economic impact of $3.1 billion in the ten years after it opens. Even if those figures are exaggerations, as such projections tend to be, it's hard to buy the professors' argument that the estimates are inflated because there's no adjacent land on which entrepreneurs could start new businesses. In reality, new uses are likely to replace current ones. The real danger is not economic stagnation, but displacement caused by gentrification.

The professors and other critics contend that the former president should have put the nineteen-acre center at an alternative site, in nearby Washington Park, thereby forestalling the present building-in-the-park brouhaha. That would have been more equitable, in their view.

But this wasn't a choice between the gritty South Side and the glitzy Gold Coast. It was a choice between two low-income African American neighborhoods—one of which, Washington Park, would likely have struggled to attract visitors, because it has one of Chicago's highest crime rates. The other neighborhood, Woodlawn, to the center's west, is at least starting to redevelop, increasing the chance that the center will become a powerful South Side growth engine.

Because this will not be a conventional presidential library that houses documents from the Obama White House (the National Archives and Records Administration will store them elsewhere), the former president's plans also have upset traditionalists who value the authenticity and gravitas artifacts convey. But such items can still be displayed in the center. The guiding idea is not a hushed treasure box. Rather, it is to create a training ground for future citizen leaders and a pleasure ground that invites people to come together. The center's urban design is integral to those purposes—a place of physical encounter that forms an antidote to the virtual relationships of the iPhone age.

By closing Cornell Drive, which grew to its current width during the highway-building binge of the mid-1960s, the proposal would open an uninterrupted swath of green space comparable to the Museum Campus, which took shape in the 1990s, when Lake Shore Drive's northbound lanes were shifted west of Soldier Field. There would be a sledding hill, plus winding bike-and-pedestrian pathways that would follow Olmsted's original contours for the park. People from the neighborhoods to the west of the center could more easily make their way to Jackson Park's lagoons and Lake Michigan.

With features like that in the offing, the notion that the center would destroy the 543-acre Jackson Park is ludicrous. Even a respected Olmsted scholar whom I consulted said so.

"There's going to be a hell of a lot of investment in this part of the park. That's a real positive," David Schuyler, a Franklin & Marshall College professor who has coedited a collection of Olmsted's papers, said during a telephone interview. "And if [the center] draws people to this part of the park, it means that the city's going to maintain it, which it hasn't been doing very much lately. So, as far as I can tell, it's a real trade-off with a very positive effect as well."

Architects Tod Williams and Billie Tsien make a convincing case for the center's tower: it would lift visitors above the park and offer, from its top-floor observatory, spectacular views of Jackson Park and nearby parks, as well as Lake Michigan. The tower also would symbolize a key theme of the center—ascension and "rising up," as personified by the story of Barack and Michelle Obama. You cannot do that with a meek building huddled below the tree line.

Yet the tower, which would be clad in a whitish-gray stone, could dwarf its environs and alter the experience of a park where nature, not buildings, are the prime focus. That's a big change, although the impact would be muted by the fact that the high-rise would be placed on the edge of the park, not at its center. Maybe it's the right change, befitting the historic identity of the first African American president. Still, the design is not yet compelling, despite recent revisions that would lighten its opaque facades with lacy stone screens and, at night, create an entrancing veillike effect. Schuyler said he found the proposed height and bulk of the severe, obelisk-like tower "a bit scary."

City officials also must answer the Cultural Landscape Foundation's charge that the Obama Center would amount to a "confiscation" of public space. But that should not be difficult. The center's outdoor space would be open to the public, free of charge. Most of its interior spaces would be, too, with the exception of the museum. That would distinguish the center from the failed proposal for the Lucas Museum, which ran into a judicial wall partly because it did not offer enough public access.

Olmsted, a beloved figure whose masterpiece is New York's Central Park, looms over the entire process. Olmsted scholars say the landscape architect generally objected to the insertion of large structures in his parks. On the other hand, he was a passionate abolitionist who might have appreciated the symbolic importance of Obama's story and accepted the need to accommodate a major new feature in his park. In the end, it's impossible to know.

What we do know is that Olmsted was a pragmatist, not an ideologue. He embraced the need to adapt his parks to changing times and circumstances. After the Chicago World's Fair of 1893, for example, he made a portion of his naturalistic landscape more formal to accommodate the Beaux-Arts fair building that is now the Museum of Science and Industry. He designed roads that could handle automobile traffic. And in a concession to more active recreational habits, he inserted oval outdoor tracks for men and women.

Olmsted did indeed write that future structures should remain subordinate to the present science museum. But that was nearly 125 years ago. Just because he might not have agreed with all aspects of the Obama Center proposal doesn't mean those plans won't have a major beneficial impact on his landscape and the lives of those who use it. The triumph of Millennium Park, whose joyous large-scale works of public art broke with the convention of a serene greensward, reveals the value of thinking big—and thinking fresh.

Improve the Obama Center plans.

Don't reject them.

Postscript: The Chicago City Council approved legislation in 2018 allowing the Obama Center to be built in Jackson Park, but that hardly quelled debate over the project. Responding to predictions from activists that the center would accelerate gentrification, the council in 2020 passed an ordinance that seeks to maintain affordable housing and prevent displacement in Woodlawn. Meanwhile, a federal review of the project dragged on through 2021, as did an unsuccessful legal challenge against the center launched by the advocacy group Protect Our Parks. By then, the project's total cost had escalated from the original $500 million estimate to more than $800 million, including $700 million for construction. Barack and Michelle Obama attended the 2021 groundbreaking, yet as the *Wall Street Journal* reported, the delays ensured that the Obama Center would set a modern record for the time between the end of a president's term in office and the completion of his presidential center.

Part Two

URBAN DESIGN

BOOM TIMES FOR CITIES, BUT WHO BENEFITS?

After the slowdown imposed by the Great Recession, the 2010s became a decade of rapid urbanization, until the worst pandemic in a century brought growth to a stunning halt. In Chicago, a wave of innovative new parks and public spaces, among them the downtown Riverwalk, built upon the popular and artistic success of Millennium Park. Ambitious transit and infrastructure projects, including new pedestrian bridges and Chicago Transit Authority stations, created valuable connectivity that took on fresh relevance during the pandemic, when stay-at-home orders and remote work drove people apart.

Yet some of these progressive initiatives—most notably, the 606 pedestrian-and-bike trail, a linear open space that was Chicago's answer to New York's High Line—led to the displacement of some of the very poor and working-class people they were meant to serve. In light of such developments, the paramount issue of Daniel Burnham's 1909 Plan of Chicago—bringing order out of urban chaos—seemed outdated or at least in need of a sharp revision. The overriding question rightly became: Who benefits from growth—if, indeed, growth is occurring at all? It was all but absent in South and West Side neighborhoods hammered by decades of discrimination and disinvestment.

Halfway across the world, images of a dystopian urban future emerged in the booming cities of China, where Chicago architects ex-

Shanghai's new skyscrapers: a skyline spectacle, but at street level, deadly dull. Photo by John J. Kim / *Chicago Tribune* / TCA.

ported their expertise in skyscrapers but discovered that a trophy skyscraper does not a good city make. Urban density, it turned out, was no guarantee of livability, architectural quality, or equity.

URBANIZATION ON THE MARCH—AND ON HOLD
BECAUSE OF THE PANDEMIC

China's Skyscrapers Are Trophies for the Nation and a Lifeline for Chicago Architects—but Growth Has Its Price

FEBRUARY 21, 2014

When Chicago architect Adrian Smith designed Shanghai's first skyscraper to crack the 1,000-foot barrier, he envisioned a glistening tower inspired by ancient pagodas—a silvery shaft topped by an exultant spire that would scrape the sky, not be hidden by it.

But the wave of air pollution that struck China's largest city late last year played an unanticipated trick on the 1,380-foot-tall Jin Mao Tower and the rest of the gigantic Shanghai skyscrapers that symbolize China's headlong rush into modernity: it made them disappear.

The smog attack, which burned throats, forced flight cancellations, and prompted a run on face masks, marked the latest twist in a little-noticed global exchange that has remade the face of Chinese cities and revitalized recession-battered American architectural practices.

As China, the boom country of the twenty-first century, builds its urban dreams, it is turning to the boom city of the late nineteenth and early twentieth centuries—Chicago. Yet this is not a simple, happy story of East meets Midwest.

It is a tale of hypersized, hyperfast urbanization that has simultaneously lifted hundreds of millions of people out of poverty and spawned dystopian living conditions: pea-soup skies, sterile new business districts, and monotonous housing blocks.

It takes time and vision to build great cities. But the strategies China has pursued mix the megalomania of Soviet-style public squares, the gigantism of American skyscrapers, and a one-dimensional Chinese focus on boosting the economy rather than the quality of life.

"The spatial design of the cities has been done in a one-size-fits-all kind of manner—the megablocks and the celebration of iconic architecture as opposed to livable space," said Jonathan Woetzel, a Shanghai-based director of the McKinsey Global Institute. The growth "was done in a hurry and was done in a way to maximize the amount of (land) you could sell for development."

The scope and pace of China's urbanization are staggering. The country has increased its urban population by about half a billion since 1980, and experts predict that the world's most populous nation will add as many as three hundred million people to its cities by 2030. As a result, a billion people—nearly one of every eight on Earth—could live in Chinese cities.

Some of the most visible symbols of this urbanization were conceived in Chicago.

The Chicago office of Skidmore, Owings & Merrill, where Adrian Smith once worked, designed the Jin Mao Tower, which reigned for nearly a decade as China's tallest skyscraper and remains one of its most iconic. Chicago stars like Helmut Jahn have their own striking Chinese towers. And the Chicago office of Gensler, a global firm headquartered in San Francisco, contributed ten architects to the team that designed the twisting 2,073-foot-tall Shanghai Tower, which, when completed, will become the world's second-tallest building, after the SOM-designed Burj Khalifa in Dubai.

But Chicago's architects and urban planners routinely find themselves powerless to direct the larger forces propelling China's growth. Their completed projects are often tinged with irony: energy-saving buildings plunked into a landscape that is anything but green; context-sensitive designs that strive to uplift their surroundings but wind up as isolated as chess pieces spread across a board.

"They buy themselves a trophy," said Jahn, whose elegant Leatop Plaza, its roof sliced on a diagonal, fronts on a grandly scaled but forlorn park in the southern Chinese city of Guangzhou.

Other Chicago architects and planners second these denunciations, though they acknowledge that China has thrown them an economic lifeline and allowed them to design projects whose scope, cost, and ambition are rarely equaled in the United States.

"We never talk about money. Never in the seven years I've been here. They just say it needs to be more luxurious," said Rick Fawell, who heads the Shanghai and Beijing offices of Chicago-based VOA Associates.

Long gone are the dark years of the Cultural Revolution, when gray Mao suits were de rigueur and cities were deemed decadent dens of the bourgeoisie. China has entered a new Gilded Age in which Chinese leaders view cities as engines of economic growth and Western architects as the latest luxury brand. Frequently, the no-holds-barred opulence leads to excess.

In the eastern Chinese city of Suzhou, an almost completed, nearly 1,000-foot-tall tower by the global firm RMJM resembles an enormous pair of jeans. Irked Chinese bloggers have nicknamed the tower, which its architects consider a monumental gateway to a new business district, "the Giant Pants."

There are many such nicknames, not all of them endearing: "the Big Shorts" (for the Dutch firm OMA's CCTV Headquarters, in Beijing); "the Bottle Opener" (for the Shanghai World Financial Center, by New York architects KPF) and "the Girl with the Thin Waist" (for the Canton Tower, a Guangzhou television tower by the Dutch firm IBA).

While the nicknames are amusing, urban planning is no game. Cities are our destiny. Paralleling China's urban rise, half of the world's 7.14 billion people now live in cities. By 2050, the World Health Organization predicts, seven of every ten people around the globe will dwell in urban areas.

China exemplifies this trend. It is no longer useful to frame its story as a tale of dazzling buildings designed by star architects. Like Chicago more than a century ago, China is a laboratory where architects, urban planners, government officials, and developers are concocting the urban future—both for better and for worse.

•

The natural affinity between Chicago and China can be expressed in two words: "big" and "fast."

In the years after the Great Fire of 1871, Chicago grew at lightning speed. Its population soared from nearly 300,000 in 1870 to 2 million in 1910, finally peaking at 3.6 million in 1950.

That's pretty impressive until you hear the story of the Chinese city of Shenzhen, near Hong Kong. Propelled by Chinese leader Deng Xiaoping's decision to spark growth by creating a special economic zone to lure factories and other businesses, Shenzhen went from a sleepy border town of 58,000 in 1980 to a sprawling urban area of more than 10 million today.

This is what is known as "Chinese speed." And it is far from isolated.

Before 1980, fewer than two of every ten Chinese lived in cities. In 2012, for the first time, more than half of China's people, 710 million, were classified as urban.

Their numbers are sure to increase as China loosens restrictions that have prevented millions of migrant workers from establishing permanent residence in cities. Rural residents who move permanently to cities, the thinking goes, will earn and spend more than they would on the farm, raising domestic demand for consumer goods.

But there's much more to urbanization than raising gross domestic product.

Where will the new urbanites live—in the already congested megacities of Shanghai and Beijing, or in smaller cities? Who will build and pay for new roads, subways, apartments, office towers, and social services? How will China provide the energy to power the buildings where the new city dwellers will live and work—with more polluting coal-fired power plants, or with a cleaner alternative?

These are urgent questions in China. Late last year, the country's top leaders, including Premier Li Keqiang, discussed them in a two-day, closed-door conference on urbanization. China's urban push has so many pervasive downsides that the language has bent to accommodate it.

Shoddy construction—like an unoccupied thirteen-story Shanghai apartment block that fell over, nearly intact, in 2009—has inspired the term "tofu-dreg project," a reference to the residue from making tofu.

Then there are "ghost cities," new housing projects that remain virtually unoccupied because no one wants to live there or can afford to.

The most telling phrase, "PM 2.5," refers to particulate matter 2.5 micrometers or less in diameter, tiny airborne particles that can cause serious health problems when ingested. Scientific studies have linked repeated exposure to the particles with reduced lung function and a rise in death rates caused by lung cancer and heart disease.

China's air pollution is so bad—and PM 2.5 is so much a part of everyday conversation—that English-language newspapers use the term in headlines. After smog woes spread from Beijing to a hundred cities in eastern China last year, the *Shanghai Daily* splashed a life-size picture of a face mask on its front page, accompanied by the headline: "Can we get rid of this today?"

The pollution affects every echelon of society. Worried parents check the PM 2.5 level before letting their children play outside. Foreign companies fret that they won't be able to recruit employees to work in China. Chicago architect Smith, who designed the Jin Mao Tower in 1993, said the air has perceptibly dulled the skyscraper's once-silvery facade of stainless steel, aluminum, and glass.

Northern China's coal-burning power plants typically get the blame for the pollution. But urban-planning practices that favor driving, not walking, also are responsible. Beijing, once a city of bicycles, now has more than 5 million cars. Car use has also skyrocketed in Shanghai.

When Beijing-based architect Chris Groesbeck of VOA Associates returns to his Naperville home from China, the blue skies seem so novel that he takes pictures of them.

"It's like coming out of a cave," he said.

•

One building in Chicago represents the burgeoning China trade: 224 South Michigan Avenue, a seventeen-story office building sheathed in white terra-cotta. It's there that legendary architect and planner Daniel Burnham had his offices and led the writing of the 1909 Plan of Chicago, which spurred the construction of such marquee public works as Navy Pier and brought order to Chicago's urban chaos.

Ringing the building's skylit atrium today are the offices of three Chicago firms with big footprints in China: Skidmore, Owings & Merrill, purveyors of sophisticated corporate skyscrapers; VOA Associates, specialists in luxury hotels and hospitals; and Goettsch Partners, whose portfolio ranges from workaday office buildings to high-rise hotels.

Seen together, the three offices form a kind of architectural export factory that reverses the usual trend of American companies outsourcing production of their wares to China. The cluster also explodes the outdated notion that Chicago architects do most of their work in Chicago.

"We typically think of Chicago in an insular way. In reality, Chicago is a hub in a global profession," said Chicago native Jonathan Solomon, associate dean of architecture at Syracuse University and former acting head of the University of Hong Kong's architecture school.

Goettsch Partners' portfolio used to be evenly divided among the US, China, and the Middle East. Last year, nearly 60 percent of the firm's billings were in China.

"We're like buffalo hunters—we go where the buffalo are," said Jim Goettsch, Goettsch Partners' chairman.

At Skidmore, Owings & Merrill, about one of every seven employees—48 out of 374—are Chinese speakers, including a half-dozen translators. Forty-three percent of the office's 2013 billings were in China.

A slowing Chinese economy could force the Chicago firms to lay off architects, but leaders of the firms insist that new projects continue to arise there. "China is saving a lot of architects' jobs in the US," said Silas Chiow, the Shanghai-based director of SOM China.

Even though Chinese architect Wang Shu won the 2012 Pritzker Architecture Prize, his field's highest honor, the Chinese need to go overseas for architectural talent. The Cultural Revolution, the late 1960s movement that forced millions of people from the cities to the country, decimated the ranks of the nation's architects, as well as their creativity.

"The ideology of the Cultural Revolution largely removed the association of art within architecture. For decades, architecture was viewed as function and economy more than aesthetics. It became this kind of machine to contain us," said Harvard University Graduate School of Design professor Bing Wang, author of *The Architectural Profession of Modern China: Emerging from the Past*.

Hiring foreign architects, like those from Chicago, is a way for the Chinese to catch up and learn from the experts, particularly when it comes to innovative skyscraper design, which, ever since tall office buildings rose in the Loop in the 1880s, has been one of the city's singular strengths.

This heritage gives Chicago architects a leg up on their competitors as they compete for lucrative high-rise jobs. "I always felt that because we were from Chicago, that made it possible," Goettsch said of his firm's move into the China market. "If we were from Minneapolis, it wouldn't have been the same."

Skyscrapers designed at 224 South Michigan have transformed the silhouette of China's cities from horizontal to vertical. By 2020, according to the Chicago-based Council on Tall Buildings and Urban Habitat, twelve of the twenty tallest buildings in the world could be in China.

China has become what Chicago used to be: a laboratory for the latest high-rise innovations.

But like other foreign firms working in China, Chicago architects regularly endure a frustrating struggle to realize their ambitions.

In Chicago, they prepare everything from concept drawings to construction documents. And they can supervise their work as it's being built. If a contractor wants to make a change, a Loop job site is a short walk away.

The rules change in China, where some construction workers have only rudimentary skills, the foreigners must partner with local firms that prepare the final blueprints, and a fourteen-hour time difference means that objectionable changes can be made while an architect in Chicago is asleep. All that necessitates ceding control, a hard thing for architects from the city that takes to heart Ludwig Mies van der Rohe's aphorism: "God is in the details."

.

God was definitely not in the details when Goettsch Partners principal Scott Seyer traveled to the eastern Chinese city of Suzhou last year to see a freshly completed office building he had designed.

The handsome high-rise, the twenty-one-story headquarters of Soochow Securities, is one of nine projects the Goettsch firm has completed in Suzhou. Its floor plan, shaped like a rounded triangle, wraps around a soaring atrium partly inspired by the one at 224 South Michigan. Seyer was excited as he neared the building. He hadn't seen it in eight months.

Then he arrived. Seyer had designed benches that would brim with plants to warm up the atrium's stone floor and create a lively gathering space. They weren't there. In their place were a few potted palms around the perimeter. At the atrium's center was a tiny and temporary picket fence surrounding Christmas decorations.

"Sometimes things change," Seyer said. "It's inevitable," he added later, "that you're not going to be able to have the same control from seven thousand miles as from seven blocks."

In the grand scheme of things, a botched detail doesn't mean much. But Chicago architects trying to address the broader problem of China's air pollution face even tougher struggles, as shown by the saga of the ecology-driven Pearl River Tower, which Smith and his partner Gordon Gill designed while both were working at SOM. They left in 2006 to start their own firm.

When the design was unveiled at a 2006 Museum of Contemporary Art Chicago exhibition, it was billed as a "net-zero energy" skyscraper that would produce as much energy as it consumed. The green billing came despite the fact that the building was to be the headquarters of the China Tobacco Guangdong Industrial Corporation, a major ciga-rette maker.

The seventy-one-story tower, which opened in 2013 in the big south-ern Chinese city of Guangzhou, has curving exterior walls that funnel the wind through four openings in its facade. The openings house spinning turbines. Inside are such green features as chilled radiant ceilings, which eliminate inefficient air ducts. The word Gill uses to describe the tower is "performance," as though the skyscraper were a race car.

A better metaphor would involve ghosts, as in "ghost building."

Just four of the tower's seventy-one floors are occupied, according to its developers. The tobacco company will not be moving into the tower for at least five years, the managing director of the firm that developed the high-rise said in an interview. The reason: the new Chinese lead-ership, which is pursuing an anti-corruption campaign, wants to limit the construction of plush administrative offices for state-owned firms.

With so few tenants, it's impossible to fully assess whether the boldly sculpted tower is a harbinger of a greener future. Even the en-vironmental elements that are in place seem more about showman-ship than sustainability. The turbines, for example, are expected to generate less than 3 percent of the building's energy.

To be sure, the project incorporates eleven of the eighteen energy-saving technologies recommended by the architects, according to the managing director, Ye Zhiming. As a result, the Pearl River Tower will use 50 to 60 percent less energy than a typical office building of com-parable size. Yet it is not close to its original goal.

"Net-zero, to me, is an ideal or a goal," Ye said. "When you put it into real life, a goal has to change."

•

For all their dazzling skylines, the new Chinese cities lack the charac-ter you find in Chicago and other pedestrian-friendly American cities. The best place to observe this regrettable phenomenon is a skyscraper-studded peninsula across the Huangpu River from the Bund, Shang-hai's celebrated row of 1910s and 1920s high-rises. It's part of a district called Pudong.

A quarter century ago, when China declared it a special economic zone, the peninsula consisted of little more than squatters' shacks and warehouses.

Today, Pudong boasts the world's only trio of supertall skyscrapers: the Jin Mao Tower, the Shanghai World Financial Center, and the Shanghai Tower. The ungainly Oriental Pearl TV Tower completes the supertall row.

Especially at night, when neon and other lights paint the towers in flashes of ever-shifting colors, the view from the riverfront pathway on the Bund is extraordinary—lower Manhattan meets Las Vegas. The spectacle promises dense, richly textured urbanity. But when you cross the river, you get something more like the car-centric sterility of Houston.

A massive street, reminiscent of the grand scale of Beijing's Tiananmen Square and its Soviet predecessors, splits the area in two. The skyscrapers are separated by oversize city blocks, rendering each an island unto itself. The three towers stand alongside one other, the equivalent, in Chicago, of putting the Willis and Trump towers alongside the John Hancock Center. This creates a spectacular skyline from afar. From up close, however, Pudong is a valley of the giants, bereft of human scale.

The area proved so dangerous that officials built a network of footbridges to connect the towers. The bridges attract pedestrians who enjoy gazing at the skyscrapers without having to worry about getting flattened by a speeding car.

The bridges are a Band-Aid. Great cities aren't just about iconic skyscrapers. They're about the spaces in between them. Big towers need small-scale buildings to leaven their gigantism. Lively streets matter as much as arresting skyscrapers. You won't find them in Pudong. American architects, thinking of suburb- and car-dominated New Jersey, refer to Pudong as "Pu Jersey."

•

Reacting to criticism of the foul air, the crammed roads, and the widespread view that they are pursuing one-dimensional growth, Chinese leaders have had what Chicagoans might call a "Burnham Moment."

Plan for a commercial center in Tianjin, China: returning to old principles to make a new downtown. Image courtesy of SOM. © Crystal CG.

After last year's conference on urbanization, they announced that they would follow a "human-centered" model of growth that would focus on sustainability and other quality-of-life goals.

A striking example of the shifting attitudes is an emerging government-backed financial district, shaped by the Chicago office of SOM. It's rising on coastal salt flats in Tianjin, about a hundred miles southeast of Beijing and thirty miles from Tianjin's downtown. Construction workers are erecting a phalanx of skyscrapers on a riverfront peninsula. But this is not going to be another Pudong.

SOM urban planner Phil Enquist designed the district to be an anti-Pudong: compact, not sprawling; walkable, not car-centric. Generous public spaces and convenient transit will be built right in.

The district's central boulevard will be only three-fifths as wide as the one government leaders wanted. To bring its scale down to a human dimension, Enquist strolled vice mayors from Tianjin down Chicago's North Michigan Avenue. He pointed out how its buildings frame the sidewalks and join with plantings and lighting to create a comfortable place to walk. Another key street in the Tianjin district will be even narrower, nearly duplicating the dimensions of Chicago's prime retail street.

City blocks will measure 328 feet by 328 feet, about a quarter of the size the officials suggested. This departure from the superblocks typical of Chinese cities promises to make it easier for pedestrians to get around and help traffic flow smoothly.

In this case, Enquist isn't designing pieces on an urban chessboard. He's reshaping the chessboard itself. His goals aren't just economic, but ecological. "If you're building this twenty-first-century economy, and you have these severe environmental challenges, who wants to be there?" he asked. "Do you want to raise a family there?"

Due to the district's remoteness, skeptics predict it will be decades before its under-construction office buildings are filled. But a new station on a high-speed rail line will bring the area within fifteen minutes of downtown Tianjin; Beijing will be less than an hour away.

Urbanologists use the term "cluster cities" to describe such interconnected centers of urban life. With high-speed rail lines compressing time and space, the theory goes, the cities will no longer exist in their own silos. They'll share infrastructure and other facilities, like art museums. That will reduce expensive duplication and make second- and third-tier cities more attractive places to live. The idea can be applied throughout China, provided turf-conscious local officials cooperate.

"The challenge is not to hold down the first-tier cities, but to pick up the third-tier ones," said Woetzel, the McKinsey Global Institute director.

Ideas like these suggest that China could fulfill its promise as a laboratory for new models of urban growth. But enormous challenges still confront China's leaders.

Will rural residents and college graduates move to smaller cities, as the government is urging? Or will they keep going to the crowded megacities of Beijing and Shanghai, where the jobs and excitement are?

More troubling, Chinese leaders at the conference made no mention of slowing the nation's growth to allow for a more deliberate approach to building cities. If the pace does not slow, it could trap ordinary Chinese in the kind of "Blade Runner" nightmare that recently struck Nanjing and a building there by Chicago architects Perkins & Will.

That building—the headquarters of Chervon, a leading Chinese maker of power tools and supplier for the Sears Craftsman brand—is a low-slung, S-shaped structure that wraps around outdoor courtyards with sculpted mounds and shallow reflecting pools. On a normal day, the seven hundred people who work inside venture into the courtyards for relaxing strolls. But due to the same smog attack that hit Shanghai, the courtyards were empty.

The foul air prompted Nan Jia, a translator in Perkins & Will's Shanghai office, to recall the fear she once felt when a sandstorm struck the northeastern Chinese province where she grew up. It turned the sky a sickening yellow and brown.

"I escaped from the sandstorm," Jia said, "but now I can't escape from the haze."

Postscript: Reacting to the aesthetic excesses of China's skyscrapers, Chinese president Xi Jinping in 2014 proclaimed "no more weird architecture," although he didn't specify what he meant by "weird." Yet Chinese cities continued to suffer the consequences of breakneck growth. In 2021, flooding in Zhengzhou and other cities in central China killed at least sixty-nine people. "The vast expansion of roads, subways and railways in cities that swelled almost overnight meant there were fewer places where rain could safely be absorbed," the *New York Times* reported.

Attacking "Plop Architecture": There's a Better, Transit-Oriented Way to Design Our Cities

MARCH 21, 2015

"Plop architecture" is the name I gave to one of the biggest urban-design faults of Chicago's pre–Great Recession building boom. The pejorative term described graceless combinations of hulking condominium towers crudely stacked atop massive parking garages. The blank-walled garages weren't just eyesores. They were energy wasters, encouraging people to drive instead of using bus and train lines that were steps away.

1611 West Division: a key step forward in the fight against car-centric architecture. Photo by Lee Bey.

While the condo towers raised the tax base and downtown's population count, their aesthetic banality and concessions to the car were a slap in the face to the push for sustainability and the vitality of city life. In New York, you looked up at the second floor of a residential building and saw windows displaying plants and other evidence of human life. In Chicago, you saw concrete.

So the city's overdue embrace of a less car-centric urban-development model is welcome, a signal that the recession wasn't just a pause but a pivot point that allowed policymakers to come to terms with a variety of shifts, especially among the millennial generation, born from the early 1980s to the early 2000s. Those changes include more bike and car sharing as well as a drop in automobile use—evidence of a changing mindset that views cars as mere transportation, not status symbols.

Now the freshly invigorated phenomenon of transit-oriented development, which encourages construction of dense residential buildings near rail stops, is adding momentum to these seismic shifts. Early signs of the trend, which include a finished residential high-rise at 1611 West Division Street with no on-site tenant parking, show it could be a major plus for the cityscape

Approved in 2013, Chicago's transit-oriented development ordinance lets developers cut by as much as half the number of required off-street parking spots if their project is within 600 feet of a CTA or Metra rail station. The same rule relaxation applies if the building is within 1,200 feet of such a station and is located along a street the city has certified as pedestrian-friendly. Back in the dark ages, before the measure was passed, there had to be one parking spot for every residential unit.

The law, which also allows developers to build more square footage if their projects are deemed transit-friendly, makes sense (and cents): it gives investors an incentive to build housing near transit. More people will live near bus and rail stops, the thinking goes, cutting energy use, pollution, and commute times. The increased population density should provide a built-in market for shop and restaurant owners, giving them a fighting chance for walk-in traffic in the age of e-commerce.

For architects, fewer parking spaces mean a chance to shape buildings that are less cloddish and more responsive to human needs. In the past, said David Brininstool, a partner at Chicago's Brininstool + Lynch, "The developer would show you the site and ask, 'How many cars can we get on it?'" Now, he added, "We start with the people, not with the cars, which is what it should have been all along."

The best place to watch these changes emerge is Chicago's Polish Triangle, a lively outdoor plaza bounded by Milwaukee and Ashland Avenues and Division Street.

Alongside the plaza, steps from its CTA Blue Line stop, you find an eleven-story residential high-rise that once would have been unthinkable: 1611 West Division, which has ninety-nine apartments, a bank branch, a coffee shop, and zero (yes, zero) tenant parking spaces. Local resident Scott Rappe, an architect, spearheaded efforts by the East Village Association, whose turf includes the Polish Triangle, to get a transit-oriented, mixed-use project at the site.

The unconventional design, led by Jon Heinert of Chicago's Wheeler Kearns Architects, consists of subtly folded facade planes and vertical panels (both transparent and opaque) that aim to counteract the building's squat, boxy mass. The seemingly random arrangement of the panels actually reflects an energy-saving layout that provides more windows for living spaces and fewer for bedrooms.

Even though the design remains chunky and two-dimensional, its quirky, kinetic composition contributes to the eclectic vitality of the Polish Triangle. The massing relates well to the classically trimmed former Home Bank & Trust Company building next door. Inside, the high-ceilinged apartments have an admirable simplicity.

Developed by Rob Buono and Paul Utigard, the year-old high-rise has been a financial success and an urban-design mold breaker, confounding skeptics who predicted that its lack of parking spaces would make it a financial flop.

In real estate, imitation is the sincerest form of flattery. Five more transit-oriented projects—1515 West Haddon Avenue, 3400 North Lincoln Avenue, 720 North LaSalle Street, 1237 North Milwaukee Avenue, and 2211 North Milwaukee—have passed the City Council, according to Peter Strazzabosco, a spokesman for the city's Department of Planning and Development. Another, at 1647 North Milwaukee, has been approved by the council's zoning committee, he said.

As in the suburbs, some neighbors have attacked transit-oriented plans as too tall and too dense, forcing developers to lop off height. Others predict the projects will accelerate gentrification. Still others have charged that the high-density projects will worsen traffic congestion and on-street parking shortages.

The changing face of the cityscape invariably produces such tensions, but the trend of transit-oriented development appears to be here to stay. That's good news for both architecture and urban design. It certainly beats the bad old days of "plop architecture."

Postscript: Transit-oriented developments have since flourished in Chicago, but with an equity-related catch: between 2016 and 2019, an estimated 90 percent of these projects were built in booming, largely white areas of the North and Northwest Sides, downtown, and the West Loop. Their landlords typically charged high rents, making it harder for low-income people, many of them Black and brown, to live near trains and take the "L" to work. In response to the lack of transit-oriented developments in struggling areas on the South and West Sides, the city in 2020 issued its first Equitable Transit-Oriented Development policy. "Without an equity lens on TOD," the policy said, "the benefits of transit—affordability, access to jobs, livable and walkable neighborhoods—end up accruing to those already with wealth and power." The policy began to bear fruit in 2021, when the Chicago Plan Commission approved a twelve-story, ninety-six-unit transit-oriented West Side development, next to the planed Damen Green Line station, that will include sixty-three low-income-housing units.

The Rise of Chicago's Super Loop: So Much Building, So Little Architecture

SEPTEMBER 9, 2017

A flock of construction cranes fills the sky. Downtown's population is soaring. The skyline is changing and so is the texture of city life.

A generation ago, West Madison Street was Chicago's Skid Row, home to winos and flophouses. It is now a chic strip of sushi joints, cycle studios, preschools, and a gourmet ice cream shop. But the architectural fare consists of bland apartment high-rises that draw complaints of monotony.

In River North, the old Ed Debevic's, a faux fifties diner best known for gum-snapping waiters and waitresses, is gone, replaced by a novel apartment tower whose cantilevered wedges of glass resemble a Jenga game in midstream. Yet that building is an anomaly amid the nondescript, form-follows-finance high-rises popping up elsewhere in the neighborhood.

So it goes in the Great Chicago Post-Recession Building Boom. A surge of tall buildings, the vast majority of them housing rental apartments, is creating a densely populated, urban core—call it the Super

Chicago high-rise construction: the downtown boomed, but creative architecture did not bloom. Photo by Lee Bey.

Loop—that's pushing far beyond the borders of the traditional down-town. But the Super Loop is patently unsuper in at least one respect: it lacks a new version of the technological and aesthetic innovations that made Chicago's reputation as the cradle of modern architecture.

As Mayor Rahm Emanuel prepares to host the second edition of a global architecture biennial that will exhibit cutting-edge design ideas, most of the new high-rises are based on tired commercial for-mulas. They are merely better versions of the exposed-concrete boxes, stacked atop parking garages, that have marred the blocks west of North Michigan Avenue. They make the leap, in other words, from awful to mediocre.

True, there are exceptions, like the under-construction Vista Tower, by Chicago architect Jeanne Gang, a staggered mountain of glass that will become the city's third-tallest building when it is completed in 2020. But the quality of a city's built environment is determined far more by the typical building than the exceptional one. And there are still too many typical buildings that are banal, graceless expressions of architect Cass Gilbert's immortal observation: a skyscraper "is a machine that makes the land pay."

Consider, though, the bright side of the building boom. For city lovers who believe that density, rather than sprawl, is the ideal path to cutting car use, saving energy, and halting the effects of climate change, these are, in many ways, the best of times.

Nearly 229,000 people now live in the central area roughly bounded by Lake Michigan on the east, the Stevenson Expressway on the south, Ashland Avenue on the west and North Avenue on the north, according to a population data analysis done for the *Tribune* by Chicago-based demographer Rob Paral.

That's an increase, since 1990, of more than 82,000—more than the population of north suburban Evanston. Three-quarters of the gain has occurred since 2000, as waves of high-rise residential construction—first primarily condominiums, then, after the recession, mainly rental apartments—remade the city's core.

Taken by itself, the Super Loop would form Illinois's second-largest city after the rest of Chicago, easily topping no. 2 Aurora, which has about 201,000 residents.

The population surge is mirrored (literally) in the skyline and its myriad glass-sheathed towers. Since 2010, developers here have erected more than seventy high-rises and started construction on at least another forty citywide—most of them in the Super Loop, according to figures compiled for the *Tribune* by the Chicago-based Council on Tall Buildings and Urban Habitat.

Because those figures are limited to structures that are at least twelve stories tall, they actually understate the building boom's impact. On the former site of Oprah Winfrey's Harpo Studios in the West Loop, for example, developer Sterling Bay is erecting a nine-story headquarters of brick, steel, and glass for McDonald's Corporation. It soars above the old meatpacking houses that give the area its grit and exemplifies, by virtue of its location west of the Kennedy Expressway, how downtown has spread far beyond its longtime borders.

The fast-growing West Loop is one of the city's three most active high-rise construction zones, along with River North and the South Loop. The Loop, home to Chicago's renowned early skyscrapers, ranks fourth.

Few would have predicted this burst nine years ago, when the Great Recession froze the city's skyline in place and left an embarrassing hole in the ground, still unfilled, on the construction site of the Santiago Calatrava–designed Chicago Spire, which was to be a two-thousand-foot-tall twisting condominium skyscraper.

As the economy strengthened, developers moved to capitalize on the demand for city living, particularly among members of the millennial generation. Telltale signs of their presence: stylish twenty-somethings walking tiny dogs, pushing baby strollers, and getting around on Divvy bikes.

"It's the reurbanization of America," said John Lahey, chairman of Solomon Cordwell Buenz, a Chicago-based firm that specializes in residential high-rises.

It's also a shift in the urban map: the once-frayed edges of downtown, previously home to the poor and working class, are now the glittering home of the affluent and well-educated. Rental rates, while less expensive than on the coasts, still leave many priced out.

It is also proving difficult to live up to the legacy of Chicago's past building booms, which in the 1880s produced pioneering steel-frame skyscrapers and in the 1960s and 1970s devised structural advances that allowed skyscrapers like the 108-story Willis Tower to rise to unprecedented heights. While the city's reputation as a wellspring of innovation derives chiefly from its tall office buildings, its residential towers, such as Ludwig Mies van der Rohe's structurally expressive high-rises at 860 and 880 North Lake Shore Drive, have been equally influential.

Very little in the pre-Recession building boom lived up to that high standard. West of North Michigan Avenue, in River North, it produced so many exposed-concrete eyesores—boxy residential high-rises stacked above blank-walled parking garages—that former mayor Richard M. Daley was forced to pledge in 2002 that there would be "no more ugly buildings."

The new wave of towers isn't ugly, but is it inspiring and innovative? Hardly.

To assess its impact, head to North Wells Street in River North, where three apartment high-rises have transformed an outpost of the fading car culture.

A Howard Johnson motel bit the dust to make way for the thirty-four-story Exhibit on Superior. A glitzy Planet Hollywood (later a Gino's East), originally adorned with fake metal versions of pink and green searchlights, has been replaced by the Gallery on Wells, a thirty-nine-story high-rise. And the theme-parky Ed Debevic's came down for the twenty-three-story 640 North Wells, the glassy eye-grabber that looks like a Jenga game.

Granted, some of these buildings introduce touches of pedestrian-oriented urbanity. Exhibit on Superior, for example, is set back from Wells, making room for greenery and restaurant seating that provides much-needed open space. Apartments wrap the perimeter of the tower's parking-garage podium, preventing the dreaded blank-walled look.

City officials have encouraged such changes with new regulations and design guidelines. "I think there have been quite a few lessons learned" from the pre-Recession building boom, said David Reifman, commissioner of the city's Department of Planning and Development.

Yet you can't legislate good design. The Gallery on Wells, by Loewenberg Architects, is essentially a reprise of the firm's elephantine towers set atop equally inelegant parking garages. It's just dressed up in brick, in a weak attempt to relate to the low-rise brick buildings of the nearby gallery district from which it takes its name.

Similarly, Exhibit on Superior, by bKL Architecture, is an ordinary box, albeit with more sophisticated brick tailoring. The 640 North Wells high-rise, by Hartshorne Plunkard Architecture, at least breaks out of the box with its eye-catching, if not entirely original, Jenga look. Such buildings are all the rage among architects today.

Alex Milanoski, development chair of the River North Residents Association, a citizens group that monitors new construction, hopes the increased density of the new towers will attract new businesses that fill empty storefronts in the area. But the new high-rises, in his view, have made this stretch of Wells "pretty cavernous."

"I appreciate the higher density," Milanoski said, "but it definitely needs to be done in a mindful manner."

City officials are trying to strike such a balance in the booming West Loop, which attracts scores of visitors to its Randolph Street restaurant row and Fulton Market district yet is struggling to retain the character that made those areas attractive in the first place.

Between 2000 and 2016, the West Loop's population surged to 10,860 from 4,409. The number of housing units skyrocketed to 6,408 from 2,111, while the number of households with children grew to 613 from 234. That's according to a recently issued draft of West Loop urban-design guidelines from the Department of Planning and Development. The guidelines call for avoiding abrupt changes in height and building taller, thinner towers to allow more sunlight to penetrate to street level.

Such an approach can make a significant difference, as illustrated by 1001 South State Street, a forty-story South Loop apartment high-rise by Solomon Cordwell Buenz.

In contrast to a blocky, brick-faced tower across the street, the building's exterior is broken into guitar-like curves, faced in glass and canted at an angle to provide residents with views of Willis Tower. Though 1001 South State's base contains a parking garage, it is sliced on a diagonal, opening up a ground-level seating area that brings a shot of street life to a section of the South Loop that lacks the vitality of River North and the West Loop.

Like 640 North Wells, 1001 South State tweaks the tower-on-a-parking-podium formula to good effect. But it remains a marginal shift, not a fundamental one. Elsewhere around the world, architects are exploring bold new paradigms.

In Milan, the wide balconies of a two-tower residential complex called the Vertical Forest contain hundreds of trees, as well as thousands of shrubs and plants. The design, by the Boeri Studio, is based on the concept of "biological architecture," which relies on a screen of vegetation, rather than conventional walls and mechanical systems, to filter sunlight, control temperatures, and save energy.

In Singapore, a residential complex called Reflections at Keppel Bay links pairs of curving towers with landscaped sky decks that are assembled at ground level and jacked into place at different levels between the high-rises. That design, by Studio Libeskind, integrates the decks into its multibuilding silhouette—in contrast to the new Chicago high-rises, where recreation decks are typically plopped atop parking-garage podiums.

While I haven't seen these buildings firsthand, it's clear that they open new doors with new thinking. Chicago architects are fully capable of such innovations, as they've shown in China and elsewhere around the world. Yet the city's architects often find their overseas clients more receptive to experimentation than the ones here.

As the 2017 Chicago Architecture Biennial prepares to open, the city occupies the unaccustomed position of boasting more innovation in the horizontal realm—evident in the vibrant landscapes of Millennium Park, the 606 trail, and the downtown Riverwalk—than in the vertical one. The growth of Chicago's Super Loop is a boon for the city. But its high-rise architecture, while an upgrade from the last building boom, remains underwhelming compared with the heights of technological and aesthetic innovation of the city's past.

Postscript: Following a trail blazed by other cities, Chicago's Department of Planning and Development in 2021 formed a new advisory group, the Committee on Design, and charged it with upholding Chicago's high architectural standards—or, at least, improving the dreadful designs turned out by hack architects. The twenty-four-member panel, which includes architects, artists, academics, and real estate professionals, reviews major development projects before they receive city approval. Yet its formation was met with hostility from developers,

A lone, masked visitor at Navy Pier: the coronavirus turned bustling downtowns into ghost towns. Photo by John J. Kim / *Chicago Tribune* / TCA.

who complained that it put an extra hurdle in an already-lengthy regulatory process, and alderman, who groused that it chipped away at their traditional power to control development in their wards.

The Things We Love about City Life—Public Transit, Urban Hustle—Are the Very Things That Put Us at Risk for COVID-19

MARCH 18, 2020

In Millennium Park, no one was reflected in the polished stainless-steel walls of the iconic *Cloud Gate* sculpture.

At Navy Pier, the promenade facing Lake Michigan was deserted except for a jogger in purple sweats and a woman pushing a baby carriage.

The ghost-town emptiness at two of Chicago's most popular attractions underscores how the fast-spreading coronavirus has temporarily turned an essential, much-praised feature of urban life—high population density—on its head.

By concentrating large numbers of people in a compact area, density allows them to walk, bike, or take transit to work. That saves energy. Density also energizes cities by pouring people—lots of people—into alluring public spaces. The Dutch architect Rem Koolhaas has celebrated Manhattan's hyperdensity, memorably labeling it the "culture of congestion."

But now, when physical proximity carries the risk of infection and spreading a pandemic, the virtue of urban density is suddenly a vice.

Shoving density off its pedestal is the mantra of "social distancing," which seeks to prevent the sick from coming in close contact with the healthy. The imperative to maintain social distancing is why Navy Pier is shuttered, and why the plaza around *Cloud Gate* has been cordoned off.

It's why Paris has closed the Eiffel Tower, why "talking" drones in Madrid are urging the public to stay home, why President Donald Trump urged Americans to limit gatherings to no more than ten people, and why Chicago felt so empty on a recent morning, with public schools closed for the first time because of the virus.

Yet the tension between density and distancing isn't limited to public spaces. These days, who wants to ride in packed elevator? Or work in one of those open-plan offices, without cubicles, where people are practically on top of one another?

The years after the Great Recession have been a boom time for central cities, with luxury apartment buildings and chic restaurants popping up like dandelions. Now, a house in the exurbs, far from the threat of infection and surrounded by dandelions, may look pretty good.

To be sure, cities aren't the only places where people come together in great numbers. All gathering places involve some risk, which is why the Illinois Department of Natural Resources just announced that it was closing state parks until further notice.

But cities like Chicago are all about dense concentrations of people, not only in skyscraper-filled downtowns but also in outlying neighborhoods packed with three-flats and graystones.

This density helps send enough customers to the shoe repairman or the corner coffee shop, enabling those businesses to be profitable. It also puts people in parks and playgrounds that provide a rare opportunity for those in a metropolitan area split on the fault lines of race and class to share the same space and to experience, if only fleetingly, their common humanity.

In this time of social distancing, social media at least gives us the chance to engage with others and reduce our isolation. But life isn't fully lived on a smartphone screen. It can't deliver the multisensory pleasures of the physical world—the sun, the breeze, the sensation of being in a large crowd, the excitement of engaging directly with a great work of art like *Cloud Gate*.

Yet for the foreseeable future, we have to bid such pleasures goodbye.

In the conflict between density and social distancing, social distancing should always win. Urban vitality is one of the great characteristics of our civilization, but it cannot take precedence over protecting human life.

The joys of density will return once this tragic chapter is over.

Postscript: Widespread vaccinations and masking would show that dense cities were not destined to fare worse than sprawling suburbs during the pandemic, but COVID-19 still had a severe impact on US downtowns, including Chicago's. With white-collar employees working remotely, offices were nearly empty and foot traffic dropped precipitously on major shopping streets. Restaurants that depended on the patronage of those employees closed. Conventions were canceled. Theaters and hotels were shuttered. Apartment rents declined. As Chicago tried to reopen in the summer of 2021, city leaders temporarily closed portions of major streets, including LaSalle Street, State Street, and North Michigan Avenue, and turned them into outdoor concert halls or opened them to restaurants and shops in an attempt to restore their prepandemic vitality. But with many companies continuing remote-work arrangements because of the Delta and Omicron variants of the virus, downtown's office-vacancy rate remained near record highs in late 2021.

PUBLIC SPACES: A BURST OF INNOVATION, WITH MIXED RESULTS ON EQUITY

Already renowned for its lakefront, Chicago in the 2010s added innovative open spaces that departed from, or reinvented, the tradition of parks that offer a pastoral respite from the harsh industrial city. In the postindustrial city, the former docks along the Chicago River became a vibrant new Riverwalk, while a former freight railroad line northwest of downtown was transformed into the 606 bike-and-pedestrian path. Elsewhere, existing open spaces were converted to new uses, including an immersive ecological boardwalk at the Lincoln Park Zoo and a vibrant children's playground at Maggie Daley Park. Yet most of these showcase public spaces were in the city's already-prosperous core or along its lakefront. And some of those in the neighborhoods sparked gentrification. It was no easy thing, urban planners found, to balance design excellence and equity.

Maggie Daley Park Is a Seed with Potential to Blossom

DECEMBER 14, 2014

At this awkward stage in its young life, the new Maggie Daley Park brings to mind a gangly teenager. Energetic? Absolutely. Graceful? Not yet.

It's strange to come upon this park, whose towering, tripod-shaped light masts resemble giant praying mantises. From a distance, it doesn't look much like a park at all. Indeed, when viewed from a passing car on Lake Shore Drive, its supersized wood fort is a bizarre departure from the Beaux-Arts grandeur of Grant Park.

But once you pierce the perimeter of the $60 million pleasure ground, witness its already joyful play areas, and realize that its trees need time (lots of time) to grow, I suspect it's going to grow on you.

A just-opened park occupies a limbo between idea and execution. It's a seed that may flower—or not. This one, with its serene landscapes, a delightful ice-skating ribbon, and a play zone packed with creative, kid-friendly features, offers ample reason for guarded optimism.

If all goes well, the fledgling park could combine with neighboring Millennium Park to provide Chicago with a powerful one-two punch: first, Millennium; then, Maggie. Even in its unfinished state, it can be deemed vastly superior to the Richard J. Daley Bicentennial Plaza, the lifeless, rigidly arranged mid-twentieth-century park it replaced.

Visitors to Millennium Park used to walk across Frank Gehry's

Maggie Daley Park: a skating loop, climbing walls, and a skyline backdrop—a respite in the city, not from the city. Photo by Lee Bey.

snaking BP Bridge, confront Daley Bicentennial's dull tableau, then turn around and head back from whence they came. Instead, when Maggie Daley Park opened, they streamed down the bridge's eastern end and kept on going, transforming it from a "somewhere to nowhere" bridge to a "somewhere to somewhere" span.

More than twenty-five acres in size and situated in Grant Park's northeast corner, the new park, like its predecessor, spreads across the roof of an underground parking garage. The old park became expendable when a waterproofing membrane below it had to be replaced to prevent structural damage to the garage. So Daley Bicentennial was torn off, trees and all, like a bad toupee. And a new park, meant to supplement the planned move of the Chicago Children's Museum to Grant Park from Navy Pier, was born.

Fortunately, the museum's ill-advised incursion into Grant Park's sacrosanct open space fell victim to the Great Recession, which hampered fundraising. But the bright idea of a park especially for children lived on, and it eventually was named for Chicago's late first lady, who died of breast cancer in 2011.

As designed for the Chicago Park District by Brooklyn-based landscape architect Michael Van Valkenburgh, Maggie Daley Park bears little resemblance to Daley Bicentennial—except for its ground-level air vents, which would have been too expensive to rebuild. When new plants grow, they will hide these minor eyesores.

Taking a cue from the coiling curves of Gehry's bridge, Van Valkenburgh has loosened Grant Park's confining corset of formal, French-inspired park design. Instead of aristocratic axes and level surfaces, he delivers meandering pathways and undulating topography. The result is an alluring hybrid of passive and active spaces.

Sylvan "lawn valleys," perfect for picnicking, slice a southwest-to-northeast diagonal that opens vistas of such nearby landmarks as Renzo Piano's Modern Wing at the Art Institute of Chicago. Van Valkenburgh lines the valleys with the light masts, which, in addition to casting a moonlike glow, are supposed to create a transition in scale between the skyscrapers that line the park and the people in it.

At this stage, the masts are a mixed blessing—clunky, but not entirely without merit.

Their legs stand astride the park's pathways, forming passages that give cadence to the pedestrian's movement. The masts also pick up on the modernist language of the Modern Wing and the monumental, lawn-spanning trellis of Gehry's Pritzker Pavilion. Once they're subsumed in a landscape of fully grown trees, which could take as long as twenty-five years, they might be OK.

A mature landscape also will enhance Maggie Daley Park's high-energy play spaces, such as the ice ribbon, which occupies the park's northwest quadrant. There, evergreens, once grown, will provide the illusion of skating through a forest. Trees might even veil the offending fort along Lake Shore Drive.

The ice ribbon, a dramatic departure from a typical rink, makes for fabulous people-watching as well as fun skating. On the park's opening day, people leaned over a concrete wall along upper Randolph Street to take in the action below. Benches line the ribbon, enhancing its identity as an urban theater. In the warm months, the ribbon will convert to a walking path with a different drama—sculpted climbing structures set in the middle of the skating loop.

In the park's southeast corner, a three-acre play garden delights with such features as the "Slide Crater," a sunken area rimmed by structures that kids climb before whooshing downward. Almost nothing in these areas, even the swing sets, is ordinary. Van Valkenburgh even reused trees from Daley Bicentennial and turned them into log benches.

Daley Bicentennial's Park District field house also got a nice freshening-up from Chicago architectural firm Valerio Dewalt Train, which brought lots of natural light—and an appropriately playful atmosphere—to the formerly drab facility.

While many small improvements are needed, such as posted maps to orient visitors, this much is clear: the Park District deserves credit for continuing Millennium Park's ambitious design agenda. And Van Valkenburgh gets kudos for shaping a democratic space that makes major strides in the ongoing effort to transform Grant Park into an everyday destination, not just a place that comes alive during the summer festivals.

In that spirit, Van Valkenburgh says, Maggie Daley Park is not an escape *from* the city, but an escape *in* the city.

It's certainly bold. And someday, it might be beautiful.

Postscript: Maggie Daley Park's popularity grew along with its landscape. As time passed, it joined with Millennium Park and the Art Institute's Modern Wing to form a new nexus of recreation and culture south of the Chicago River, where relatively few tourists had ventured before. New hotels and residential high-rises followed, particularly in the once-moribund stretch of Michigan Avenue south of the DuSable Bridge. The park's maturing landscape also began to conceal its initial awkwardness.

Chicago's Downtown Riverwalk: A New Phase of the City's "Second Lakefront" Takes Shape, a Model of Waterfront Urbanity

JUNE 5, 2015

Chicago's downtown Riverwalk keeps getting better and better.

The latest stretch of this already-popular public space consists of a monumental flight of stairs between Clark and LaSalle Streets that lets the city's energy spill down to the Chicago River's south bank.

Expect to see the people on those stairs sunning themselves, munching on their lunch, holding hands, and taking selfies. They'll be taking in the river's open-air theater of water, tour boats, and skyscrapers. And they'll be part of the play, too. People, after all, flock to public spaces to watch other people, not just the scenery.

Dubbed the River Theater, this new section of the Riverwalk follows two other just-opened blocks in what ultimately will be a $110 million extension of the prime public space. When three more blocks are completed next year, the project will create a continuous, 1¼-mile pedestrian-and-bike path reaching from Lake Michigan to Lake Street.

Yet the new sections don't repeat the ones that opened six years ago. They raise the Riverwalk to a higher level of urbanity, furthering its transformation from a hard-edged industrial waterfront to a welcoming postindustrial amenity.

The project is poised to become a signature achievement of Mayor Rahm Emanuel, who financed most of it with a federal loan.

Designed by the landscape architects of Watertown, MA–based Sasaki Associates and Chicago's Ross Barney Architects, the River-

The downtown Riverwalk's River Theater: how to turn industrial-era infrastructure into a splendid postindustrial amenity. Photo by Lee Bey.

walk is, at root, an engineering feat, one achieved in collaboration with structural engineers at Chicago's Alfred Benesch & Company.

To bring pedestrians closer to the water, decades-old dock platforms were lowered several feet. With the Coast Guard and the Army Corps of Engineers signing off, the shoreline was extended twenty-five feet into the river's roughly two-hundred-foot-wide channel. Landfill brought in by barge was dumped between new sheet piles and the existing shoreline. During construction, two of the barges sank.

For Sasaki's Gina Ford and Chicago architect Carol Ross Barney, the challenge posed by the Riverwalk's linear space was to create a satisfying mix of visual consistency and variety. They struck this balance in the new sections, improving upon a previous stretch of the public space that opened in 2009, when Richard M. Daley was mayor.

That stretch, chiefly designed by Barney's firm and running from east of the landmark DuSable Bridge to State Street, has an appropriately civic character, principally expressed by a monumental flight of stairs that descends from street level to Chicago's Vietnam Veterans Memorial. Thin stainless-steel railings lend the waterfront space a subtle nautical character.

The three new sections resemble a retail arcade, with plans calling for the Beaux-Arts arches lining Lower Wacker Drive to be filled with shops ranging from a winery to a Belgian-beer-and-fries joint. But the new stretch is not tawdry and overcommercialized. Nor does it descend to the level of theme-park cutesiness, even though its room-like outdoor spaces, bracketed by the muscular, burgundy-colored bridges across the river, are based on water-related themes.

The first and most successful of these rooms, known as the Marina Plaza, is located between State and Dearborn Streets. It comes with high-backed, elegantly detailed teak benches that offer prime spots from which to view Marina City's corncob-shaped towers and the boats docking beneath them. A ledge protruding from the back of the benches provides people standing behind the stylish seating with a convenient spot to place a laptop or a drink. The benches and precast-concrete planks near the river underscore the space's linearity. Thin maple trees should blaze with color come fall.

In a surprise for those accustomed to previous stretches of the Riverwalk that sit well above the water, steps in this section descend from the main path to nearly river level. There are no protective railings. Attorneys who think all public spaces should be designed to avoid lawsuits may hate this arrangement, but visitors seem to love it. On a recent warm day, some sat as close to the cool water as they could. Round life preservers will hang nearby in case anyone falls in.

The same intention—to connect to the water—informs the section of the Riverwalk between Dearborn and Clark Streets, which is called the Cove and was inspired by beach landscapes.

The Cove features a looser, less formal geometry than the Marina Plaza, epitomized by low-slung, rocklike benches where people sprawl like seals drying themselves in the sun. Kayaks and other small boats will be able to tie up here, just as larger boats will be able to dock (for an hourly fee) at the Marina Plaza. This sort of interactivity with the river is a good thing—as long as the big boats don't park forever and block views.

The soon-to-open River Theater, which will be able to seat more than 750 people, has a fitting formality, given its location along La-Salle, one of the most formal streets leading into the Loop. Here, the designers took the bold step of removing the balustrade separating Upper Wacker Drive from the flight of stairs leading down to the river. A beautifully detailed switchback ramp slicing through the stairs offers access to people with disabilities. Honey-locust trees provide shade. The space is grand, an imposing but inviting cliff.

The designers also deserve credit for their deft handling of the pathways that lead beneath the bridges and connect the Riverwalk's roomlike spaces. These paths, essentially U-shaped and extending into the river, seem like bridges unto themselves. They also serve the important function of slowing down cyclists, denying them a speed-encouraging straightaway. And they provide a shaded perch for fishermen.

Someday, advertising could blight the Riverwalk's pleasingly commercial-free character if the city is desperate for revenue to pay back its nearly $99 million federal loan.

For now, though, the latest stretch of the Riverwalk marks a significant step forward in achieving the ideal—originally voiced by Daley and vigorously adopted by Emanuel—of transforming the once-neglected downtown riverfront into a showcase public space that creates the equivalent of a second lakefront. Here, in bold strokes worthy of Daniel Burnham, Chicago is confirming and renewing its identity as a civilized metropolis.

Postscript: The Riverwalk turned out to be a major success, activating the once-dull waterfront. Its third phase, located between LaSalle and Lake Streets and also designed by Sasaki and Ross Barney, opened in 2016, while the renovation of an older stretch from Michigan Avenue to Lake Michigan was completed in 2020. The renovation, designed by architects Muller2 and landscape architects of the Site Design Group, endowed the older section with plazas and playful seating that harmonized with the new sections west of the DuSable Bridge. The combined projects created a great new public space and a new way to experience downtown. The Riverwalk became Chicago's "Low Line," a linear public space below street level where one simultaneously escapes from the city and gains a heightened awareness of it.

The 606, Two Years Later: As Its Landscape Grows, So Do Concerns about Displacement

JUNE 6, 2017

Growing in. With growing pains. That summarizes the state of the 606, Chicago's signature rails-to-trails project, two years after its much-ballyhooed opening.

"Growing in" alludes to the 606's nicely maturing, but not yet magical, landscape of 224 species of trees, shrubs, grasses, vines, bulbs, and herbaceous flowering plants known as forbs.

The "growing pains" are the 606's unintended consequences: rising rents and a wave of expensive new developments threaten to force out some of the very middle- and working-class people to whom the elevated park was supposed to deliver much-needed open space. Here and nationwide, such tensions have prompted open-space advocates to search for ways that future park plans can incorporate affordable housing and avoid displacement.

"In the past, parks were perceived exclusively as a net good," said Adrian Benepe, director of city park development at the Trust for Public Land, the San Francisco–based nonprofit that joined with the City of Chicago and the Chicago Park District to bring the 606 into being. "Now you do have some pushback. You have people saying: 'It's a net good until it displaces me.' And then it's a net bad."

The 606, a former freight line whose 2.7-mile-long Bloomingdale Trail wends its way through the Bucktown, Wicker Park, Humboldt Park, and Logan Square neighborhoods, is one of Mayor Rahm Emanuel's most visible public works and part of a trend, epitomized by New York's High Line, of turning outdated infrastructure into elevated parks.

The 606: an old freight line becomes a bike-and-pedestrian trail, but sparks gentrification and displacement. Photo by Lee Bey.

Like the urbane downtown Riverwalk, the $95 million project is part park and part transportation route—a sliver of land meant for walking, jogging, and biking as well as sitting, socializing, and contemplating. But unlike the Riverwalk, the plant-heavy trail through the North and Northwest Sides did not emerge camera-ready. Landscape architecture never does.

When a new building opens, "It will never look that good again," said Matthew Urbanski, a principal at Michael Van Valkenburgh Associates, which designed the 606. "The day of the opening of a landscape, it will never look worse—unless it's abused."

When the 606, which is named for Chicago's zip-code prefix, opened on the carefully selected day of June 6, 2015, it was almost embarrassingly bare. Trees and wooded plants had yet to grow. Sedges and prairie grasses hadn't been planted. Some spots had more pavement than plantings. "The 606: Is that all there is?" asked *Crain's Chicago Business*.

The picture looks very different today. Trees and shrubs are growing. Grasses are spreading. A pleasing variety of textures and colors combines with a consistent palette of soothing green. The amount of enclosure is increasing, courtesy of trembling aspens, thin oaks, and smoke trees that pop up from the planter boxes on the trail's expansive Humboldt Boulevard overlook.

As good as these moments are, the 606 still lacks the overall level of quality we've come to expect from the Van Valkenburgh firm, which designed Maggie Daley Park and is the landscape architect for the forthcoming Obama Presidential Center.

Some areas along the trail didn't get mesh fencing, allowing people and dogs to trample fragile grasses. Dirt patches blight the sides of the spiraling Exelon Observatory on the trail's west end. It clearly will take time for the 606 to fulfill its promise as a kind of plant gallery—a botanical array that unfolds as bikers, skateboarders, joggers, and others pass by.

Nonetheless, the 606 drew 1.3 million visitors last year, according to Vivian Garcia, the Chicago Park District's 606 manager. A sensible layout underlies the trail's popularity and growing horticultural allure.

Even though the 606 is just fourteen feet wide, it allows cyclists and people on foot to peacefully coexist. Walkers and joggers tend to stick to the blue rubberized paths on the trail's flanks. People unfamiliar with bike-path etiquette have learned to move out of the way when an approaching cyclist yells, "On your left!" When the trail opened, "A lot of people from the community did not know what that means," Garcia said.

But the 606 also has become a flashpoint for controversy, as developers tear down modest homes and apartment buildings alongside or near the trail and replace them with luxury apartments and expensive single-family homes.

Three alderman—Proco "Joe" Moreno (First), Roberto Maldonado (Twenty-Sixth), and Carlos Ramirez-Rosa (Thirty-Fifth)—recently introduced an ordinance that would increase the demolition fee for residential properties near the 606 and charge a deconversion fee when multiple-unit buildings are turned into single-family homes.

Benepe, of the Trust for Public Land, maintained that it's unfair to single out parks as the lone cause of displacement. For the 606, he said, the nonprofit convened a "working group in the neighborhood anticipating this exact issue," but it was powerless to build affordable housing in tandem with the trail.

The trust is trying to do better as it spurs the creation of urban parks elsewhere. Benepe cited its plan to build affordable housing next to a large park in Bozeman, Montana.

As the 606 shows, it is not enough to address the simple question of geographic equity—whether people on one side of town have access to the same level of amenities as those on the other side. A new park invariably changes real estate dynamics. The big question is whether park advocates and public officials should intervene—beforehand—on behalf of those most likely to be displaced.

"As benign as a park sounds, a park can have unintended consequences," Benepe said. "We need to anticipate those."

Postscript: In 2021, the City Council approved "anti-deconversion" ordinances that seek to preserve affordable housing and slow the gentrification that displaced many longtime middle- and working-class residents of neighborhoods along the 606 and in the Near Southwest Side's Pilsen district.

Rating Chicago's Latest Wave of Parks and Public Spaces by the Three "E"s: They're Better on Entertainment and Ecology than Equity

DECEMBER 24, 2019

Beginning with the triumphant opening of Millennium Park, in 2004, a remarkable collection of new public spaces has sprung up, like spring blossoms, in Chicago. It is hard to imagine the city today without that

Cloud Gate sculpture in Millennium Park: the epitome of parks as art and entertainment. Photo by Blair Kamin and Lee Bey.

park and other public spaces, among them Maggie Daley Park, the downtown Riverwalk, the 606 trail, and Northerly Island Park.

Created in the last fifteen years, these landscapes are new fixed points on our mental map. It's no exaggeration to say they've had a greater impact on daily life than knock-your-eyes-out buildings, like the seemingly teetering, tuning-fork-shaped 150 North Riverside office building, that have gone up in the same period. People don't just look at these public spaces. They use them, inhabit them, and make them their own.

But these are not ordinary parks if, by "park," we mean a serene oasis for escaping the pressures of urban life. Some place a new emphasis on visual spectacle and entertainment. Others devote attention to improving the habitat of plants and animals as well as humans—in short, to ecology.

Yet despite their worthy efforts to bring the natural and the humanmade into harmony, the new parks and public spaces have sometimes emerged as disruptive forces, accelerating gentrification and displacement. The 606, which cuts through four Northwest Side neighborhoods, is the prime culprit.

Boil this trend down to the three "E"s—entertainment, ecology, and equity—and the new open spaces score better on the first two "E"s than on the third.

The classic American parks of the great nineteenth-century landscape architect Frederick Law Olmsted, who designed Chicago's Jackson and Washington Parks as well as New York's Central Park, were a progressive response to the late nineteenth-century megatrends of urbanization and industrialization. They provided a naturalistic refuge from polluted air, filthy streets, and packed tenements.

But Olmsted's parks were less about preserving existing natural features than about bringing a range of soothing elements (humanmade meadows and meres, lagoons and rock formations) close to those who could not afford to travel to the country. The rigid city-street grid stopped at the edge of such parks, replaced by meandering pathways that intentionally slowed people and horses. Nature and the city were separated, not intertwined.

"That was that era's Green New Deal," said Harvard urban-design professor Alex Krieger, alluding to the proposed federal legislation that calls for dramatic steps to curb climate change and create high-paying jobs in clean-energy industries. "Their Green New Deal was sewage and clean water and tenement controls and bringing the healthfulness of nature into the city."

"Olmsted wished the city to recede," Krieger added. "We now wish the city to impress us and entertain us and make us more urbane and cosmopolitan."

Sally Chappell, author of the 2007 book *Chicago's Urban Nature: A Guide to the City's Architecture + Landscape*, sounded a similar note about the changing face of urban parkland: "The Olmsted approach and even some things thereafter were kind of 'the city versus nature,' 'nature versus the city.' Lately, we've been going with architecture and landscape conceived together as a conceptual whole."

These shifts are no accident. Chicago is a different city than it was during its industrial-age heyday of butchering hogs and stacking wheat. Fewer than one of every ten Chicagoans now work in manufacturing; in 1960, more than one of every three did. As a result, park designers feel less pressure to hold the city at bay. Many now recycle industrial infrastructure, like the muscular concrete retaining walls of the 606, to evoke a shared, if sentimentalized, "Big Shoulders" past.

The environmental movement has also had an impact. The Chicago River is far less polluted than it once was, even though you would be ill-advised to swim in it. "If you had the river you had in the 1970s, you wouldn't have a Riverwalk. No one would go there," said Carol Ross Barney, codesigner of the downtown promenade.

Digital technology has propelled further change, in ways both positive and negative. It enabled the complex curves of Millennium Park's glistening, skyline-reflecting *Cloud Gate*, by Anish Kapoor. Yet park designers struggle to satisfy the public's seemingly insatiable desire for Instagrammable moments without dumbing down their designs.

"The things we're driven by these days are just amazing," said Ernest Wong, who endowed the West Loop's Mary Bartelme Park with an Instagrammable moment of off-kilter stainless-steel arches.

What does all this add up to? A new paradigm for the urban park, for which Millennium Park is Exhibit A.

Built on tiered concrete decks atop working commuter-railroad yards and the roof of a below-grade parking garage, the park invites the city in. Its paths along Michigan Avenue extend the geometry of straight-lined Loop streets right into the park. Large-scale objects like *Cloud Gate* become focal points for crowds that see, smile, snap selfies, then move on. The trees that frame that park's outdoor rooms, if not quite an afterthought, are certainly not the main event.

This is the park as urban spectacle rather than as a soothing escape from the city. The adjoining Maggie Daley Park, with its delightful skating loop and out-of-the-ordinary children's playgrounds, extends the fun. The downtown Riverwalk, a series of outdoor rooms (some for sipping wine, others for fishing or lounging on monumental flights of stairs), provides its own menu of amusements.

"We don't need bathhouses (in parks) anymore. But you need something else. I think it's entertainment and I think it's open space," said Barney. "You need that type of relaxation. It's as much an expression of today as Olmsted's parks were expressions of their time."

If Millennium Park represents the park as a focal point for urban spectacle, a smaller, lesser-known project, the Nature Boardwalk at Lincoln Park Zoo, exemplifies a different impulse: the park as a hub of urban ecology.

Designed by Chicago architect Jeanne Gang and completed in 2010, the boardwalk revitalized Lincoln Park's South Pond, a picturesque but outdated Victorian-era water feature across which paddle boats once glided.

The redesign made the pond twenty feet deep instead of the original three feet and tore out its concrete edges, replacing them with a "soft edge" of grasses and greenery. The benefits are both practical and aesthetic: the pond's greater depth lets it hold more rainwater, alleviating pressure on the city's stormwater system and allowing the pond to serve as a true habitat. Fish can stay in the pond year-round instead of being removed in winter, as they were before. The plants clean the water. Migrating birds that come to the pond eat insects.

Instead of walking along a sterile concrete edge, visitors traversing the South Pond's boardwalk are enveloped by nature. The project serves a new zoo program that promotes the study of urban wildlife. Gang shaped an elegantly curving, wood-framed pavilion, now a much-photographed landmark, that provides an outdoor classroom for the program.

As Gang acknowledges, the boardwalk, like Olmsted's parks, is a "totally created" environment." But it's not just for aesthetic value and not solely for people. Instead, it's a place where the city and nature, people and plants, fruitfully coexist.

"We're not the only kind of life in cities," Gang said. While Chicago may be less industrial than it used to be, "We still crave and want the relationship to nature and green space and all the benefits it brings."

Nature Boardwalk at Lincoln Park Zoo: turning a picturesque Victorian pond into an immersive ecological experience. Photo by Lee Bey.

In the same spirit, at four-year-old Northerly Island Park, Gang turned an old and outmoded lakefront airport into a cluster of human-made hills, grasslands, a savanna of trees and shrubs, a lagoon, and other features, including walking and biking paths, that place visitors at a serene remove from city life. Located on the Lake Michigan Flyway, Northerly Island also serves as a buffer against the glass-walled buildings of downtown, which migrating birds often run into, killing themselves.

In this case, however, coexistence with nature hasn't been entirely successful. Because Northerly Island Park lacks offshore reefs and barrier islands that Gang proposed but the US Army Corps of Engineers and the Chicago Park District deemed too expensive, Lake Michigan's rising water levels have overwhelmed the park's eastern edge. That led the corps to remove a portion of the park's looping path, frustrating pedestrians, joggers, and cyclists.

Despite such flaws, the new parks and public spaces are a major achievement, continuing a tradition of leadership epitomized by Chicago's "City in a Garden" motto and Daniel Burnham's visionary Plan of Chicago. They creatively recycle aging industrial infrastructure and heal urban wounds inflicted during the postwar era, when planners like Robert Moses prioritized the needs of "car people" over "foot people," in the memorable phrasing of Jane Jacobs.

The trouble is location: most of these projects are along parts of the lakefront lined by affluent neighborhoods or in areas of Chicago that have gentrified or are gentrifying—in part due to the presence of these alluring public spaces. Their benefits need to be spread to other parts of the city, particularly the South and West Sides, which Mayor Lori Lightfoot and her chief planner, Maurice Cox, have targeted for revival.

Ideally, too, the new open spaces will be part of green networks, not isolated destinations, encouraging people of different races and classes to mix. That was Olmsted's goal: to break down economic stratification and forge bonds that would build a better democracy. Despite changing circumstances and enlightened new designs, his aim remains as relevant as ever.

TRANSIT AND INFRASTRUCTURE: AFTER A BUMPY START, SOLID ADVANCES

One of Mayor Rahm Emanuel's singular strengths was the attention he devoted to transit—not just getting riders from point A to point B, but upgrading the quality of the journey and using transit stations to encourage economic development and, with it, equity. That focus was visible in new or renovated Chicago Transit Authority stations, like the boldly revamped Ninety-Fifth Street station in the middle of the Dan Ryan Expressway, which made it easier for poor and working-class people to get to their jobs. Also in these years, attractive, albeit long-overdue, pedestrian bridges enhanced access to the South Side lakefront from nearby Black neighborhoods. During the pandemic, under Mayor Lori Lightfoot, Chicago went a step further in reinventing infrastructure, inaugurating a street-closure program that turned roads into public spaces shared by cyclists, pedestrians, and slow-moving vehicles. All of these enlightened efforts, however, were preceded by a high-profile stumble that happened early on Emanuel's watch.

Signs Uglify Our Beautiful Bridges

NOVEMBER 15, 2011

Tasteless. Clueless. And—thank God—only temporary.

The new Bank of America signs that were just plastered onto the Wabash Avenue Bridge represent a grotesque cheapening of the public realm. As the first products of Mayor Rahm Emanuel's shortsighted plan to raise $25 million by selling ads on all types of city property, they offer a nightmarish hint of what the plan might deliver: the uglification of the City Beautiful.

About the only good thing I can say about the astonishingly awkward display, which reminds me of a bleached white T-shirt layered atop a finely tailored gray suit, is that it will be gone in a few weeks.

What's next?

Flashing neon signs on the Water Tower?

A warehouse-store promotion on the Picasso?

A pork-and-beans ad on the Bean?

"I can't understand why, in a city supposedly so proud of its archi-

Bank of America signs on the Wabash Avenue Bridge: a graceless grab for revenue by the City of Chicago. Photo by Chris Walker / *Chicago Tribune* / TCA.

tecture, defacement of iconic structures would be allowed. Is corporate graffiti any different than tagger's work?" asked Jim Phillips, who runs the website chicagoloopbridges.com.

Yes, these are tough times, and Chicago is desperate for cash. "We want to find innovative ways to bring new revenues into the city to protect critical city services," said Kathleen Strand, a city spokeswoman.

But the public instinctively understands that marring civic icons in the name of balancing the books is a self-destructive act, one that sacrifices Chicago's matchless architectural identity. Indeed, more than 96 percent of those responding to an online *Tribune* poll gave the bridge ads a thumbs-down.

With its multitiered mansard roofs and chiseled limestone facades, the single-deck Wabash Avenue Bridge is an essential part of the Paris-on-the-Prairie tableau inspired by Daniel Burnham and Edward Bennett's 1909 Plan of Chicago. It's not as grand as the lavishly decorated, double-deck DuSable Bridge to the east, but it's mighty fine nonetheless.

A plaque on the bridge, which was designed by a team that included

Bennett, shows that the American Institute of Steel Construction in 1930 named it the most beautiful steel bridge. It is now part of the graceful urban sequence of the Chicago Riverwalk, which Daley got underway in 2009.

All the more ironic, then, that Daley, supposedly the great beautifier, was the one who floated the idea of allowing corporate advertising on downtown Chicago River bridge houses. Emanuel is now running with the idea, confident he can sell ad space on everything from city-owned buildings to garbage cans.

This is what that blinded-by-dollars thinking has given us: signs that look like they're touting the opening of a bank branch.

They appear to have been painted onto the limestone walls of the bridge houses, but the head of the company hired by the city to sell the sponsorship rights reports that the signs are vinyl, not paint. Tests were done to ensure that the signs would stick to the limestone but come off, said Philip Lynch, president and owner of Lincolnshire-based Fresh Picked Media.

Strand, the city spokeswoman, said the signs would not leave a residue, though she declined to say how much revenue the city will get from the ads.

Whether the material leaves a mark or not, it's hard to imagine a more visually insensitive treatment.

The seven banner-like signs—four on the south bridge house, three on its northern counterpart—don't blend in. Instead, their white backdrop offers a grating contrast to the subtle, refined elegance of the limestone-faced towers. The blue letters and the American flag–like B of A logo only add to the visual cacophony.

The deeper problem here is not corporate sponsorship; it's how the sponsor is recognized. There are more discreet ways to do this, like the unobtrusive, chiseled-in-stone recognitions of donors in Millennium Park. Sticking a corporate name on a beautiful object disparages both the object and the company whose name goes on it.

Yet few hurdles blocked the bank and the city from mauling the bridge. Unlike the DuSable Bridge, its Wabash counterpart is not an official city landmark protected from demolition or defacement. Last year, the City Council approved an ordinance giving the city and the Chicago Department of Transportation the authority to place signs, banners, posters, and other promotional materials on the bridge houses.

Though there has only been one taker so far, Strand foresees ads on more bridge houses.

"As you know, municipal marketing and sponsorship is a major initiative of the 2012 budget that is looking at a number of new opportunities that also include light boxes and garbage cans," she wrote in an email.

But there's a crucial difference between sticking a corporate logo on a garbage can and putting one on a priceless work of civic infrastructure. One is merely utilitarian. The other is civic art that expresses the city's highest aspirations and should not be subject to commercial clutter.

Your ad here?

No way. No how.

Postscript: After the temporary Bank of America signs were removed, Emanuel did not repeat the mistake of selling advertising space on Chicago River bridges. However, the city proceeded with selling advertising space at less prominent sites, like the inside of "L" stations.

First New Loop "L" Station in Twenty Years Creates Curvy Gateway to Millennium Park

AUGUST 30, 2017

Wave hello to the Loop's striking new elevated station. It's going to wave back.

The first new Loop elevated stop in twenty years, the $75 million Washington-Wabash station stands out because the canopies covering its passenger platforms appear to undulate, like the skeleton of a skinny reptile.

Opening after more than two years of noisy, traffic-halting construction, the festive station is meant to serve as a gateway to the crowd-pleasing spectacle of nearby Millennium Park. And an impressive gateway it is, though it seems to copy global architect and engineer Santiago Calatrava, whose works range from the poetic, birdlike addition to the Milwaukee Art Museum to the overblown, budget-busting World Trade Center transit hub.

Yet the designers, Chicago-based EXP, have created an authentic blend of form and function, not a superficial exercise in Calatrava Lite.

Chicago Transit Authority's Washington-Wabash station: Calatrava-esque curves that enliven the often-bleak world of public transit. Photo by Lee Bey.

Chicago Transit Authority riders are getting a clean-lined, visually dynamic transit station whose platform level feels remarkably open. The cityscape also benefits because the light and airy modernist design rejects the heavy-handed postmodernism of the elevated station at the Harold Washington Library Center, built in 1997 and the most recently erected Loop elevated stop before this one.

Located in the Jewelers Row historic district and funded by the federal government, the Washington-Wabash facility replaces two aging elevated stations—one at Madison and Wabash, already demolished; the other at Randolph and Wabash, which will soon close. The new station will serve the CTA's Brown, Green, Orange, Pink, and Purple Lines.

The practical challenges faced by the architects and their client, the Chicago Department of Transportation, were enormous. Elevated trains had to keep running while the Madison-Wabash station was torn down and the new one was built. The new station had to be erected around the existing train structure, which dates back to 1897 and needed shoring up.

But the bigger challenge was to accommodate riders' needs while satisfying Mayor Rahm Emanuel's directive that the new station be an iconic design. Too many recent buildings, especially Calatrava's World Trade Center transit hub, have been built on the flimsy foundations of grandiose thinking rather than growing organically from practical necessity. EXP's team, led by architect Tom Hoepf and structural engineer Shankar Nair, avoided this trap.

Take the canopies, which nearly cover the entire length of the 425-foot platforms—the only elevated station in the Loop to provide that much shelter. They don't just protect riders from the rain and snow. They endow the station with visual élan, making it a fitting entry for such icons as Millennium Park's glistening *Cloud Gate*.

The canopies' distinctive skeletal structure consists of ellipse-shaped steel columns that support a spinelike element running parallel to the platform edge. Angled steel ribs spring upward from the spine and hold up glass panes that sweep over the platforms.

None of the elements curves, but their varied lengths and angles create the illusion that the canopy undulates both from top to bottom and from side to side. Architects and artists call this sort of thing "trompe l'oeil" (fool the eye). LEDs at the tips of the ribs accentuate the illusion.

The architects say the curves express the movement of the CTA's trains, provide a lacy counterpoint to the Loop's muscular buildings, and anticipate the soft, naturalistic forms of Millennium Park and Lake Michigan. Such rhetorical justifications can be taken for what they are. It matters more that the station is designed to improve the experience of both the passenger and the passerby.

Great care was put into the laser-cut pickets that serve as guardrails for the station's platforms, mezzanine, and stairs. Their curves, which are real, echo the way the canopies seem to curve. In a nice riff, the pickets sheathing the station's elevator towers are cut so they portray the CTA's circular logo when viewed at an oblique angle. Throughout, functional elements like gutters, electrical wiring, and speakers are carefully tucked into the structure rather than clumsily applied.

The mezzanine, though cramped, is well-handled, with a corrugated-steel ceiling that doubles as a gutter. Backlit directional signs and mural-like glass walls that depict pedestrians also enliven this area of the station. Thin, poured-in-place concrete floors hang from handsomely detailed structural elements, eliminating the need for thick beams that would have obstructed truck traffic on Wabash.

The platforms are ten to thirteen feet wide, a major improvement on the seven-foot-six-inch width of the old stations. The canopies' upward tilt adds to the platform's feeling of expansiveness, while their glass ceilings admit daylight and open views of the sky and surrounding buildings.

One can quibble with the station's Calatrava-esque aesthetic—not because it's a copy, but because the canopies are a bit flouncy, a vestige of the pre–Great Recession era and its infatuation with architectural spectacle. Yet even though the station lacks the compelling directness of the West Loop's Morgan station by Chicago's Ross Barney Architects, it is a considerable achievement, one that brings Chicago's storied Loop fully into the twenty-first century.

Along the Dan Ryan, an Eye-Grabbing CTA Terminal Reaches beyond the Ordinary

FEBRUARY 10, 2019

You're likely to notice the CTA's new Ninety-Fifth Street terminal even if you never set foot inside. The ultralong building is an eye-grabber wedged in the middle of the busy Dan Ryan Expressway.

Bright red walls wrap around the terminal, seemingly holding together its disparate pieces like a taut ribbon. The entrances on the terminal's flanks jut outward at a sharp diagonal. Through color and shape, the building asserts itself amid the earsplitting rush of cars and trucks that whoosh through the Ryan's brutal concrete trench.

Chicago Transit Authority's Ninety-Fifth Street terminal: bold design uplifts underserved South Side neighborhoods. Photo by Lee Bey.

But a CTA terminal isn't a piece of sculpture. First and foremost, it has to satisfy the demands of function—and all the better if it combines that need with pleasing form. So how well does this building serve its twenty thousand daily rail and bus commuters and the scores of CTA, Pace, and Greyhound buses that use it on the average weekday?

Pretty well, it turns out.

The most expensive station project in CTA history, the $280 million terminal takes the passenger experience up several notches by attending to the architectural basics—good proportions, ample natural light, broad paths, and (for the most part) clear signage.

It's a solid effort, elevated by a dose of flair; the aforementioned red-ribbon treatment is a fitting flourish for the CTA's Red Line. Though the terminal does not match the aesthetic outcome of the finest new

CTA stations, it easily bests them when it comes to spreading the infrastructure wealth.

Designed by Chicago-based architects and engineers EXP and built with federal, state, and local funds, the terminal provides rapid-transit service to Chicago's Far South Side. Its surroundings are largely African American neighborhoods, some poor and plagued by violence. Infrastructure like this pays dividends beyond itself. Because good jobs often follow good transit facilities, the terminal could turn out to be a much-needed economic engine, not just a way to get around.

EXP, whose team was led by architect Tom Hoepf and engineer Shankar Nair, cleverly responded to the practical and aesthetic challenges posed by the sprawling complex.

Major track work takes into account the planned extension of the Red Line south to 130th Street. New bus bays were built, raising the total to twenty-six from the previous twelve. The station's once-cramped north terminal, dating from the 1960s and originally designed by Skidmore, Owings & Merrill, is being rebuilt, complete with high ceilings and skylights. A new south terminal accommodates CTA offices as well as passenger facilities.

A truss-supported pedestrian bridge over Ninety-Fifth Street connects the terminals and enables people to cross Ninety-Fifth without having to worry about getting hit by cars and buses. The bus bays that ring the terminals are arranged in a saw-toothed pattern that allows buses to pull up without blocking traffic. Large digital-display screens, like those in airports, let passengers know how long it will take for their bus to arrive and where the bus will be stopping.

Unfortunately, not all the signage, which was designed by the CTA's in-house customer-information team, is clear.

Some arrows directing people to bus bays point at a downward angle, suggesting that passengers need to go downstairs to get where they're going. What the arrows really mean is that passengers need to turn around—the stops are behind them.

Despite such faults and the fact that construction of the north terminal isn't yet complete, the overall design can already be deemed a success. That's because EXP conceived of the terminal as a local landmark as well as a regional transportation hub.

The ribbonlike red walls, which consist of thin aluminum panels, visually connect the north and south terminals, turning what could have been two static and separate buildings into a dynamic whole. The exterior's linear look echoes the motion of vehicles streaming down the highway.

Old-school modernists might fault the red-ribbon treatment because the aluminum panels are applied to the terminal rather than expressing its internal structure. But connecting a building to its context matters just as much as structural honesty.

Still-to-come features, including two public art pieces by Chicago native Theaster Gates, should reinforce such connections, both physically and culturally. The south terminal's upper level already contains one of Gates's displays—a pair of tapestries, made from strips of decommissioned fire hoses, which evoke the fire hoses that shot powerful jets of water at African American demonstrators during the civil rights movement. In the north terminal, a manned DJ booth will broadcast music over its public-address system that seeks to appeal to the station's users.

The prospect of sound animating space is exciting, suggesting that public art can be aural as well as visual and that it can express the identity of a community that transit serves. So there's more to come at the Ninety-Fifth Street terminal. But what's already there is worth celebrating, especially because the building spreads the benefits of well-designed infrastructure to an area that truly needs it.

Postscript: The DJ booth, called *AESOP (An Extended Song of Our People)* and billed by the CTA as the first of its kind, opened in 2019 and was a hit with riders, some of whom danced to the tunes that DJs broadcast. "Art has an ability to heal and be therapeutic and to reach the people of this community," Ronald Ale, program director for AESOP 95th, told WTTW–Channel 11. In 2021, US Secretary of Transportation Pete Buttigieg visited the station, citing the long-discussed extension of Chicago's Red Line south to 130th Street as a reason to support President Joe Biden's $1 trillion bipartisan infrastructure package. After Biden signed the bill, in late 2021, Gov. J. B. Pritzker and Mayor Lori Lightfoot said that extending the Red Line from Ninety-Fifth Street to 130th Street was among their top priorities for projects to be funded by the law.

Forty-First Street pedestrian bridge: at long last, improved South Side access to Lake Michigan. Photo by Lee Bey.

On Chicago's South Lakefront, a Curving Pedestrian Bridge over Lake Shore Drive Also Bends toward Justice

APRIL 26, 2019

A buoyant pedestrian bridge on Chicago's south lakefront isn't a structural masterpiece, but it still brings to mind a famous line of Martin Luther King Jr.: "The arc of the moral universe is long, but it bends toward justice."

The nearly complete $33 million bridge, which spans Lake Shore Drive and the railroad tracks at Forty-First Street, flaunts tilting arches, curving railings, and a deck shaped like a backward "S."

But its most important curves aren't literal. The bridge bends Chicago toward urban-planning justice by opening a welcoming, at times scintillating, path to the shoreline from predominantly African American neighborhoods to the west.

Two decades ago, in contrast, Chicago had a separate and unequal lakefront.

To the north, Lincoln Park, lined by mostly white and affluent neighborhoods, was easy to reach and packed with amenities—a zoo, ample restaurants and restrooms, museums, and more. In contrast, the South Side's Burnham Park, rimmed by neighborhoods that were mostly poor and Black, was a bleak and narrow expanse, littered with trash, broken glass, and a shattered sea wall.

Burnham Park also was difficult to reach on foot or by bike, because of the enormous barrier raised by Lake Shore Drive and railroad tracks that run parallel to the roadway. Pedestrian bridges built in the 1930s—ugly, rickety, and not accessible to those in wheelchairs—were better at repulsing people than encouraging them to cross.

In recent years, however, the Chicago Park District, the Chicago Department of Transportation, and other public agencies have poured hundreds of millions of dollars into Burnham Park.

New lake fill created more parkland. A marina, fishing piers, and beaches were added, along with a handsome suspension bridge at Thirty-Fifth Street. These upgrades, especially the bridges, have woven this once-isolated stretch of the lakefront and the adjoining North Kenwood and Oakland neighborhoods into the fabric of daily life.

The bridges "bring more people into the community. There are so many people who thought this community never existed," said area activist Shirley Newsome, who lives a block from the Forty-First Street span.

To be sure, the improvements and the construction of attractive homes have not shielded North Kenwood from the gun violence that has plagued Chicago's South and West Sides. In 2013, fifteen-year-old Hadiya Pendleton was shot to death in a park in the 4400 block of South Oakenwald Avenue, three blocks to the south.

Still, the sight of cyclists and pedestrians crossing the nearly 1,500-foot-long Forty-First Street span suggests that things are slowly changing for the better. "It's easy to just come outside and walk right across," said Destiny Brown, twenty-three, who lives in an eight-story building next door.

The bridge's designers—John Clark of the Chicago office of Cordo-

gan Clark & Associates and the Chicago office of AECOM, a global infrastructure specialist—were among the winners of a city-sponsored
competition for lakefront bridges whose outcome was announced all
the way back in 2005.

The need to wring funds out of Washington and Springfield delayed construction, angering residents and real estate developers who
counted on the bridge to be finished sooner. A companion span at
Forty-Third Street, also by Cordogan Clark and AECOM, only recently
won approval from the Chicago Plan Commission.

Both bridges exemplified a reaction against the spectacular yet
often-domineering spans of Zurich-based architect-engineer Santiago
Calatrava. In contrast to Calatrava's "bridge as object" approach, the
planned bridges promised to almost blend into the landscape. Renderings showed spans that echoed the gently curving walkways of the
lakefront's parks.

As built, the Forty-First Street Bridge both achieves and strays from
this ideal.

The most obvious departure is the bridge's color—a bright blue
that was pretty much forced on the designers because it is one of two
colors that the Chicago Department of Transportation, always concerned about ease of maintenance, uses to paint bridges. (The other
is burgundy.)

No matter how you rationalize the color—a match for the waters
of Lake Michigan, a hue that will fade into the sky—it's visually aggressive and verges on garish. It also accentuates the awkward meeting of the bridge's arches with the ground. An extra leg was needed to
support the arches, resulting in a stubby, wishbone-like arrangement.

Yet while the bridge is a less-than-perfect object, it succeeds as
a work of urban design and in elevating human experience.

The curving abutments leave ample room for a children's playground on the city side and mature trees on the lake side. Because the
bridge is essentially a giant ramp, people in wheelchairs and cyclists
can easily use it. At the same time, stairs at the bends of the bridge's
reverse "S" curve allow pedestrians to cut directly across the span.
That journey is a delight.

In contrast to the 1930s lakefront bridges, whose straight lines
made the walk over Lake Shore Drive and the railroad tracks intimi-

dating, the deck's curves create the perception of shorter—and thus more manageable—distances. The curves also lead you to wonder, as on a winding street, what's coming up around the bend.

The procession culminates at the curving arches, which are tilted to create openness to the sky. The arches and their steel cables frame spectacular views of the downtown skyline and the Forty-First Street Beach. Here, the bridge becomes a balcony, a belvedere, a viewing platform. It invites you to pause and ponder, taking a break from the business and busyness of everyday life. In doing so, the span becomes an extension of the leisurely landscape of the park, not just a route to it.

The designers deserve credit for small touches, like curving rail supports and arced light standards, that accentuate the overall design. And CDOT gets a tip of the hat for not cutting such details, as penny-pinching bureaucrats are wont to do.

A bridge, this project reminds us, can be much more than a way to surmount a barrier. It can invite shifts in the fate of neighborhoods, in our patterns of movement, and even perhaps in our region's long-standing divisions of race and class. The last feature may take generations to change, but what better way than a bridge to symbolize, and bring about, the closing of that gap?

Postscript: Even as construction proceeded on the Forty-Third Street Bridge, expected to be complete in late 2022, new problems plagued the one at Forty-First Street. Motorcycle gangs, loudly revving their engines, rode over the bridge at night. Partiers added to the clamor. Some launched fireworks from the bridge. Instead of improving their quality of life, neighbors said, the bridge was destroying it. They demanded more policing and surveillance cameras from the local alderman, Sophia King (Fourth).

Chicago's New "Shared Street" Tilts the Balance in Favor of Pedestrians, Cyclists, and Social Distancing, but It's Tinkering, not Structural Change

JUNE 11, 2020

Before the brutal killing of George Floyd, this column would have been a routine assessment of the first "shared street" Chicago has created

A "shared street" on Leland Avenue: the pandemic pushed Chicago to turn more streets into public spaces, not just drag strips for vehicles. Photo by Brian Cassella / *Chicago Tribune* / TCA.

in response to the coronavirus pandemic. Yet it would be foolish to write such a column now.

Foolish because Floyd died in public space and the protests against the police brutality that took his life have erupted in public space.

Foolish because many white Americans have begun to realize that the public space they experience is less dangerous than the public space navigated by Black Americans.

Foolish, in short, because urban design can't be stuffed into a neat little box, separate from the tumult that is shaking American society.

The racism that killed Floyd is deep-seated, systemic, and structural. The new shared street on Leland Avenue, which closes the road to through traffic and lets pedestrians and cyclists share the pavement with slow-moving vehicles, won't change that.

So let's keep this nice new wrinkle in perspective.

Providing welcome relief from pandemic-crowded sidewalks, the project is the latest manifestation of an urban-design movement that seeks to turn streets into something other than drag strips for vehicles. Chicago opened its first shared street on Argyle Street in Uptown in 2017.

Located in the North Side's Ravenswood neighborhood, the new shared street was opened late last month by Chicago's Department of Transportation—well after other US cities had responded to the pandemic with their own traffic-calming measures. City officials call it a temporary response to the pandemic rather than a permanent change.

The shared section of Leland extends a little more than a mile from the charming Lincoln Square shopping district on the west to Clark Street on the east. Most of the stretch is leafy, flanked by well-kept wood-frame and brick homes. The neighborhood is largely white.

The design elements are rudimentary. On the flanks of the shared street, fence-like barriers indicate that the road is only open to local traffic. Signs attached to orange drums in the middle of the street urge drivers to slow down and yield to pedestrians.

More signs, on light poles, tell people on foot or riding bikes to stay six feet apart and keep moving. A notice posted by Forty-Seventh Ward alderman Matt Martin adds that people shouldn't congregate and that they should wear masks.

"It's not a block party—It's a public health benefit," the alderman's sign says.

It's always interesting to see how simple changes like this encourage people to behave in new ways. Emboldened by the absence of through traffic, people walk and jog in the street. One of them, Esley Stahl, strolled with her almost two-year-old son Felix, who was pedaling a small blue toy car.

"It's easier to social distance," Stahl said, adding that the shared street frees her from worrying about getting hit by fast-moving runners, cyclists, and cars.

The vast majority of Leland's residents and those in the Forty-Seventh Ward like the arrangement, Josh Mark, Martin's director of infrastructure and development, told me.

Parents are less fearful that kids playing in the front yard will run into trouble on sidewalks that became crowded after Mayor Lori Lightfoot shut down the Lakefront Trail. Neighbors are sitting on their front porches to watch the passing parade.

"There's a sense of freedom and happiness that comes from being able to walk in the street," Mark said.

Delivery trucks and emergency vehicles are still allowed on the shared street, and people who live on Leland can park there. The arrangement doesn't need to be monitored by police, freeing them to go where they're needed.

Even so, a small number of residents have complained that some drivers don't slow down. Others are unhappy with parents who don't closely monitor children; the kids turn the revamped street into a playground. "People have to remember that this remains a road," Mark said.

People also should remember the smart planning goal set by Transportation Commissioner Gia Biagi: the shared street should be part of a broader network of bike paths and car-free getting around, not an isolated amenity.

Fortunately, that's still possible. The city plans to convert the shared-street stretch of Leland into a bike-friendly "greenway" that would link to an existing greenway east of Clark Street. Typically, the greenways have speed bumps and pavement markings that encourage drivers to slow down and share the road with bikes.

Even so, any enthusiasm about the shared-street initiative must be tempered by the reality, underscored by Floyd's death, that Chicago and other American cities face much deeper questions about their sharp divisions of race and class.

If the program only benefits gentrified neighborhoods on the North Side or fuels more gentrification citywide, it won't meet Mayor Lori Lightfoot's noble goal of promoting social equity. It will only prove itself worthy if, as city officials promise, it benefits struggling areas as well as those that are already thriving.

Shared streets should remind us of our shared destiny.

Postscript: The Chicago Department of Transportation opened more than thirteen miles of shared streets, located throughout the city, in 2020. Many were popular with residents, staying open for months. At some locations, however, pedestrians and cyclists complained about aggressive driving and a lack of police enforcement. The transportation department brought the shared-street program to new locations in 2021, while Choose Chicago, the city's tourism arm, expanded a successful 2020 pilot program for outdoor dining with an equity-focused initiative, Chicago Alfresco; it provided $2.3 million in grants to fifteen community groups, many on the South and West Sides. While the programs did not fundamentally alter Chicago's race and class divides, they still revealed the positive change that can occur when officials view streets as opportunities for place-making and community-building.

Part Three

ARCHITECTURE

ARE BUILDINGS GOOD CITIZENS?

Whether it is new or old, modest or monumental, every urban building can be measured with this yardstick: Is it a good citizen? If it's tall, does it etch a memorable silhouette on the skyline? If it's privately owned, does it solely serve the owner's right to make a profit, or does it also recognize his or her responsibility to give something to the city around it? It is not enough to evaluate buildings as aesthetic objects. They should be seen instead as contributors to—or detractors from—the shared space of the public realm.

Yet today, good architectural citizenship isn't as simple as it was in the 1980s, when postmodernists preached the virtues of buildings that address their urban context rather than stand in icy isolation. Good architectural citizenship now covers a vast array of technical, cultural, and social, as well as formal, concerns making the architect's job (and the critic's) as complex as a game of three-dimensional chess.

Because buildings and their construction produce nearly 40 percent of annual energy-related carbon-dioxide emissions, every building has an impact on the global project of reducing the impact of climate change. Likewise, every building can be viewed through the lens of whether it advances the goal of building a more livable, equitable city. If it's a redevelopment of public housing, how much low-income housing does it actually provide? If it's a museum, is it an egotistical expression of its patron or a people's palace? In Chicago and beyond,

such issues came to the fore during the post–Great Recession building boom—in museums and public buildings, in flagship stores, and,
most visibly, on the skyline.

TALL BUILDINGS: HIGHS AND LOWS

150 North Riverside May Look Like It's Teetering, but There's a Method to Its Madness

APRIL 20, 2017

You know a new building has struck a nerve when people give it nicknames like "the Tuning Fork" or "the Guillotine." Or when the building
appears alongside the likes of Willis Tower and Marina City on tour-
boat posters that tout a chance to see Chicago's architectural icons.

The just-opened high-rise at 150 North Riverside, a slope-bottomed
office tower along the Chicago River's South Branch, is the boldest,
most attention-getting Chicago skyscraper since Jeanne Gang's cur-
vaceous Aqua Tower made its much-praised debut in 2009. The new
high-rise's base, which flaunts sloping diagonal columns and glass
walls that look blade sharp, raises the question: Why did they do it
that way? People have been heard to wonder whether a strong puff of
wind might blow the high-rise over.

The most important question, though, centers on whether this fifty-
four-story high-rise is a genuine synthesis of structure, function, and
form, not just eye candy.

I'd say it meets that bar, though I wouldn't call it a masterpiece on
the level of the Bertrand Goldberg–designed Marina City. This building nonetheless yields real benefits: development of a prime riverfront
parcel once considered unbuildable, more than an acre of landscaped
open space, and a powerfully sculpted office tower that writes the latest chapter in the fabled Chicago story of successfully integrating engineering and architecture.

Like doctors and lawyers, architects are said to "practice," with each
commission yielding lessons that inform the next one. And so it is
here. The tower's architects, Chicago's Goettsch Partners, and their
structural engineers, Seattle-based Magnusson Klemencic Associates,
have played this game before, though not always to critical acclaim.

150 North Riverside: a slope-bottomed high-rise that flipped the skyscraper script and up-graded the riverfront. Photo by Lee Bey.

Forty years ago, Magnusson Klemencic collaborated with World Trade Center architect Minoru Yamasaki on Seattle's Rainier Tower, a willfully eccentric design that stacked office floors atop a flaring pedestal. The unusual look sparked nicknames—"the Golf Tee Building," "the Wine Glass," and "the Beaver Building"—as well as disparagement. In 1977, *New York Times* critic Paul Goldberger slammed the design for its "self-aggrandizing, narcissistic flamboyance."

More recently, Goettsch Partners completed an Abu Dhabi office and financial complex that contains four office buildings that, while shorter than 150 North Riverside, look much the same. Thus, when 150's design was unveiled, some accused the Goettsch firm of ripping off its own work. Yet the slope-bottomed Abu Dhabi buildings, like Seattle's Rainier Tower, arose from choice. The unusual form of 150 was birthed by necessity.

For decades, the two-acre site—bounded by the Chicago River's South Branch, the viaducts of Lake and Randolph Streets, and the beefy brick condo building at 165 North Canal Street—was a dusty pit. Trains rumbled through the parcel's western third, which was owned by Amtrak. More trains ran through the middle slice, owned by the City of Chicago. Anyone who wanted to build on the eastern third had to leave at least thirty feet for a city-mandated riverwalk.

Those constraints left veteran Chicago developer John O'Donnell, a former John Buck Company president who left to found Riverside Investment & Development, little room to maneuver. But the architects and engineers came up with an ingenious solution, pushing 150 North Riverside to the site's eastern side and developing a structural system that yields multiple benefits.

An extra-thick concrete elevator core braces the building against the potentially toppling force of the wind. On the upper floors, a steel frame attached to the core carries the weight of the building and its contents, or "gravity load," downward. But the frame's columns never reach the ground, as they do in a typical structure.

Instead, beneath the eighth floor, massive steel columns slope inward to the core. The core, in turn, brings the gravity load down to 110-foot-deep caissons that reach to bedrock. The design, which the engineers call a core-supported structure, leaves the railroad tracks undisturbed and makes room for the required riverwalk.

To further prevent the thin high-rise from being buffeted by the wind, the engineers inserted two enclosed concrete vaults near the building's top. The water in the vaults, which are called "tuned liquid dampers," is not for swimming. When the wind pushes the high-rise one way, the water sloshes the other way, damping wind-induced sway and eliminating the threat of rattling chandeliers and whitecaps in the toilets.

The beneficial outcome of these structural acrobatics is immediately evident when you approach 150 North Riverside. More than three-quarters of its site is open space, much of it attractively landscaped with swirling curves that play against the building's insistent right angles and diagonals. Chicago's Wolff Landscape Architecture handled that part of the project.

The open space appears user-friendly, with a tiered amphitheater along the river and a raised park built atop a seventy-two-space parking garage on the site's western side. Office workers going to and from nearby train stations already are streaming through the building's street-level plaza and riverwalk. Curving glass walls that extend outward from the high-rise are supposed to prevent downdrafts from knocking over pedestrians.

The broader benefit is that 150 North Riverside effectively joins with the landscaped plaza of the recently completed River Point office building, a fifty-two-story high-rise at 444 West Lake Street, to enhance the downtown riverfront's "confluence district" (so called because it lines the meeting, or confluence, of the Chicago River's north and south branches). In some ways, 150's plaza improves upon its River Point counterpart, which had to be raised several feet above street level to leave room for trains below. Here, in contrast, much of the plaza is right at ground level, enabling the smooth flow of pedestrians.

The abundant open space also works to the advantage of the building, serving as a forecourt for 150's boldly sculptural, yet structurally grounded, form. The design, by Goettsch Partners' Jim Goettsch and the firm's Joachim Schuessler, takes advantage of the highly visible riverfront site with a series of projections and setbacks that distinguish the building from an ordinary box and create multiple corner offices on each floor.

Undulating vertical fins lend much-needed texture to the broad east and west facades. The fins also suggest the ever-shifting character of the river's waters.

The building's strong verticality, emphasized by metal panels that express its structural columns and granite cladding that suggest its core, sets up a winning architectural conversation with the dominant horizontality of nearby River Point. The two make a fine early twenty-first-century pair.

Still, there are faults. The underside of 150's sloping eastern facade, where louvers for mechanical systems are plainly visible, looms awkwardly above the new riverwalk. The high-rise's north and south flanks appear flat when seen head-on. Most important, the building's structural innovations are largely limited to its base. Above the eighth floor, it is essentially a conventional office building. At Goldberg's Marina City, in contrast, the big structural idea—a circular core surrounded by modules that resemble the petals of a flower—informs the entire design, from pie-shaped apartments to balconies.

I'll give 150 North Riverside this much in comparison to Marina City: it's got a riverwalk (Marina City has none) and it meets the ground far more effectively, especially the high-ceilinged, glass-sheathed lobby that adorns its west side. This enclosure, which includes structural columns made of glass, is bracingly transparent, albeit somewhat cool. Yet it's warmed up by a digital light sculpture of thin vertical strips and a second-floor overlook that will contain a Starbucks. The Lake Street "L" train shoots by seating for the coffee shop, like a kinetic sculpture.

Perhaps 150 North Riverside is unnerving, challenging our desire for buildings that not only are stable but look stable. But I suspect you'll come to appreciate its gravity-defying design. This is a gutsy building, one that rises to the challenge of its site. Goettsch and O'Donnell should aim to equal or exceed it in a planned office tower across the river at 110 North Wacker Drive. What they've achieved at 150 is not perfect, but it's very good indeed—a persuasive blend of the pragmatic and the dramatic.

Postscript: When the fifty-six-story, 817-foot Bank of America Tower opened in 2020 at 110 North Wacker in 2020, it was Chicago's tallest office building in thirty years—and almost empty because of the pandemic. The design turned out to be an unsatisfying mix of reflective-glass banality and structural drama, the latter provided by three massive three-pronged structural elements ("tridents," the architects called them) at the tower's riverfront base. While the bold arrangement lent a feeling of expansiveness to the building's riverwalk, it was visually at odds with the rest of the ordinary high-rise and appeared precarious, as if the structural elements were a waiter's fingers balancing a stack of plates.

When Bad Things Happen to a Good Architect: The Saga of 151 North Franklin

JUNE 14, 2018

Something's definitely amiss when an architect arrives for an interview with an architecture critic, looks at his building, and says bluntly: "We did not design that box."

The architect, Chicago's John Ronan, has won acclaim for such subtly elegant works of modernism as the Poetry Foundation headquarters in River North. His latest design, 151 North Franklin, is his first office building. But given the rocky road it traveled from conception to completion, I wonder if it will be his last.

The talents Ronan displayed at the Poetry Foundation are fully evident at the base of 151 North Franklin. An outdoor room, carved into the lower portion of the high-rise, offers a civilized respite from downtown's bustle. After that enticing introduction, it's maddening to gaze up to 151 North Franklin's bland exterior walls, which lapse into could-be-anywhere, glass-box mediocrity.

The forces acting on this building reveal the ever-present tension in commercial architecture between the building and the budget, aesthetics and economics. Well-endowed institutions like the Poetry Foundation don't have to worry about profit and loss. But even very successful developers like Chicago's John Buck, the financial force behind 151 North Franklin, do.

"We had to work to the budget," Buck said when I asked about the crucial ways the finished building departs from Ronan's design. To illustrate the point, he recalled a warning he once issued to the late architect Philip Johnson.

151 North Franklin, also known as the CNA Center: where sticking to the budget led to high-rise banality. Photo by Lee Bey.

"The boss is the budget," Buck said.

Johnson's reply: "Mr. Buck, if you can't afford to build it, I'm out of work."

Despite that caution, the Johnson-designed 190 South LaSalle (now called the US Bank Building) turned out to be a lavish postmodern affair, flaunting a multigabled roof and a towering lobby with a vaulted gold-leaf ceiling. Such extravagance, typical in the 1980s, was enabled by the building's prestigious location and the high rents it commanded. But Franklin Street, a block west of the elevated tracks, is no LaSalle Street. A scruffy little Walgreens used to occupy the 151 North Franklin site, the northeast corner of Franklin and Randolph streets.

Ronan's design for the thirty-five-story speculative office building, whose lead tenants are insurer CNA and the Hinshaw & Culbertson law firm, was modest but promising. It called for a high-rise slab with a taut skin of whitish glass covering its underlying steel frame. Details like rounded corners, vertically proportioned panels of glass, and a ceramic frit pattern would have elevated the skin above the glass-box norm. But such refinements were ultimately discarded because, in Buck's view, the projected rents didn't justify the cost.

To meet the budget, Buck turned to Toronto-based Adamson Associates Architects, a firm that has worked on skyscrapers around the world. As 151 North Franklin's executive architect, Adamson was charged with turning Ronan's design into drawings that contractors would use to build the high-rise. Yet its attempt at striking a balance between form and finance, style and spreadsheets, falls flat.

The glass panels lack Ronan's fine proportions. The corners are right-angled, not round. The color is the typical sky-reflecting blue, not that arresting white. The surface of the glass is uniform, not fritted.

The heat-reflecting walls of this glass box surely will meet Chicago's tough energy code, but they fall far short of the city's high design standards. The only architectural feature of interest is an extra-large structural column, sheathed in polished metal, that carries the load borne by three upper-level columns to the ground to free up the outdoor room's open space. Yet even the head-turning column looked better in the original design.

Yawn.

Here, less really *is* a bore.

At least Buck and Adamson Associates faithfully carried out Ronan's vision for the base of 151 North Franklin.

The high-rise skillfully extends the public space of the neighboring 155 North Wacker office building, which has a forty-five-foot-tall arcade and pocket park along Randolph Street. Ronan takes this thread and weaves it into something special: the aforementioned outdoor room, which is about forty feet tall and raised above the sidewalk by small steps.

The room has a strong sense of enclosure, framed on one side by granite walls and, on the other, by the building's elevator core, which is clad in luminous panels of sandblasted mirror glass. Thin birch trees subdivide the room, giving it an intimate scale and a welcome touch of greenery. The granite walls, done in varying shades of gray that reflect three different finishes of the material, add further visual richness.

The room feels connected to the city but removed from it. The idea behind it is Ronan's rejection of what he calls "the spectacle of solitude"—skyscrapers that simultaneously dazzle you with their exotic silhouettes and rebuff you with their sharp division between inside and outside. He's also no fan of mausoleum-like lobbies that inspire awe rather than invite human interaction.

Unfortunately, due to an absence of edifying signs, passersby may not realize that 151 North Franklin's public space extends inside to an expansive multilevel lobby outfitted with conversation nooks, plus a grand stair that leads to a second-floor food kiosk and an outdoor terrace reachable by stair from the street. As long as security guards don't shoo people away, these spaces will provide an amenity for the public as well as office workers who like to move around rather than being chained to their desk.

A rooftop terrace, shielded from the wind by tall walls, offers views of nearby skyscrapers and another place where tenants can refresh themselves without leaving the building. Typical offices have ceiling heights of nine feet, six inches—six inches less than Ronan designed but still generous.

Ground-level graciousness saves 151 North Franklin from being a complete bust, but the project still represents a lost opportunity— and, for Ronan, a painful learning experience. In light of the skill and intelligence he's exhibited in previous work, I hope it won't be his last attempt at the high-wire act of the commercial high-rise.

A Celebrated New Yorker's New Chicago Tower: The Peak of Urban Luxury, not the Height of Skyscraper Style

JULY 31, 2019

Very tall and very thin, One Bennett Park looks from certain angles like the numeral one—a fitting resemblance, since it's a building for the 1 percent.

The sixty-nine condos cost anywhere from $1.87 million to $15 million. The most expensive of the 279 apartments, a four-bedroom with a private terrace, rents for (brace yourself) $22,500 a month.

Such stratospheric prices seem destined to make One Bennett Park a target for critics of income inequality, but it is undeniable that buildings like this keep popping up as more of the ultrawealthy choose to live in cities. We may not like them or wish they incorporated affordable housing, yet we ignore them at our peril.

So some basic questions are in order: Do these buildings add to, or detract from, the skyline? What do they deliver at street level to people of all income levels? Seen through that clarifying lens, One Bennett Park, the first Chicago high-rise of celebrated New York architect Robert A. M. Stern, can be judged a mixed bag.

This tradition-minded tower is easily superior to its mediocre modernist neighbors. But it doesn't match the skyline élan of the Art Deco and classically influenced skyscrapers that inspired it. It's a case study in how difficult it can be, even for the most skillful of architects, to transform the designs of the past into a compelling new synthesis.

Related Midwest developed the sixty-eight-story, 837-foot tower, which is located at 451 East Grand Avenue, a few blocks west of Navy Pier. As part of the deal that allowed Related to build to such heights, the developer remade a previously little-used public space next door. It's now an attractive, 1.95-acre privately owned park, designed by Michael Van Valkenburgh, that leavens the tower's formality with funky plantings, spongy blue-green play surfaces, and rustic play areas. But Stern's design, which was carried out by Chicago's GREC Architects, is the core of this enterprise.

One Bennett Park: no match for the setback skyscrapers that inspired it. Photo by Lee Bey.

Nattily dressed, often acerbic, and a prolific producer of books as well as buildings, Stern already has made an impact on Chicago and its suburbs. His previous commissions here include single-family houses on the North Shore as well as Chicago's ubiquitous bus shelters, a heavy-handed combination of classical design elements and industrial-age infrastructure. Architects, he is fond of saying, need to look backward in order to move forward. In that spirit, One Bennett Park's name honors the late Edward Bennett, Daniel Burnham's coauthor on the influential 1909 Plan of Chicago and a significant architect in his own right.

Given the skyscraper's jaw-dropping condo and apartment prices, it may seem hard to believe that Stern and Daniel Lobitz, a partner at his firm and his codesigner on the project, faced cost constraints. But they did, at least in comparison to Stern's best and best-known residential high-rise—15 Central Park West, a two-tower 2008 condo development off Manhattan's Central Park that cost nearly $1 billion and counts assorted CEOs, hedge-fund heads, and celebrities among its residents.

Reflecting Manhattan's supercharged real estate market, prices at 15 Central Park West are even higher than they are at One Bennett Park. That enabled Stern to clad the New York tower in Indiana limestone, a material widely admired for its texture, subtle coloring, and durability. At One Bennett, in contrast, projected sales per square foot only justified covering the bottom 50 feet of the tower in a Kansas limestone the architects selected for its visual warmth and rich veining. The rest is clad in less expensive (and less alluring) panels of precast concrete.

Using that lesser material on this prominent tower practically invites unflattering comparisons with some of Chicago's finest Art Deco skyscrapers—333 North Michigan Avenue, the Palmolive Building, and the Chicago Board of Trade. Those 1920s standard-setters are chiefly clad in Indiana limestone and benefit from the setback silhouettes, strong vertical lines, and elegant facade decoration that are hallmarks of the Art Deco style. A comparable level of quality infuses the grand New York hotel towers, like the Waldorf Astoria, that also influenced Stern's design.

Did Stern avoid the trap of producing an unsatisfactory imitation? Sometimes yes and sometimes no.

If nothing else, One Bennett Park is a civilized work of urban design. Owing to the presence of an underground garage beneath the aforementioned park, no ponderous parking-garage podium blights the cityscape. The tower comes straight down to the surrounding sidewalks and does much to enliven them with precisely honed, chamfered arcades of limestone as well as gracefully linear Art Deco decoration. Motor courts for the apartment and condo entrances (the former on the small street called Peshtigo Court, the latter on Grand) are a pleasure to behold even if you don't own a Rolls-Royce to pull into them.

Higher up, though, the architecture is a disappointment, and not simply because of the less-than-ideal materials.

While the broad outlines are solid—the tower's mountain-like massing, achieved by notched corners and setbacks, creates a kind of campanile for the Streeterville area west of Navy Pier—God is not in the details. Stacks of dark-metal window surrounds strive to create powerful vertical lines, but resemble skin blotches. Between the surrounds, precast-concrete panels bulge outward, a cosmetic visual trick. The overall effect is leaden instead of soaring, mannered rather than direct. While a certain amount of quirkiness is desirable in a residential high-rise, quirkiness is no substitute for quality.

The tower's west-facing crown, a stumpy reprise of 333 North Michigan's elegantly sculpted top, is equally underwhelming. You might think an enormous penthouse sits behind the double-height windows up there. Actually, the windows conceal mechanical equipment and a tuned liquid damper, or "slosh tank," that helps the tall, thin tower maintain equilibrium in the face of high winds.

While the vast majority of the public will never experience One Bennett Park's interior, it should be noted that Stern and his team have done superior, even exquisite, work there. A prime example occurs in the high-ceilinged condo lobby, which comes with elegant walnut paneling and granite portal surrounds. An airy, hanging installation by artist Tomás Saraceno, his first permanent work in Chicago, keeps the traditional design from feeling stodgy.

The same can be said for the condominiums, which occupy the forty-second to sixty-sixth floors; the apartments, which go from the fourth floor to the thirty-ninth; and separate amenity areas for the condos and apartments. Throughout One Bennett Park, Stern uses skills he honed designing single-family homes as well as his understanding of how affluent families in Chicago prefer to live.

You don't feel like you're in an anonymous high-rise when you encounter an elegant formal stairway that connects two amenity floors. The condos and apartments, like many Chicago homes today, have island kitchens that open to family rooms. They also have discrete window openings rather than continuous ribbons of windows, as in modernist buildings. The views are still extraordinary.

The amenities, like a saltwater pool and a "cordials room" where condo owners can have drinks with guests, offer the bells and whistles you expect with the high prices. You know you're in rare economic air when a Related Midwest executive refers to a stone-clad loggia, outfitted with grills, as "the cathedral of the barbecue."

Beautifully furnished and city friendly it may be, but as a skyline statement, One Bennett Park is a flawed transformation of tradition. How ironic that a tower notable for its sky-high prices winds up being an aesthetic let-down.

The Vista Tower, Now Chicago's Third-Tallest Building, Brings Stirring Curves and More to a Squared-Off Skyline

NOVEMBER 23, 2020

Chicago's nearly complete Vista Tower comes wrapped in superlatives—the city's third-tallest building and the world's tallest building designed by a woman—as well as seemingly curving, multicolored glass. But the hype would be meaningless if the $1 billion, 101-story tower didn't merit a more important distinction: it's a stirring work of skyline artistry.

Vista's architect, Jeanne Gang, already has given Chicago the eighty-seven-story Aqua Tower, whose spectacularly wavy balconies were inspired by the layered topography of limestone outcroppings along the Great Lakes. Vista, in contrast, appears as liquid as it is solid, as if the waters of Lake Michigan had burst upward and transformed themselves into fluid, undulating tiers of glass.

The tower represents a decisive break from the muscular, industrial-age modernism of Willis Tower and 875 North Michigan Avenue (the former John Hancock Center). And it doesn't simply show that women

St. Regis Chicago (originally Vista Tower): a striking sculptural presence that makes significant contributions to the public realm. Photo by Lee Bey.

can play the male-dominated skyscraper game. They can play it, literally and figuratively, at the highest levels.

Located on a multilevel riverfront site at 363 East Wacker Drive that belongs to the same Lakeshore East development as Aqua, Vista will house a 191-room hotel and 393 condominiums once it's complete. For now, as COVID-19 rages and office cubicles remain empty, the tower sends the upbeat message that downtown has a future, and it's not just for the 1 percent. Vista's ground-level amenities will benefit ordinary citizens as well as those who can afford the tower's condos, which start at around $1 million.

The lone fault comes on the eighty-third floor, which has been left empty to let Chicago's famous winds whip through. This so-called blow-through floor will reduce unnerving sway, but it disrupts the tower's upward sweep.

Beginning with internal frames of steel that allowed skyscrapers to reach new heights in the late nineteenth century, Chicago has long been a center of innovative architectural design. Yet the formulaic apartment high-rises of the current building boom demonstrate little interest in breaking out of the box.

As a result, many of the city's top architects have been exporting their best ideas to fast-growing parts of the world, like China, that are more receptive to innovation. Now, ironically, Chinese money has brought leading-edge design concepts back to Chicago. Vista's developers were China's Dalian Wanda Group and Chicago's Magellan Development Group.

Sharp-eyed observers have noted a similarity between Vista's suggestion of endless verticality and sculptor Constantin Brancusi's *Endless Column*, a Romanian war memorial whose stack of truncated pyramids symbolizes infinity and infinite sacrifice. But the Chicago tower—which Gang designed with Juliane Wolf, a principal at her Chicago-based firm of Studio Gang, and the architect of record, Chicago's bKL Architecture—is no copycat.

Unlike the single-columned Brancusi sculpture, Vista consists of three connected high-rises, or stems, the highest of which reaches 1,191 feet—a level topped in Chicago only by the 1,451-foot Willis Tower and the 1,389-foot Trump International Hotel & Tower.

The stems reflect Gang's desire to make the tower a good neighbor as well as an alluring object. Their underlying structure—concrete cores in the outer stems, linked by a spinelike wall in the middle one—frees the central stem to bridge over the ground. That opens the way for Vista's chief ground-level amenity: a well-lit, visually enticing passageway that leads from the handsome park at the center of Lakeshore East to the downtown Riverwalk, just to the north.

In another urban-design plus, Vista is turning what used to be the dull dead end of East Wacker into a small park, open to the public, that will overlook the river and Navy Pier. OLIN landscape architects of Philadelphia are handling that part of the project.

The tower also enlivens the continuous row of buildings, or "streetwall," of East Wacker, with a glass-walled projection, which the architects call "the cube." Among other uses, it will contain the hotel's restaurant and glow like a beacon, beckoning pedestrians from Michigan Avenue.

Vista's architecture is as persuasive as its urban design.

At Aqua, Gang began with small units—the curving concrete balconies, which captured views—and organized them into mesmerizing stacks. She follows a similar path at Vista, where her building block is a series of truncated pyramids, called "frustums," that create different floor sizes and form the building's stems

The stems grow in height from east to west, making an effective transition between the wide-open horizontality of the lakefront and the soaring verticality of downtown's skyscrapers. Following the angled path of East Wacker, the stems also are offset, giving the tower eight corners instead of four—a plus for the developers, who rely on panoramic views to sell condos.

It all adds up to a tower that does exactly what a skyscraper is supposed to do: appeal to the viewer at many different scales.

Seen from a distance, Vista's stepping silhouette recalls the pronounced setbacks of the Willis and Trump towers. Because it shifts from a broad base to a narrow top, it is very much a Chicago building—a powerful presence, unlike the freakishly thin, cigarette-shaped towers that rise from Manhattan's Billionaires' Row.

Viewed at closer range, Vista goes from the familiar to the spectacular, owing in part to an optical trick. The stems seem to curve in and out even though the structural columns on the tower's perimeter are, in fact, straight.

Gang creates that illusion with a steplike progression in which each column is placed five inches inward or outward from the one below it. It's a small move, but, multiplied hundreds of times, it equals the difference between a bland vertical stalk like the neighboring Aon Center and a dramatic sculptural form.

Two close-up views are particularly memorable. From the Lake Shore Drive Bridge over the Chicago River, Vista is a stunning presence, with deep shadows accentuating the curves of its three stems. Seen from South Lake Shore Drive around the Field Museum, the tower looks flatter but is still striking, rising directly ahead of the driver as Gang takes full advantage of its location on the same line, or axis, as the drive.

In a significant refinement, the glass exterior is sheathed in six types of energy-efficient, blue-green coating—darker for the smaller floors of the truncated pyramids, which should prevent them from overheating, and lighter for the larger floors, which are less vulnerable to solar heat gain.

Made in Germany, the multicolored glass will join with the curving exterior and low reflectivity to lessen the likelihood that migrating birds will crash into the tower. Fortunately, there is not a discernible difference in views from apartments with darker glass and those with lighter glass.

The overall result combines noble simplicity with a dynamism appropriate to the digital age. Vista is not fussy and backward-looking, like architect Robert A. M. Stern's One Bennett Park. And it's more emphatically vertical than Skidmore, Owings & Merrill's Trump Tower, whose setbacks resemble the stacks of a wedding cake.

But the blow-through floor, a double-height space at the tower's eighty-third level, is not ideal. The first of its kind in Chicago, it had to be added after wind-tunnel tests revealed that high winds could cause the tower to sway, making people inside uncomfortable or even sick.

From ground level, the blow-through floor looks strangely unfinished, a scar that interrupts the upward sweep of Vista's curves. Gang calls it a "focal point." I liken it to a hole in a forehead. Still, it's not a fatal flaw. The tower's form is strong enough to absorb it.

The interior is very much a work in progress. My tour included an eighty-fourth-floor penthouse, whose drop-dead views of the lakefront and skyline make it seem like a private observatory, as well as a forty-seventh-floor outdoor deck for residents, complete with a pool, that will keep Vista competitive in the amenity arms race fought by luxury towers.

There is one extraordinary interior space: the hotel's restaurant, which flaunts thirty-eight-foot ceilings and massive, dramatically canted concrete columns that are pulled back from the facade to maintain riverfront views. Metal window frames subdivide the cube's exterior into truncated pyramids, further breaking down the tower's scale.

Through such features and its ground-level amenities, Vista stands poised to become an active part of Chicago's daily life as well as a skyline symbol. It is one of Chicago's finest skyline giants—not as strong architecturally as the X-braced former Hancock Center, but still a great success. With its sleek curves and sophisticated environmental approach, it refreshes Chicago's historic role in tall-building design and charts bold new directions in skyscraper style.

Postscript: Days after this review appeared, the Magellan Development Group announced that the Vista Tower would be renamed the St. Regis Chicago, recognizing the chain that will operate the hotel in the tower's base. The announcement was the latest name change among Chicago's tallest towers. The skyscraper originally known as Sears Tower is now Willis Tower. Similarly, the John Hancock Center is 875 North Michigan Avenue, while the Standard Oil Building is the Aon Center. (Among the city's five-tallest buildings, only the Trump International Hotel & Tower has not been renamed.) The changes reinforce the notion that, when it comes to the names of Chicago's tallest towers, almost nothing is sacred and practically everything is for sale. In New York, in contrast, the Empire State and Chrysler Buildings retain their original names.

Fifty Years Later, Lake Point Tower Is a Singular Achievement—Let's Hope It Stays That Way

SEPTEMBER 20, 2018

It's Chicago's only high-rise east of Lake Shore Drive—dark, suavely curving, subtly reflective, a world unto itself whose impact extends far out into the world.

Lake Point Tower: a shoreline stunner that pushed Chicago to safeguard its lake-front. Photo by Lee Bey.

As Lake Point Tower, once the world's tallest all-residential high-rise, celebrates its fiftieth anniversary, it's an apt time to reflect on its legacy. The seventy-story condominium tower, which sits just west of Navy Pier at 505 North Lake Shore Drive, is both hero and villain, though it is more the former than the latter.

It is, by all accounts, a spectacular and rare object—a poetic expression of curves in a city that worships the right angle, as well as a vertical marker for the horizontal sweep of Navy Pier. There is no other skyscraper quite like it, though there are imitators, which is the sincerest form of real estate flattery.

Its three-winged floor plan helped inspire the design of the tallest building on Earth, Dubai's Burj Khalifa. Along with Marina City, it pioneered a new kind of downtown living at a time when Chicagoans were fleeing to the suburbs. Today's generation of apartment high-rises outfitted with rooftop terraces, complete with swimming pools and greenery, follows its sybaritic lead.

Yet five years after its 1968 opening, Chicago passed the Lakefront Protection Ordinance, which prevented further commercial construction from marring the city's shoreline. And now, the urban renaissance that Lake Point Tower helped to begin, and new attitudes about urban design, have made its self-contained character seem fortress-like, standoffish.

If this iconic condominium tower were not so beautifully designed, it might be widely reviled for hogging a piece of the lakefront and turning blank walls to the street.

But look at it from afar and it melts your heart, standing, as it does, in splendid isolation from the forest of skyscrapers across Lake Shore Drive. There's the city and there's the lake, as different as earth and water, and then there's this lovely thing that perfectly draws them together.

In 1967, as contractors put the finishing touches on Lake Point Tower's walls of glass and aluminum, the land to its west was filled with gritty factories, warehouses, silos, and docks. Along with surface-parking lots, they were what was left of an industrial park that began in 1857, when William Ogden, who had been Chicago's first mayor, established the Chicago Dock and Canal Company, with help from his lawyer Abraham Lincoln.

By the early 1960s, Ogden's successors could see that the future of this land lay in real estate development—specifically, a high-rise district of offices and apartments. To jump-start growth, Chicago Dock leased a choice piece of lakefront property to two young developers, William Hartnett and Charles Shaw. Their architects, George Schipporeit and John Heinrich, both in their thirties at the time of Lake Point Tower's 1965 groundbreaking, had studied at the Illinois Institute of Technology, where they were imbued with the less-is-more philosophy of the school's leader, Ludwig Mies van der Rohe.

People often wrongly assume that Schipporeit and Heinrich based Lake Point Tower on Mies's visionary but unbuilt 1921 plan for a triangular, glass-sheathed high-rise in Berlin. In fact, the architects initially conceived the skyscraper as a cross-shaped design, with four wings, not three.

To make the project fit the budget, the developers lopped off one of the proposed wings. That led the architects to work out a three-winged, purely curvilinear design that was further distinguished by its sleek, continuous surfaces—a "skin" architecture as opposed to the X-braced "bones" of the John Hancock Center. The difference between the final design and the original was the difference between poetry and prose.

"George [Schipporeit] told me several times that every night when he said his prayers, he thanked the Lord that the first one didn't get built," said Edward Windhorst, coauthor with Kevin Harrington of *Lake Point Tower: A Design History*.

As constructed, Lake Point Tower resembles a large-scale version of the Constantin Brancusi sculptures Schipporeit admired: a sensuous object atop a base—in this case, the tower sitting atop a multistory parking garage, or podium, whose roof was topped with a park designed by noted landscape architect Alfred Caldwell.

Schipporeit had worked for Mies, designing exterior "curtain walls" of glass and aluminum, so he knew how to put God in the details. The tower's elegant exterior walls of bronze-tinted glass and bronze-anodized aluminum drew from the vocabulary Mies brought to perfection at Manhattan's bronze-clad Seagram Building, of 1958.

The building's appearance and affluence (its isolated location has long made it a favored home for celebrities) both caused a stir. Some praised the way it took Mies's less-is-more language in a new direction. Others branded it a sellout departure from the modernist credo that architecture should serve the masses, not just the privileged. Lake Point Tower was talked about in the 1970s, Harrington said, as "the culmination or ruination of the modernist movement."

The tower's visual drama is not reserved for faraway vistas. Pulling up to the podium—the designers assumed that residents would drive, not walk—the visitor is greeted with a circular cutout that affords a view, straight up, to the tower's soaring curves.

The travertine-clad walls of the ground-floor lobby follow the understated Miesian manner. On the second floor are shops and offices, including businesses where you can get a vasectomy or have your nails done.

Outside the third floor is Caldwell's 2.5-acre Skyline Park, a green roof before anyone used that term. It's a private version of the landscape architect's renowned Lily Pool, in Lincoln Park, with layered limestone outcroppings lining its lagoon, an artificial waterfall, and, in a concession to modern tastes, a kidney-shaped swimming pool. Residents can gaze out from this artificial, but still compelling, wonderland at cars stuck in rush-hour traffic on Lake Shore Drive.

Not surprisingly, the 857 condominiums (the tower went condo in 1988) boast panoramic views that are especially prized during the annual Air and Water Show, when the Blue Angels zip by. "They go below you sometimes. You can see their eyeballs, practically," said Marcia Stanton, who lives on the fifty-first floor.

Ceilings are only eight feet high, which is substandard in today's condo market of nine- and even ten-foot ceilings, but the views of vast Lake Michigan compensate.

On the sixty-ninth-floor roof, railroad-like tracks guide an automatic window-washing machine around the tower. The views from up there are even more stunning—and they testify to the tower's disparate urban impacts.

By demonstrating that a residential high-rise far to the east of North Michigan Avenue could be profitable, Lake Point Tower encouraged Chicago Dock to clear the low-rise industrial buildings that remained on its land and make way for a new wave of high-rise apartments and offices.

The tower's influence also is evident in what you *don't* see from the rooftop: other high-rises east of Lake Shore Drive.

Even before the developers broke ground, in 1965, they asked Schipporeit and Heinrich to prepare plans for two more three-winged towers on land to the south. When the plans were made public, critics charged that two more giant high-rises would crowd the shoreline. That controversy—and the one surrounding the 1971 construction of the Lakeside Center at McCormick Place—led to the passage of the Lakefront Protection Ordinance, which banned any more commercial construction east of Lake Shore Drive.

But the most notable example of Lake Point Tower's impact can be found halfway around the world—in Dubai.

When Chicago architect Adrian Smith, then at Skidmore, Owings & Merrill, sought inspiration for the Burj Khalifa, he looked out from the window of the SOM offices at 224 South Michigan Avenue, glimpsed Lake Point Tower in the distance, and said to himself, "There's the prototype."

The tower's thin wings, which bring inhabitants close to the windows, proved an apt model for a supertall skyscraper containing a hotel and apartments. Views, after all, are what sells the units. The under-construction Jeddah Tower in Saudi Arabia, by Smith and Gordon Gill, which is supposed to be about 3,280 feet tall and replace the 2,717-foot Burj Khalifa as the world's tallest building, also uses the three-wing model.

That Lake Point Tower has had such broad influence testifies to Chicago's ongoing ability to export its architectural expertise. Yet in the city itself, the tower remains a singular achievement.

For the sake of the lakefront, let's hope it forever stays that way.

FLAGSHIP STORES, FROM FINE-GRAINED TO FLASHY

Flagship stores exist not just to sell the product, but to promote the brand. Not surprisingly, then, they typically eschew architectural understatement for conspicuous self-promotion. But if all stores strive to be showstopping, attention-getting "wow" buildings, the inevitable result is "every building for itself" architectural chaos. In Chicago during these years, new flagship stores for Apple and McDonald's rose above this pitfall, serving up quietly appealing designs that enlivened the public realm, albeit with varying degrees of success. Meanwhile, in north suburban Skokie, a new flagship for the Greenhouse cannabis company stuck with the architectural "wow" formula, largely to good effect.

Apple's New Flagship Store an Understated Gem on the Chicago River

OCTOBER 20, 2017

Chicago's new Apple store is thrillingly transparent, elegantly understated, and a major plus for the city's riverfront.

With its huge sheets of laminated glass and an ultrathin roof of lightweight carbon fiber, the store is simultaneously present and absent, there and not there. From North Michigan Avenue, you look through its glassy membrane and see the river's blue-green waters and passing tour boats. A plaza of tiered granite steps spills down to the riverfront.

And because there's no Apple logo on the roof—a kitschy move the computer giant considered and wisely rejected—the store, thank goodness, doesn't resemble an oversized laptop.

Even accounting for possible problems, like the glare that invaded a portion of the interior during a preview, the store is a gem, realizing the vision of the late Chicago architect Ludwig Mies van der Rohe for buildings that would be reduced to their essence—an architecture of "almost nothing."

Yet "almost nothing" does not come cheap.

Located in the Pioneer Court plaza at 401 North Michigan and fronting the Chicago River's north bank, the $27 million store cost an astounding $1,350 per square foot. Apple, which has a market capitalization of more than $800 billion, can easily foot that bill.

While there is no architectural revolution in this building, the latest in Apple's global rollout of new stores, it represents a skillful evolution of the company's architectural brand: a clean-lined, seemingly effortless modernism that suggests the precision and beauty of Apple's products. In location and quality, it's certainly an upgrade from the company's former Chicago flagship, a converted four-story building at 679 North Michigan that opened in 2003.

North Michigan Avenue Apple store: bracing transparency and a stepped plaza that formed an attractive gateway to the riverfront. Photo by Lee Bey.

The architects, London-based Foster + Partners, have produced such global landmarks as London's pickle-shaped 30 St. Mary Axe skyscraper, fondly nicknamed "the Gherkin," as well as Apple's ring-shaped, spaceship-like headquarters in Cupertino, California, which has drawn criticism for übersuburban isolation. Yet the partner in charge of the Chicago project, Stefan Behling, conceived of the store not as a stand-alone object, but as a landscape that would simultaneously respect and enliven a historic yet moribund stretch of riverfront.

The respect is evident in the store's low-slung profile and placement on the site's eastern end. That means it only minimally obstructs views of 401 North Michigan, the handsome modernist office high-rise to its east, and Tribune Tower, the neo-Gothic skyscraper to its north.

The injection of new life can be seen in the way the store reconfigures its environs.

Previously, a cliff-like Beaux-Arts wall separated Pioneer Court from the riverfront. To get from street level to the water, you had to gingerly make your way down a curving staircase. Once you arrived, you encountered a bleak expanse of pavement.

Today, the cliff and the stair have been replaced by a gently tiered outdoor plaza that provides a much-easier and more inviting transition between street level and the riverfront. (An elevator inside the store will provide access to those in wheelchairs.) In addition, the stairs form an amphitheater like the one on Chicago's downtown Riverwalk. Now it's up to Apple to book concerts and other programs lest the space become as dull as the river-level plaza at the nearby Trump International Hotel & Tower.

Whether or not that transpires, the store's transparency is a stunner, blowing away fears that Apple would block visual access to the riverfront. The building's sheets of ultraclear, low-iron glass—ten feet wide and ranging in height from fourteen to thirty-two feet—give new meaning to the word "see-through." At the corners, curving sheets of glass, which do not come cheap, make clear that the building isn't just another box.

There is muscle in the membrane. The thin sheets are laminated together like "glass plywood," Behling said, so they provide structural support. The main heavy lifting is done by the building's four interior columns—two thin columns of stainless steel and two much-thicker, steel-supported columns encased in Italian stone. They hold up the carbon-fiber roof, whose overhangs are supposed to offer cooling shade.

Apple's decision to jettison the rooftop logo was the right call. The logo made the building look cheesy, like a small product enlarged to giant scale. The logo was placed instead on one of the building's large interior columns, where it is easily visible to passersby.

The store's interior is equally compelling, not only because of its openness but also because relatively little of it is devoted to pushing product.

At street level, the visitor encounters a "genius gallery," a row of bleacher-like seats that overlooks a projection screen on the lower level. On the flanks, granite stairs lead down to what Apple calls a "forum," a meeting area with wood stools in front of the big screen. The sales floor, pleasantly column-free, occupies the underside of the genius gallery. There, one finds the familiar wood tables on which products are displayed and some new wrinkles, including smartly designed niches called "avenues," where you can buy things like earphones.

I like the way the plaza's tiered granite steps extend inside, a move that marks the latest chapter in the modernist tradition of blurring the distinction between interior and exterior. Still, questions abound.

There are no curtains or blinds, so glare may be a problem in the area immediately around the projection screen. And will birds unwittingly crash into the glassy exterior? The architects say no. In case you were wondering, they've also installed fine wires on the building's roof to discourage sea gulls from pooping on it.

The bigger issue has to do with the way Apple and its retail head, Angela Ahrendts, identify this and other new stores as "town squares." Critics, also noting the use of the words "forum" and "avenues," have accused the company of co-opting the language of public space. Apple's real mission, they say, is to sell products. In this view, features like the plaza have a hidden agenda: To encourage people to linger. And the longer they linger, the more they will buy.

But Chicago has a long tradition, dating back to the old Daily News Building at 400 West Madison Street of privately owned riverfront buildings that provide top-tier architecture and public space. Apple's new store extends and enriches that tradition, even though it's replete with unintended irony. The very company that has caused us to stare endlessly into our smartphones is now issuing an invitation to look up and come together in a shared space—its space. More than inside and outside are merging here. So are the civic and the commercial realms. It's the latest twist of the digital age.

Postscript: The architects' prediction that the glassy Apple store would not cause bird deaths turned out to be wildly inaccurate. Shortly after the store opened, members of the Chicago Bird Collision Monitors, a volunteer group that rescues migrating birds that collide with buildings, said they had found numerous dead birds outside the store. To prevent additional deaths, Apple announced it would dim the store's lights at night.

McDonald's New Flagship in River North: Not Ketchup Red or Mustard Yellow, but Green

AUGUST 9, 2018

Behold the new McDonald's flagship in Chicago!

This temple of the Big Mac is billed as a model of energy-saving architecture—sustainability! It's supposed to bring people together—community! It even aims to be visually subtle, which amounts to a revolution for a company whose stores, once decked out in ketchup red and mustard yellow, blighted America's highways and byways.

"I defy you to find another McDonald's on Earth as beautiful as this one," said downtown alderman Brendan Reilly (Forty-Second), at a press preview.

That's a lot of hype to live up to. But as good as the new flagship is, it doesn't always deliver.

The building, a white pavilion with pencil-thin steel columns, environmentally friendly timber, and an array of 1,062 rooftop solar panels, is architecturally adventurous—the antithesis of the supersized, retro McDonald's it replaced. Its airy, plant-showcasing interior is miles better than the artificial, plastic-heavy McDonald's of old. Yet the flagship's outdoor plaza isn't nearly as inviting as it should be. And its green credentials, while impressive, are undercut by the fact that it remains tied to the energy-wasting car culture.

I give this building, whose costs were largely shouldered by McDonald's rather than franchise owner Nick Karavites, an "A" for effort and a "B" for execution.

Holding down the block bounded by Ohio, Ontario, Clark, and La-Salle Streets, the McDonald's occupies a strange spot in Chicago—a place I once dubbed "the blurbs," for the way its blurs the line between authentic urban character and the tacky suburban strip. The

McDonald's flagship in River North: the fast-food giant embraced forward-looking architecture, but couldn't completely shake the energy-wasting car culture. Photo by Lee Bey.

original McDonald's on this site, a low-slung affair that opened in 1983, played a leading role in this visual cacophony.

Its interior display of rock 'n' roll memorabilia bestowed a sheen of glamour on the grubby business of serving up burgers and fries. Affectionately nicknamed "the Rock 'n' Roll McDonald's," it lasted until 2004, when it was demolished for an on-steroids version of the McDonald's that company mastermind Ray Kroc built in northwest suburban Des Plaines in 1955. The 2004 building and its massive Golden Arches meekly looked backward. The new one, with a commendable push from McDonald's CEO Steve Easterbrook, boldly looks forward.

The architect, Chicago's Carol Ross Barney, is widely recognized for her work on the Chicago Riverwalk, one of the city's finest new public spaces. It's less well known that Barney's eponymous firm assisted

London-based Foster + Partners on the design of Chicago's new Apple flagship store. Both flagships don't just aim to project a brand identity. They seek to give something back to the community in the form of usable public space—a fitting gesture for McDonald's, which recently moved its headquarters to the city's hip Fulton Market district from the sleepy confines of west suburban Oak Brook.

For Barney, the company's directive about "community" meant striking a new balance (for McDonald's) between cars and pedestrians. She sought to create an urban oasis where people could eat, drink, and meet. On the site's west side, she got McDonald's to cut the amount of parking by about one-third. She also increased the number of trees and shrubs and replaced ugly asphalt with permeable concrete pavers that cover the site like a gray rug, giving it the feel of a sophisticated outdoor plaza. Even the drive-through lanes have those pavers, making them resemble a "shared street," where pedestrians, cyclists, and drivers have equal claim to the road.

But the outdoor space disappoints, even though, admittedly, it's unfinished. In contrast to the Riverwalk, there aren't enough places to sit, apparently because local officials were concerned that homeless people would turn benches into makeshift beds. In addition, city regulations aimed at concealing ugly surface-parking lots required Barney to wrap much of the site with fencing and shrubs. This treatment forms a visual barrier that makes the new flagship less open and inviting.

The building itself, which occupies the site's east side, cleverly interprets McDonald's desire to associate itself with environmental sustainability. In contrast to the sign-plastered, decoration-slathered eyesores around it, it relies on the essentials of architecture, columns and beams, to convey its message. The result is a shade-providing, energy-producing structure—a "solar pergola," Barney calls it. Company executives expect it to meet at least 60 percent of the store's electricity needs.

Perhaps the pergola looks a little industrial. (Is it a factory or a mini power station?) It also will strike some observers as a rough-edged knockoff of the Art Institute of Chicago's elegant Modern Wing (Barney denies any influence). And you wonder how the open-to-the-elements structure will fare when brutal winter winds blow.

Still, the understated exterior, which has only six small versions of the McDonald's arches affixed to the structure, comes off well. The pergola draws together the store's disparate elements—the kitchen, the drive-through lanes, and a new dining area—into a visually unified whole. The impressive canopy, in keeping with the Chicago tradition of celebrating structure, has enough visual oomph to stand up to ever-larger buildings rising around it. And the dining area is a little jewel, a minimalist glass box that reveals the wood structure that helps support it.

Experienced from within, the dining zone is roomy and light-filled even though the 19,000-square-foot store is 20 percent smaller than the previous flagship and has one level of seating versus the old store's two. Enhancing its expansiveness is the obligatory "wow" feature—a hanging, glass-sheathed garden, set below the roof and filled with river birch trees. Cross-laminated timber, an advanced form of plywood that requires less energy to make than concrete or steel, supports the roof—reputedly, the first commercial use of the material in Chicago.

Barney worked on the interior with the Sydney firm of Landini Associates, which did a fine job on the appropriately modern furniture and legible layout. Like the exterior, the interior has a calm palette, consisting of cool grays and warm woods. Ketchup red is notably absent, though there are traces of mustard yellow.

The store is a showcase in McDonald's' effort to convert its roughly 14,000 US locations to an "experience of the future" model that features ordering kiosks, table service, and increasing use of the mobile app. With the store expected to use half the energy of a typical restaurant, McDonald's is seeking the highest level in the Leadership in Energy and Environmental Design ratings, platinum, for the project.

Some things don't change, though. About half the store's business comes from its drive-through lanes (in a typical McDonald's, that share can be 70 percent). So while the materials and building systems of the new McDonald's point to an environmentally enlightened future, its car-culture business model remains stuck in the past.

That inconsistency doesn't make the store an exercise in "greenwashing," an epithet cast at buildings that are better at presenting the image of reducing energy use than actually doing it. But it does show that architecture must adapt to slowly changing habits even as it points the way to new ones.

Hurdles abound on the road to eco-utopia.

Curaleaf (originally Greenhouse) cannabis dispensary in Skokie: farewell, homely old head-shop. Photo by Blair Kamin.

In Skokie, an Architecturally Arresting Pot Shop Reveals How Marijuana Has Gone Mainstream

AUGUST 16, 2020

Chicago and its suburbs have long been fertile ground for cultivating architectural superlatives. Now they're vying for a new one: the world's most visually arresting pot shop.

To say that the soon-to-open Greenhouse flagship cannabis dispensary in north suburban Skokie is startling would be an understatement. Amid the banality of a suburban commercial strip—the Old Orchard mall is across the street—a bright white, pleated facade sweeps across the building's front like a rising theater curtain.

The exuberant design is even more surprising when you realize that this is not a new building, but the renovation of an old one: a former Bank of America branch that, according to Skokie associate planner Mike Voitik, was a Maurice L. Rothschild & Company clothing store when it was built in 1956. Around 1971, after the building had been turned into a Vignola furniture store, it was a laughably bad example of the Colonial Revival style, complete with a cartoonish clock tower and weather vane.

How the times, our attitudes toward a once-illegal drug, and architecture, have changed.

As the *Tribune*'s Ally Marotti recently reported, sales of recreational marijuana have exceeded expectations since Illinois made them legal this year. The drug has moved out of the shadows and into the mainstream.

With dispensaries opening around the country, architects and designers are abandoning the cluttered look of hippie head shops for clean-lined interiors that have been compared to Apple stores, art galleries, and high-end ski lodges. But those are interiors, tucked into quiet facades. Now we have a dispensary that fairly trumpets its identity. It's no masterpiece, but its energy and presence are undeniable.

Designed by CT architects of Des Plaines, the roughly $3.5 million renovation is at its most striking at night, when a thin white LED light accents the lip of its curtain-like facade. But whether it's viewed at night or during the day, it's a head turner for drivers passing through the busy intersection of Skokie Boulevard and Old Orchard Road.

The architects, Peter Theodore and Stephen Coorlas, clearly were inspired by the fluid forms of the late Iraqi-born British architect Zaha Hadid, the first woman to win the Pritzker Architecture Prize. They also credit their client, Mitchell Kahn, cofounder of Chicago-based Grassroots, which owns the Greenhouse brand, for encouraging them to do something outside the box.

There is definitely no box here.

Handed the vacant Bank of America branch, the architects sheared off its faux peaked roof and gutted most of the interior. Yet they wisely retained a tall, light-emitting wall of steel and glass that faces the intersection, as well as flanking towers that now contain restrooms and other uses. Most important, they kept the building's curving geometry, though they used computer-aided design and digital fabrication techniques to give it an entirely new look.

The contractor, Chicago-based Pacific Construction, cut foam into hundreds of pieces of varying widths, lengths, and depths. They were arranged like a jigsaw puzzle, then covered with an acrylic-based finish that hides seams between the pieces and keeps out the rain. As the building took shape, the architects began to speak of it metaphorically, as if they were lifting the curtain on what once was an underground business. Thus, the building's theatrical facade.

But the metaphor is less important than the outcome: a jolt of creativity in a context where that quality is conspicuously lacking. Some may complain the building doesn't "fit in." Yet what's the point of replicating boring commercial design? Curving landscaping by the architects, which consists of stripes of blue slate and fescue grass, extends the building's dynamism beyond its facade.

The design also strikes a successful balance between projecting a sense of openness and maintaining security—no small thing in light of the fact that looters have recently struck several Chicago-area dispensaries. The tall steel-and-glass wall, for instance, is covered with films that make it both opaque and hard to break. Yet the building appears anything but fortresslike.

If there's a fault here, it's that the dazzling wall is essentially decorative. It's a stage set applied to the building behind it, not a true integration of form and function.

At the former Crate & Barrel flagship on Michigan Avenue, now the world's largest Starbucks, the big architectural move, a glass-enclosed corner cylinder, serves as both an entrance and a circulation route. At the dispensary, in contrast, the wall's archlike form suggests a grand gateway, but you actually enter the dispensary through a modest foyer off the parking lot.

Still, retail design is not forever, as the just-announced closing of the twenty-seven-year-old downtown Rainforest Cafe—and the loss of the hideous green frog on its roof—reminds us. The architects deserve credit for bold strokes, including the dispensary's interior, a two-level space that possesses far more visual oomph than a typical store.

The first floor features display cases filled with imitation versions of cannabis products (the real thing is kept in vaults) as well as a demonstration area (shades of Apple stores) where customers can learn how to do things like infuse their food with cannabis. Walk-up sales occur at a long counter. Customers go to the second floor, a mezzanine, to pick up preordered merchandise.

Smooth white walls that frame a curving staircase and the mezzanine's edge seem to float, extending inside the exterior's lighter-than-air appeal. The walls, which owe a debt to Frank Lloyd Wright's spiraling Guggenheim Museum in New York, also are likely to distract customers from the myriad security cameras that train an eye on them.

Even so, the interior lacks the refinement of a 2015 Chicago medical marijuana dispensary, Perimeter Architects' Dispensary 33 in the city's Andersonville neighborhood, which won a small-projects award from the Chicago chapter of the American Institute of Architects. Among that dispensary's signature features: specially cut white-oak counters that create an atmosphere that's healing, not sterile.

Nothing could be more different from the homely head shops of the past. For better or worse, pot has gone mainstream, and architects are both expressing and enabling what amounts to a major cultural change.

Postscript: In 2021, Massachusetts-based Curaleaf, a publicly traded company, purchased Grassroots, owner of the Skokie dispensary, for $830 million. Soon after, the Greenhouse signs came down, replaced by those touting Curaleaf.

MUSEUMS: REACTING AGAINST, AND REACHING BEYOND, "STARCHITECTURE"

As cities sought to duplicate the smashing 1997 opening of Frank Gehry's Guggenheim Museum in Bilbao, Spain, the museum building boom of the pre-Recession years offered an endless series of "look at me" designs. But things changed after 2008, not just due to the economic slowdown but also because digitally driven architectural pyrotechnics came to be seen as overheated and, in some cases, unnecessary. Just because the computer enabled architects to design wild, off-kilter shapes didn't mean they had to. A new restraint and respect for the old informed the renovation of Chicago's Museum of Contemporary Art, while the National Museum of African American History and Culture in Washington, DC, presented a bracing departure from the capital city's neoclassical temples, as well as a preview of Chicago's Obama Presidential Center. Along the city's lakefront,

First design for the Lucas Museum of Narrative Art: an out-of-place mountain for the horizontal expanse of the lakefront. Image credit: MAD Architects / Lucas Museum of Narrative Art.

however, self-indulgent architectural spectacle persisted as *Star Wars* creator George Lucas unveiled the design for a museum that would have wreaked havoc on the city's greatest public space.

George Lucas's Museum Proposal Is Needlessly Massive

NOVEMBER 6, 2014

I think I can explain the widespread public revulsion toward the just-released design for the Lucas Museum of Narrative Art. This isn't the typical shock of the new. People are mad because they instinctively get that this cartoonish mountain of a building would be glaringly out of place amid the horizontal sweep of Chicago's lakefront.

With its broad, uninterrupted vistas, Lake Michigan is Chicago's greatest natural asset—a sublime work of nature that never ceases to inspire with its vast swaths of sky and ever-changing waters. By civic custom, the buildings that rim the lake or reach into it, from the mighty temple of the Field Museum to the low-slung Navy Pier, hew to its overriding horizontality.

Which is why the mountain-like mass of the Lucas plan is so jarringly off-key—and why people are likening it to other vertical structures they despise, from nuclear cooling towers to the remade Soldier Field.

The plan represents a fumbled essay in "blob architecture," a school of design that uses computer modeling to achieve amorphous, amoeba-like buildings that defy conventional, right-angled geometry. Overly abstract and underdetailed, it looks, from some angles, like a giant lump.

Fortunately, the project is at an early, conceptual stage, and Mayor Rahm Emanuel pointedly has yet to embrace it. That leaves time for rethinking the building and its surroundings. A dose of restraint is in order for this showcase shoreline site. As we know from the polarizing case of Soldier Field, one person's bold vision is another's overwrought eyesore.

It is tempting to blame the plan's faults solely on the syndrome of the "starchitect" who zips around the globe so quickly that he lacks the time to grasp local nuances. But that would be unfair to Ma Yansong, the promising, thirty-nine-year-old Chinese architect whom *Star Wars* creator George Lucas picked for this plum job.

The underlying problem is that Lucas has saddled Ma with an overly ambitious program that calls for the museum to house everything but a re-creation of the fictional *Star Wars* bar habituated by freighter pilots, bounty hunters, alien misfits, and other dangerous characters.

In addition to galleries for Lucas's eclectic collection of paintings by artists like Norman Rockwell, *Star Wars* memorabilia, and digital art, the museum would contain archives, an education center, four movie theaters, and, atop all that, a circular restaurant and a halo-shaped observation deck. At four hundred thousand square feet, it would be more than four times the size of the one that Lucas tried and failed to build in San Francisco.

This is more than mission creep. It's "mission ooze," as *San Francisco Chronicle* urban-design critic John King tweeted. While Lucas has promised to pay for the building, which is projected to cost at least $300 million, and no charge is envisioned for the observation deck, the many other uses suggest a desire to maximize revenue. Whatever their raison d'être, they present Ma with a daunting challenge: how to cram all that stuff on the lakefront.

The architect's response is to stack the myriad elements on the seventeen-acre site's southern half and arrange them as a collection of bulbous peaks. Voilà—Mount Lucas!

This is the Temple of George, a monument to its patron rather than a modest addition to a democratic public space.

Ma compounds that mistake by proposing to sheathe his mountain in blocks of whitish-gray stone or a fancy form of concrete, not the sleek metal skins with which he's draped his previous museums. As his own renderings suggest, the outcome would be leaden and lumpy.

The narrow, deeply inset windows he'd slice into his mountain only add to its sense of impenetrability. They also have the unfortunate effect of evoking the leering, reptilian eyes of Jabba the Hutt, the fat, toad-like crime boss in the *Star Wars* saga.

Like the bloated Jabba, the building needs to be put on a diet—or rethought altogether.

In its present state, it's an abstract outline without convincing details, a representation of a city rather than the real thing. Lucas has conjured imaginary worlds that are more persuasive.

In real-world Chicago, the burden is on the filmmaker to demonstrate that he's enhancing the lakefront, not just luring tourists. And yet, the plan doesn't appear to transform the site's twelve acres of parking lots into new parkland, as city officials said it would. Emanuel even predicted that the project would complete Chicago's Museum Campus, the cluster of natural science museums consisting of the Field Museum, the Shedd Aquarium, and the Adler Planetarium.

Instead, the proposal, which discards promised underground parking and retains a two-level parking deck on the site's north half, looks to be giving us more "museum" than "campus." The project will add "significantly" to lakefront green space, the Lucas camp claims. But it offers no hard estimate to back up its assertion.

Plunk down Ma's mountain and you have an imposing row of five structures along South Lake Shore Drive—the Field Museum, Soldier Field, the aforementioned parking deck, the Lucas Museum, and the McCormick Place Lakeside Center. Their cumulative effect would be at war with one of the policies set out in the city's lakefront plan: "Maintain and enhance the predominantly landscaped, spacious, and continuous character of the lakeshore parks."

The ultimate issue is the site. Can the lakefront accommodate what

Lucas wants and can Lucas, in turn, enhance the city's shoreline? It may be that no reconciliation is possible, which may push Emanuel to offer the movie mogul another, less contentious, spot, like the former Michael Reese campus on Thirty-First Street.

For now, this much is clear: confronted by the prospect of a weird blob along the lakefront, it's time for Rahm to tell George: "Take Two."

Postscript: Lucas later unveiled detailed landscape plans for the museum, but refused to consider alternative sites, leading the advocacy group Friends of the Parks to challenge the proposal in court. The fight reached a turning point in 2016 when US District Judge John Darrah rejected the City of Chicago's motion to dismiss the group's lawsuit. Finding that the museum site was formerly submerged lake bottom that belonged to the State of Illinois, not the city, Darrah wrote that Friends of the Parks had made a plausible claim that the museum would violate the "public-trust doctrine." The purpose of the doctrine is "to police the legislature's disposition of public lands," Darrah explained, pointedly noting that state lawmakers can't relinquish control of such land "to satisfy a private interest." Frustrated by the prospect of a long-running court battle, Lucas withdrew the proposal and announced he would build the museum in Los Angeles. Also designed by Ma Yansong, it is scheduled to open in 2023.

MCA's Renovation Is No Hostile Takeover. It Reflects How Audiences Interact with Art and Each Other

SEPTEMBER 6, 2017

There are two ways to freshen an old museum: with a sledgehammer or a scalpel.

The sledgehammer approach imposes the will of the renovation architect on the original design. It is, in effect, a hostile takeover. In the scalpel method, the new updates and improves upon the old rather than overwhelming it. It makes a virtue out of not striving for attention-getting virtuosity.

In their modestly scaled $16 million renovation of the common spaces inside the Museum of Contemporary Art Chicago, Los Angeles architects Sharon Johnston and Mark Lee have wielded a scalpel with

Museum of Contemporary Art Chicago interior: warming up, but respecting, a chilly design. Photo by Kendall McCaughtery, Hall+Merrick Photographers.

admirable precision. Yet their revamp, which was done in cooperation with other designers, is anything but clinical.

Highlights include a ground-floor restaurant by the British painter Chris Ofili and a second-floor gathering space by the Mexican design studio Pedro y Juana. Both introduce much-needed warmth and color, and even elements of fantasy, to the MCA's coolly gridded rationalist interior. Multiple voices, the project suggests, can be as compelling as a single vision.

The new elements pay heed to how the museum-going experience has changed in the twenty-one years since the MCA opened its off-putting home by the late Berlin architect Josef Paul Kleihues ("about as inviting as a chancellery," I commented at the time). But they still manage to be deeply respectful of the Kleihues design—a surprise, given that the building's intimidating exterior might have invited a wholesale makeover.

The stolid five-story structure at 220 East Chicago Avenue was based on the traditional idea of the museum as a temple and treasure house. It was all symmetry and monumentality, fronted by a steep, intimidating flight of steps. The inside, though more appealing (especially its skylit, barrel-vaulted galleries), remained focused on the individual's passive and private contemplation of works of art. The design sought to be timeless rather than giving artists the opportunity to change it over time.

Madeleine Grynsztejn, the MCA's director since 2008, took a different tack. Research showed that museum audiences wanted more interaction with works of art and with each other. She also rejected the model of Frank Gehry's Guggenheim Museum Bilbao, whose 1997 debut triggered a wave of pre–Great Recession museums that trafficked in the often-false currency of architectural spectacle.

Instead, the MCA sought for the activities within the building, not an Instagram-ready architectural container, to drive its renovation. The fact that the project *was* a renovation, rather than an expansion (the default option for many museums today), itself projected a certain modesty.

In Johnston and Lee—joint artistic directors of the 2017 Chicago Architecture Biennial—the MCA selected architects perfectly suited to this approach. Their title for the biennial, "Make New History," suggests the value of a continuum that builds quietly on the past rather than indulging in radical ruptures. Their MCA renovation vividly demonstrates the idea's value.

The project, which remakes 12,000 square feet within the museum's 151,000-square-foot footprint, consists of a reconfigured ground floor on the museum's north side; a second-floor "engagement" space, called the Commons, on the museum's east side; and, directly above the Commons, a third-floor classroom and meeting space. A new, almond-shaped interior staircase in the museum's northeast corner leads directly from the remade ground floor to the Commons.

The staircase's configuration is the most obvious sign of the sensitivity Johnston and Lee have shown to Kleihues even as they have improved upon his original. It clearly pays homage to an elliptical, multilevel staircase in the museum's northwest corner that exemplified Kleihues's theory of "poetic rationalism."

Other elements also balance respect and change. Made of precisely honed acoustic plaster, the vaulted ceilings in a renovated ground-floor corridor evoke the sharp-edged barrel vaults in the MCA's top-floor galleries. They also create visual rhythms, comparable to those in an arcade, that join with the new staircase's elegant curves and the natural light that brightens it to lure you forward. The corridor, still lined by the museum's theater, is no longer a dead end.

The Ofili-designed restaurant, called Marisol and designed in cooperation with its chef, Chicago's Jason Hammel, is the focal point of the journey down the arcade. The restaurant features a secluded dining room, topped by a vaulted ceiling that frames a colorful mural depicting a fantastic sight—two human figures riding a beast over a red cave. The room is a hip crypt. Ofili's sinuous lines, which run from walls to windows, further the appealing fantasy.

The Commons represents a Chicago reprise for Pedro y Juana, the Mexico City studio founded by Ana Paula Ruiz Galindo and Mecky Reuss. Their temporary Randolph Street lobby in the Chicago Cultural Center, with its movable lamps and rocking chairs, was one of the delights of the 2015 Chicago Architecture Biennial. It's good to see the MCA draw on their talent.

They, too, have warmed up the Kleihues original with hanging "plant lamps" that evoke Mexican paper cutout art and introduce a note of greenery. A small stage, able to fold out of the wall like a Murphy bed, will allow for small-scale talks or performances in the Commons. In five years, Grynsztejn said, other designers will likely be invited to remake the space, furthering the MCA's goal of an evolving, artist-driven interior.

As a fan of high-ceilinged, handsomely proportioned interiors, I was disappointed to see the two-story restaurant at the back of the museum disappear to make way for the one-story Commons and the new classroom/meeting spaces above it. Yet the new elements largely retain the transparency of the museum's fifty-five-foot-tall atrium and promise to enliven that space with a view of human activity. That's a better sight than empty spectacle.

The National African American Museum Still Stirs the Soul—and Drops Hints of What to Expect at the Obama Presidential Center

JULY 11, 2018

The line to see the open casket that once held the tortured body of Emmett Till, the fourteen-year-old Chicagoan whose 1955 murder in Mississippi helped ignite the civil rights movement, is long and moves oh-so-slowly. But scores of visitors to the National Museum of African American History and Culture in Washington, DC, still queue up.

The visitors file by, paying their respects, as though they were at the South Side's Roberts Temple Church of God in Christ, where thousands gazed into this casket to see Till's mutilated face.

The display marks an emotional high point of the museum, which has drawn more than 3.5 million people since its 2016 opening. To venture through it is a charged experience, entirely different from a stroll through a decorous place like the National Portrait Gallery. Many visitors, particularly African Americans, bring a palpable intensity to the displays, lingering over them as though they were poring over a freshly discovered scrapbook of family photos.

Critics typically assess buildings before they open, without people in them. To visit after the inaugural hoopla, as I did during a recent family trip, may be the best way to determine whether a design has staying power. This one does, fusing architecture and exhibits into a powerful, provocative whole, one that drops hints about what visitors will experience in the museum tower of Chicago's Obama Presidential Center.

Louise Bernard, director of the Obama museum, was part of the design team that developed the exhibits at the acclaimed African American museum. And there are certain architectural similarities between it and the Obama museum tower—more about those in a moment.

National Museum of African American History and Culture: inclusive modernism that draws on diverse sources to tell a powerful story. Photo by Alan Karchmer.

In 2015, an illuminating Art Institute of Chicago exhibition about the African American museum's chief design architect, the Tanzanian-born, London-based David Adjaye, foreshadowed the building's success.

Adjaye, who collaborated on the project with the Freelon Group,

Davis Brody Bond, and SmithGroupJJR, practices a different kind of modernism than the steel-and-glass abstractions of Ludwig Mies van der Rohe. He wants his buildings to tell a story. To him, ornament is not a crime but a way to communicate. His buildings respect their surroundings but don't hesitate to challenge them with something new.

So it is with the African American museum, which rises along the National Mall, not far from the Washington Monument's iconic white obelisk.

I first saw the museum at night, a fleeting drive-by encounter that revealed how the design differs from its neoclassical neighbors. The museum isn't an opaque mass of marble. It's a reliquary of light, which shines through the bronze-colored filigree of aluminum that sheathes its stacked, crown-like tiers. The tiers seem to float above the museum's glass-sheathed, ground-level floor. The effect is beacon-like, a visual tease that makes you wonder what's inside.

The Obama Center's architects, Tod Williams and Billie Tsien, hope to achieve a similar effect, with screenlike walls of letters that symbolize Obama's ability to transform ordinary words into soaring rhetoric. Following Adjaye's template, they have crafted a design that emphasizes an ascending path, both physical and symbolic, that culminates with panoramic views.

Some critics have complained that the African American museum's three-tiered crown, which was inspired by a wood sculpture made by an early twentieth-century Yoruba artist, turns a dull brown when there's no sunlight to make the aluminum sparkle.

But on the bright day that I visited, the crown was a shimmery, patterned mix of browns and golds, like chain-mail fabric without the bling. Its ornamental panels, which pay tribute to decorative ironwork on buildings crafted by slaves and free African American artisans in cities like New Orleans, possessed a delicate beauty when viewed at close range. Just outside the south-facing entrance, people clustered in seats beneath a broad canopy that provides much-needed shade and evokes the social role that porches played in African American culture.

The exterior is a multicultural monument, expressing cultural diversity instead of concealing it beneath a cloak of orthodox neoclassicism or modernism.

Inside, the story of the African American experience unfolds in three searing belowground galleries that proceed chronologically from the Atlantic slave trade that began in the 1400s to the 2008 election of President Barack Obama. Above these galleries, but still underground, is an atrium, with an adjoining café and a theater named for Oprah Winfrey. The aboveground portion of the museum includes galleries devoted to such subjects as the African American experience in music, the military, and sports.

Throughout, the architecture subtly frames the narrative, as in the dark, low-ceilinged spaces, whose exhibits relate how Africans were abducted, enslaved, and shipped across the Atlantic. With the sound of water echoing in the background, occupying these spaces feels like being in the belly of a slave ship.

Even when you're released from this constricted environment, moving into a dramatic, high-ceilinged space that coincides with the founding of America, the mood is dark, the story focused on the paradox of a society that was founded on the ideal of liberty but still sanctioned slavery. A prevailing theme, presented pointedly but without rancor, is how Black labor helped build the benefits of white society.

Ramps lead up to the two other belowground galleries, one of which includes the moving display of Till's open casket. The ramps not only accommodate the movement of people with disabilities but also carve out vertical expanses that create anticipation for what's ahead. Above one of the ramps hangs an open-cockpit plane that the legendary Tuskegee Airmen used to train for combat in World War II.

The spatial drama continues on the upper floors, where visitors can gaze down canyon-like expanses to the building's atrium. Or they can look outside, through the filigree, to the Mall, the Washington Monument, and other landmarks.

Adjaye had audaciously promised a new perspective on those landmarks, raising the risk of great but unfulfilled expectations. Yet his design delivers. After journeying through the museum, we're invited to view these iconic structures—and the national narrative they symbolize—in a newly complex manner. We can see them, literally and figuratively, through an African American lens.

Here, in contrast to museums that dazzle us with a flashy shell that bears little relation to what's inside, the building and its exhibitions, the container and the contained, reinforce each other to tremendous effect.

The design stirs the soul and pricks the conscience.

PUBLIC BUILDINGS: THE BENEFITS—AND LIMITS—OF GOOD DESIGN

Public buildings have a special obligation to enhance the public realm, not just because they are funded by taxpayer dollars, but also because they are, at least theoretically, free of the economic pressures that lead some developers to strip designs to the bare minimum. "Theoretically" is the key word. Under former mayor Richard M. Daley, Chicago took a shortsighted, one-size-fits-all approach to public buildings that lowered costs but robbed neighborhoods of their distinctive sense of place. Mayor Rahm Emanuel wisely reversed Daley's policy, leading to outstanding projects like a Jeanne Gang–designed boathouse along the Chicago River. But the issue of equity still cast a shadow on such efforts and loomed over the remake of a North Side public-housing project where a private developer and two nonprofits handsomely restored Depression-era buildings, yet the number of public-housing units fell dramatically.

Chinatown Library Breaks the Cookie-Cutter Mold and Builds Bonds of Community

SEPTEMBER 7, 2015

After years of building cookie-cutter public libraries that failed to live up to Chicago's reputation as the first city of American architecture, the city has finally broken the mold with an elegant new branch in Chinatown.

This rounded triangle of steel and glass, its exterior lined with bronze-colored aluminum fins, is everything its banal, prototype-based predecessors are not: tailored to its physical surroundings and cultural context; a vessel for stirring spaces and abundant natural light; functional and efficient but also inspiring.

Public buildings can be as innovative and memorable as private ones, this one reminds us. And they don't have to break the bank.

Chicago Public Library's Chinatown branch: tailored to its physical surroundings and cultural context. Photo by Lee Bey.

The two-story, $19.1 million branch of the Chicago Public Library at 2100 South Wentworth Avenue has been attracting about 1,500 people a day since it opened, according to its managers. That's more than a twofold increase over the average daily attendance at its former home, an aging, overcrowded branch at 2353 South Wentworth.

The numbers tell only part of the story. Patrons seem to love the building, from a first-floor children's area that encourages active learning to upstairs reading areas that offer prime views of the downtown skyline.

"I get lots of thumbs up," said Brandy Morrill, the branch's first assistant, explaining that many Chinese-speaking patrons use that gesture, rather than English words, to convey their appreciation.

The library's distinctive form arose from a distinctive process that departed from past practices.

Under former mayor Richard M. Daley, the city used prototype designs for libraries, police stations, and other public buildings. Officials argued that the standardized plans saved money and increased efficiency. But the prototypes resulted in a stultifying sameness.

Now there's an alternative, backed by Mayor Rahm Emanuel.

Instead of ordering up a conventional rectangular library, which would have been out of place on the oddly shaped site, Chicago Public Library Commissioner Brian Bannon invited competing teams of architects and builders to think anew.

The winning "design-build" team consisted of the Chicago office of architects Skidmore, Owings & Merrill and the Chicago office of the Darien-based Wight & Company, which executed the Skidmore design. While the need to hold down costs compromised certain details, the overall plan by Skidmore design partner Brian Lee was strong enough to survive these trims.

Lee's key idea transformed the rectangular floor plan of the prototype libraries into something closer to a circle. That makes for less perimeter wall, reducing costs. Corridor space is minimized. Natural light entering one side of the glassy building can easily make its way to the other side. A central atrium serves as a flexible space for reading, exhibitions, and receptions.

Fortuitously, this hole-in-the-doughnut diagram subtly evokes the layout of traditional Chinese houses, which wrap around a courtyard. It also cost only about 5 percent more than a comparable prototype, according to the Public Building Commission of Chicago, which oversaw the library's construction.

But such economies would be meaningless if the library didn't play another, easily overlooked role: upgrading the cityscape with a memorable design.

The shape, scale, and articulation of the exterior separate the branch from the ordinary, squared-off commercial buildings around it. The bronze-colored fins bring much-needed visual warmth and delicacy to the cool walls of steel and glass. They also act as sunscreens, reducing both energy costs for the city and distracting brightness for users.

In another plus, the library's glass walls reveal the bones—in this case, white-painted steel columns and diagonal braces—that hold the building up. This X-ray look hews to the Chicago tradition of revealing and celebrating a building's structure.

Granted, there are faults. In daylight hours, the tinted walls are less transparent than Lee wanted, undercutting the library's ability to express activities inside. Even so, the library has a strong civic presence. You wouldn't mistake it for a chain store, as you would its cookie-cutter predecessors. And things get even better inside.

The two-story atrium, topped by a circular skylight and flaunting a dynamic curving staircase, is further enlivened by a brightly colored CJ Hungerman mural. Showstopping but not over-the-top, the space offers a refreshing change from the grim entry hall of Chicago's main library, the Harold Washington Library Center.

At the Washington library, only the Winter Garden on the building's top floor is bathed in natural light. In Chinatown, by contrast, natural light is everywhere, and the atrium, outfitted with chairs and other furniture, feels like an indoor piazza.

In addition to breaking from the tomb-like libraries of old, the spaces that revolve around the atrium appear to function well. In the children's area, designed to encourage interaction, kids romp through openings in undulating bookshelves or gather in a semi-circular story-telling area. Upstairs, a special media room for teenagers can be cordoned off with an acoustical curtain. Elsewhere on the second floor, stacks are arranged to form open reading areas and intimate nooks. Study rooms allow for group work.

On both floors, high ceilings and the presence of natural light make for an alluring sense of spatial generosity. Yet there's an underlying sense of order due to Skidmore's careful placement of ceiling fixtures. Shades can be drawn to filter out the sun.

You might think this open-plan, light-filled design would pose acoustical and glare issues. But Morrill and Si Chen, the branch manager, said they've had only two complaints from patrons about noise and just one request to lower the shades.

Clearly, libraries are changing, becoming centers of community as well as places where individuals curl up with a book. In this one, Lee and his colleagues at SOM have used common, off-the-shelf materials

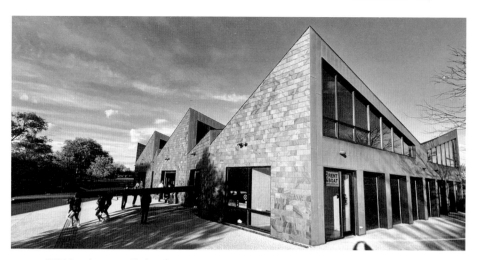

WMS Boathouse at Clark Park: an exemplary integration of structure, function, and expression. Photo by Blair Kamin.

to achieve uncommon results. The Chinatown branch possesses some of the grandeur of great old libraries, but none of their stodginess.

Let's have more like it—in other words, throw away the architectural cookie cutter.

A New Boathouse along the Chicago River Turns the Motion of Rowing into an Instant Landmark

OCTOBER 20, 2013

Few sights in sport are more stirring than eight rowers propelling a thin racing shell across the water. Legs drive forward. Arms pull backward. Oars carve through the water in perfect, V-shaped synchronization. It's visual poetry—and in some cities, it extends to the buildings where rowers gather and their boats are stored and dried.

Philadelphia boasts Boathouse Row, a string of elegant Victorian boat clubs along the Schuylkill River, including one designed by the great Frank Furness. Outside Boston, along the Charles River, there's the Community Rowing Boathouse, an exuberant contemporary structure that draws inspiration from such diverse sources as tobacco sheds and covered bridges.

Chicago is poised to join this tradition with the upcoming dedication of an exceptional boathouse along the north branch of the Chicago River. The building is the work of Jeanne Gang and her Chicago firm Studio Gang, who are no strangers to maritime themes. Gang made her name with a downtown condo-hotel tower, called Aqua, whose undulating concrete balconies seem to ripple across its glass surface.

The new boathouse features a serrated roof that announces its presence and shelters inspiring light-filled spaces that represent a major step up from the typical boathouse barn. It's also a welcome shift from the stuffy, dark-paneled elitism of old boathouses. Yet Chicago being Chicago, the democratic design comes with a clout-related twist.

Though the $8.8 million boathouse was principally sponsored by the Chicago Park District, which will run a variety of rowing programs there, it had the chance to become an architectural showpiece because it was built with $3.2 million in private funds. They include $2 million from the WMS Gaming company whose offices are across the river; $1 million from North Park University, whose rowers will use the facility; and $200,000 from the Chicago Rowing Foundation, a nonprofit that will offer most of the boathouse's youth rowing programs.

Meanwhile, amid the hard-edged, industrial landscape of South Side Bridgeport, plans for a similar, Gang-designed boathouse are lagging, with funds still to be raised, no groundbreaking set, and a 2015 completion target that seems optimistic. The disparity sends a clear message: if you live in or near the right zip code, you get access to top-drawer public works. If not, prepare to wait.

Situated at 3400 North Rockwell Street, two miles west of Wrigley Field, the new facility is the second of four boathouses Mayor Rahm Emanuel wants to build along the Chicago River. His aim: transform the long-polluted river into a recreational showplace.

The first Emanuel-backed boathouse, a small facility in Chinatown that rents canoes and kayaks, got the mayor's riverfront push off to a solid start last year, with a gutsy, modern design, by the firm Johnson & Lee, that relates well to its gritty surroundings.

The new North Side boathouse is not only bigger than the Chinatown facility, but better, because it successfully integrates the architectural triad of structure, function, and expression.

It has two parts: a sprawling, one-story boat-storage shed that doubles as a canoe-kayak rental outlet; and a compact, two-story field house with such advanced training facilities as an indoor rowing tank. Both buildings are clad in durable slate shingles and zinc panels, giving them a taut, continuous surface that enhances their sculptural presence.

An entry court between the buildings is wide enough to allow visiting crews to carry their shells through the space to a floating dock, but narrow enough to create a framed passage that enhances the visitor's sense of arrival. Along the river itself, Gang drew upon memories of her graduate student days at Harvard, where the historic Weld Boathouse has an expansive boat-launch apron that doubles as a public space. Cascading steps help to re-create the effect in Chicago.

To Gang's credit, though, the boathouse never reverts to a skin-deep, postmodern take on tradition. Instead, it represents her latest essay in transforming simple, rational needs into expressive aesthetic forms. At Aqua, she did it with the balconies. Here, she and her project architect, William Emmick, drew inspiration from time-lapse photographs of rowers and the rhythmic motion of their strokes. The result, a series of steel roof trusses that alternate between "M" and inverted "V" shapes, works both formally and functionally.

Among other things, the arrangement floods the storage shed with natural light and should save energy by warming the shed's concrete floor in winter. At the same time, the light accentuates the visual drama of intentionally warped plywood ceilings that swoop between the shed's trusses and echo the complex curves of the sleek racing shells.

From the outside, the shed's roofline assumes ever-changing profiles—sometimes serrated like an old-fashioned factory, sometimes faceted, as though it were a diamond. Here is the rare building that simultaneously shapes space and works as an object in space.

The fieldhouse achieves the same effect, though it employs a different internal structure as well as heating and cooling systems necessitated by the fact that its primary occupants will be people, not boats.

Its first-floor rowing tank, which will allow an entire eight-person crew to practice as though they were on the water, benefits further from the fact that it overlooks the Chicago River. The fieldhouse's second-floor training room, which has its own warped plywood ceiling and ample natural light, should soothe rowers after their exhausting "ergometer" workouts. A porch just outside this room offers a prime spot for watching races.

An instant landmark, the boathouse promises to serve its users well and invigorate Emanuel's push to transform the river into a major public space. But if the mayor and his Chicago Park District really believe in social equity, their job is only half done. That means full steam ahead on building a comparable boathouse in Bridgeport.

Postscript: The Bridgeport facility, called the Park No. 571 Boathouse and located at 2828 South Eleanor Street, opened in 2016, a year behind schedule.

Chicago Shows How Public Housing and Public Libraries Can Coexist and Be Visually Striking. Now We Need More of These Creative Combinations

AUGUST 22, 2019

Let's dispense with the obvious, shall we? Three new Chicago buildings that combine public libraries and public housing are head and shoulders above the Robert Taylor Homes, Cabrini-Green, and the rest of the city's dehumanizing, now-demolished public-housing projects.

How could they not be? The library-housing combos are modest-sized structures rather than enormous complexes built to warehouse the poor. They're physically integrated into neighborhoods instead of isolated. And they're produced by skilled developers and architects, not hacks following bureaucrats' orders that public housing shouldn't just *be* cheap—it should *look* cheap.

In these works, architects John Ronan, Ralph Johnson, and Brian Lee have turned in performances that range from solid to stellar. The buildings are bright, optimistic, and city enhancing. And their libraries—brimming with activity, although too noisy for some—form a new kind of civic commons, drawing together people of different races, ages, and income levels.

The outcome reveals architecture's oft-ignored potential as a social art. Yet in light of how few apartments the developments actually provide, I'm compelled to ask: Will these models be replicated or are

Independence Branch Library and Apartments: a creative exercise in "co-location," mixing a public library and public housing. Photo by Lee Bey.

they three beautiful drops in the bucket? The question takes on fresh relevance after the abrupt resignation of Eugene Jones, the head of the Chicago Housing Authority, who spearheaded the projects.

Located in the neighborhoods of Irving Park, West Ridge, and Little Italy, all on the North and Near West sides, the library-housing fusions are offshoots of an innovative concept, "co-location," which joins a library with another type of building to lower construction costs and

boost library attendance. Chicago is in the forefront of US cities exper-
imenting with the concept, already used in England, because of the
political backing of former mayor Rahm Emanuel.

"People were asking me for more libraries, and I knew we needed
to bring affordable housing into good neighborhoods so they're not
so concentrated," Emanuel told a reporter last year. "If you can't solve
a problem, make it a bigger problem and see if you can solve it."

In other words, the Chicago Public Library didn't have enough
money to build new libraries on its own. Combining the proposed
libraries with public housing freed up funding from state and federal sources, including the US Department of Housing and Urban
Development. According to the CHA, the total cost of the projects
was $109.9 million—$41.3 million in Little Italy, $35.3 million in West
Ridge, and $33.3 million in Irving Park.

In light of that sizable bill, the total number of apartments to
emerge from the three projects, just 161, is positively paltry. It represents a tiny fraction of the more than 58,000 applicants on the CHA's
public-housing waiting list.

That fraction gets even smaller when you account for the fact that
that only about three-fifths of the new units (97) are for CHA residents.
The rest are rented at market rates or at reduced "affordable" prices.
In addition, all the public-housing units in Irving Park and West Ridge
are for seniors. Only 37 units, all in Little Italy, are for CHA families,
a group traditionally relegated to Chicago's poorest, most segregated
areas.

Such statistics reflect a long-running tension in public housing:
the need to build as many units as possible versus the desire to make
those units safe, sanitary, and, at best, life-affirming. Yet the designers
of the three projects still have performed admirably.

For starters, the exteriors of their buildings vary widely in appearance—a significant break from the cookie-cutter libraries favored by
former mayor Richard M. Daley. Unlike postmodern designs that tried
to make public housing "fit in," the library-housing combinations deliver a sophisticated shot of modernity even as they relate to the scale
and character of the buildings around them.

At the Little Italy Branch Library and Taylor Street Apartments, developed by Related Midwest, Lee and his Skidmore, Owings & Merrill

Northtown Branch Library and Apartments: a visually assertive design that expresses the importance of public buildings. Photo by Lee Bey.

colleagues nod to neighboring brick facades with corrugated metal panels of red and orange. The panels give the building a pleasing sense of texture and shadow patterns. A section of the apartments is wisely set back from the street, reducing the impact of the building's potentially overwhelming seven-story mass.

At West Ridge's Northtown Branch Library and Apartments, backed by the Evergreen Real Estate Group, Johnson and his Perkins & Will team engage a very different context: Western Avenue's auto row / gas station strip. Their cantilevered box, supported by V-shaped concrete columns, creates a monumental presence. A curving extension of the box snakes to the north. Yellow-green walls accentuate deep recesses that give the four-story building a strongly sculptural look. As at Taylor Street, the single-level library is topped by a planted roof that residents can use.

At the just-completed Independence Branch Library and Apartments on Elston Avenue in Irving Park, also developed by the Evergreen firm, Ronan and architects at his eponymous firm make the boldest—and best—statement of the three. Their design has a clarity of expression that lifts it above the other two.

Two stories tall and clad in glass as well as handsome precast concrete, the library projects outward to the sidewalk, engaging passersby and echoing the scale of nearby buildings. Monolithic but not oppressive, its dark mass engages in a visual dialogue with its brightly colored apartment block, whose recessed balconies are wrapped in hues right out of a Crayola crayon box. The design individualizes each apartment, so a resident can point to his or her balcony and say, "That's mine." It's a way of encouraging residents to feel like they live in an individualized home, not generic housing.

Very well, you might say, but how do these buildings work? So far, so good, based on what I saw.

Each library hummed with activity. Patrons took advantage of free Wi-Fi, children's play areas, and media zones especially for teens. Airy, clean-lined interiors ennoble the activities they contain. So do memorable design elements, like a glass-sheathed reading courtyard at the Northtown branch and amphitheater-like seating that unites the two floors of the Independence branch.

Some library patrons complain that the noise emanating from such features makes the buildings indistinguishable from day-care centers. But the branches have enclosed study rooms for those who like their reading rooms to be as quiet as a church.

Tours of the apartments and conversations with residents also painted an optimistic picture. In the corridors of the Independence apartments, Ronan ingeniously repeated the bright colors of the balconies, giving each apartment the equivalent of a doormat. That helps bring these typically dreary spaces to life. At each site, the apartments are modest but attractive, with some at Taylor Street even offering views of Willis Tower and the downtown skyline.

"I love the place," said Taylor Street resident Ricarda Coleman, sixty-two, who formerly lived in the economically struggling Austin

Little Italy Branch Library and Taylor Street Apartments: weaving a big building into the fabric of its neighborhood. Photo by Lee Bey.

neighborhood. She goes downstairs to the library, she said, to get DVDs. Although some residents of Little Italy vociferously opposed the project, calling it a monstrosity, people in the neighborhood are "friendly," she said.

But caution is in order. The history of public housing is littered with examples of buildings that were camera-ready on opening day, then descended into chaos when housing authorities in Chicago and other cities failed to maintain them and allowed gangs to overrun them. These buildings should be different because they're run by private managers, not the CHA.

It's also too early to tell if the libraries are achieving their goal of mixing public-housing residents into the broader community.

In an interview before his resignation, Jones said such interaction is already occurring. Residents "now have a place in which they can meet new members of the community and bond," he said. "The only thing I'm mad about is that I didn't put in some kind of restaurant or coffee shop."

The bigger issue, especially in light of Jones's departure and the priority that Mayor Lori Lightfoot is putting on redeveloping economically struggling parts of the South and West Sides, revolves around equity: Will the CHA and the Chicago Public Library spread the wealth of library-housing combinations to those parts of town?

Plenty of South Side communities would like a new library to go with their subsidized housing. The libraries should be more than a way to sugarcoat public housing so it's palatable to residents of already-stable communities.

The new projects are impressive fusions of good design and good works, but their location on the North and Northwest Sides and their meager output of new public housing reveals that they are no panacea for the ills of racial and economic segregation that ail Chicago and other American cities.

Postscript: In 2021, Lightfoot opened another public library that uses the co-location concept, this one in the Far South Side's Altgeld Gardens public-housing development. Designed by Chicago's KOO architects, the building includes a day-care center and a community meeting room as well as a library.

A Former North Side Public-Housing Project Is Beautifully Remade, but at What Cost?

FEBRUARY 6, 2020

Millennials peer into glowing laptops at a coffee shop. A jogger runs across a walkway that swoops over the Chicago River. Handsome brick buildings have been painstakingly restored.

Renovation of the former Julia C. Lathrop Homes: new life for Art Moderne gems, but not enough public housing. Photo by Lee Bey.

River North? Bucktown? Guess again.

This is a remade public-housing project on Chicago's North Side—the former Julia C. Lathrop Homes, which once was the antithesis of the Chicago Housing Authority's high-rise hells, but later spiraled into physical decay and worse.

"It was very violent," a thirty-three-year-old resident, Lashaunda Brownlow, who grew up at the Lathrop Homes, told me. Now, he said, "it's a lot nicer. You don't see violence like before. The buildings are clean. The grounds are clean."

Hearing endorsements like that and touring the Lathrop Homes' transformation, I was tempted to label the project, at the intersection of Diversey Parkway and Clybourn Avenue, a great success.

After all, the redevelopment preserves a trove of historic buildings and creates a "mixed-income" neighborhood that includes people from different socioeconomic groups—a major shift from the isolated concentrations of poverty that were the root cause of public housing's woes.

The redevelopment also provides an alluring new stretch of riverwalk designed by landscape architect Michael Van Valkenburgh.

Here's the catch: when the remake is done, the redeveloped Lathrop will have a total of 1,116 housing units, yet just 400 of them will be public housing—525 fewer than before. The other units are rented at market rates or those deemed "affordable."

That shortcoming raises broader questions: Are mixed-income developments like this one a new form of gentrification, saving historic buildings but shifting poor people out of desirable locations? Or, in the long run, are they smart public policy?

Completed in 1938 and named for a Rockford-born social-welfare worker whose methodical techniques and hands-on dedication led to significant improvements in urban living conditions and childcare, the Lathrop Homes reflected the progressive thinking of New Deal reformers.

Providing an enclave that stood apart from packed slums, polluting factories, and the polluted Chicago River, its low-rise brick buildings gathered around generous open spaces designed by renowned landscape architect Jens Jensen.

The buildings, shaped by an all-star team of economically struggling architects including a son of Daniel Burnham, conferred dignity upon residents with Georgian and Art Moderne details—the polar opposite of dehumanizing plainness. Narrow floor plans maximized the amount of light and air coming into apartments.

By 2016, though, the Lathrop Homes had gone from model to mess, and the housing authority approved a three-phase redevelopment plan, backed by a large commercial developer, Related Midwest, and two nonprofits, Bickerdike Redevelopment Corporation and Heartland Housing. (The CHA still owns the land at Lathrop; the developers have a ninety-nine-year lease to the property.)

The $140 million first phase, which is mostly north of Diversey and delivers 414 apartments, skillfully puts today's design principles to work. The idea is to connect the development, now known as Lathrop, to the city and to nature rather than making it an enclave. The big move, the riverwalk, reverses Lathrop's original stance of turning its back on the river but remains faithful to Jensen's nature-inspired aesthetic.

The riverwalk offers stylish contemporary benches, a launch for nonmotorized boats, a circular dog walk, and a delightful, curving stretch that extends out over the river. A restored, two-acre "great lawn" in the heart of the project provides an expansive link between Clybourn and the riverwalk as well as a prime setting for community events like outdoor movie nights.

Smaller public spaces, like a raised outdoor plaza overlooking the Diversey-Clybourn intersection, also invite outsiders to enter a project that neighbors once strove to avoid. Behind the plaza, for example, is the busy Hexe Coffee Co. café, which occupies Lathrop's former administration building.

Working with historic-preservation consultants McGuire Igleski & Associates of Evanston, Chicago architectural firms HED and JGMA have carefully rehabbed sixteen historic buildings north of Diversey.

Paned metal windows and restored brickwork have brought the exteriors back to their original look. Interiors have been gutted and given de rigueur amenities, like quartz countertops and stainless-steel appliances. South of Diversey, a six-story, fifty-nine-unit apartment building by Chicago's bKL Architecture puts a compelling new spin on the brickwork of the older buildings.

The entire redevelopment received about $20 million in historic-preservation tax credits, according to Related Midwest. Given Lathrop's historical and architectural significance, that was money well spent. It's hard to believe now that the housing authority once proposed tearing down the entire complex.

But if the design of the new Lathrop deserves high marks, the jury is still out on its social architecture.

Will residents find jobs by networking with their neighbors? Will living in such a neighborhood provide role models for the children of public-housing residents? It will take years to know. In any event, there's not much room for large families that once lived at Lathrop, given that most of the new units have only one or two bedrooms.

Equally important, the housing authority has yet to fully make good on its promise to replace Lathrop's 525 lost public-housing units with new ones on the North Side, which traditionally has had far less public housing than the South and West Sides.

So far, according to the CHA, 290 replacement units either have been built elsewhere on the North Side, are under construction, or have been approved for development. That leaves the agency well short of its goal.

The story at Lathrop is far from over. The redevelopment's second and third phases, south of Diversey, are still to come while the CHA continues the difficult effort to build more public housing on the North Side—a move that has run into bitter opposition in some neighborhoods.

The architecture and landscape at Lathrop deserve high praise. But it's too early to tell if the architects of public policy have succeeded at the greater, far more daunting task of integrating public-housing residents into society.

Part Four

HISTORIC PRESERVATION

WHAT GETS SAVED AND WHY?

In light of the ever-present tension between those who seek to save Chicago's extraordinary stock of old buildings and those who seek to send them to the scrap heap, historic-preservation battles in the city are as inevitable as the sun rising over Lake Michigan. But these fights had very different outcomes after the Great Recession. Buildings of the distant architectural past, like Frank Lloyd Wright's masterful Robie House, generally fared far better than those of the recent past, like Bertrand Goldberg's Prentice Women's Hospital, which came down despite protests from some of the world's top architects.

The demise of the Brutalist hospital illustrated the particular danger faced by buildings that haven't yet reached the age of fifty or sixty: they're too old to be new and too new to be old, so many are prematurely dispatched to the architectural graveyard—before time and historical perspective allow them to become valued and protected. Helmut Jahn's James R. Thompson Center proved a notable exception—saved in part by the record amount of vacant downtown office space that the pandemic produced, greatly diminishing the allure of replacing the controversial postmodern structure with a massive office tower.

In the post-Recession era, new perspectives on race, class, and gender joined with existing government financial incentives to broaden the spectrum of buildings considered for protected status. As the reinvention of beloved, once-endangered buildings like the old Cook County Hospital showed, the trend was a plus for an increasingly diverse society because it expanded the range of stories that architecture tells. Yet such efforts were not without controversy, as the failure of a proposed landmark district for the once Czech, now Latino, neighborhood of Pilsen revealed. Revisionist thinking also complicated the identity of iconic buildings like the Ludwig Mies van der Rohe–designed Farnsworth House, whose patron long had been overshadowed by its architect. Looming over all these concerns was a fraught political matter: Who gets to decide if an aged building lives or dies?

WHO SHOULD DETERMINE A BUILDING'S FATE— THE EXPERTS, THE COMMUNITY, OR THE CLOUT-HEAVY?

Changes Will Erode Foundation of Landmarks Commission

JULY 8, 2011

Dr. Anita Blanchard is widely known as the obstetrician who delivered Barack and Michelle Obama's two daughters, Malia and Sasha. Her husband, Chicago businessman Martin Nesbitt, is a basketball-playing buddy of the president and has been described as one of his closest friends.

Blanchard, an associate professor of obstetrics and gynecology at the University of Chicago Medical Center, may well have saved lives through her work. But is she qualified to decide which Chicago buildings should be spared from the wrecker's ball?

Mayor Rahm Emanuel has nominated Blanchard to serve on the Commission on Chicago Landmarks, the panel entrusted with safeguarding the city's architectural treasures. Could the fact that Nesbitt donated $5,000 to Emanuel's mayoral campaign have anything to do with the nomination? This is Chicago, after all.

Blanchard, it turns out, is not the only bewildering nominee put up by Emanuel.

At the latest commission meeting, it became clear that the mayor is not going to reappoint four highly respected members of the panel,

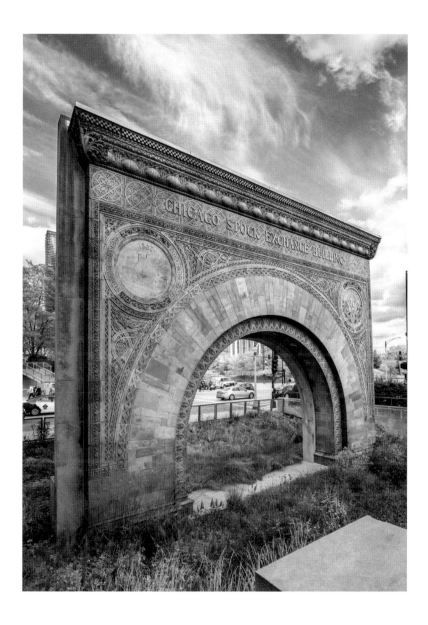

Chicago Stock Exchange Building arch at the Art Institute of Chicago: the city's landmarks commission is often the last line of defense against such outcomes. Photo by Lee Bey.

including two architects, a National Park Service official with a master's degree in historic preservation, and a preservation-minded financial-services consultant.

Instead, he's backing Blanchard and a well-known local chef, Chinatown's Tony Hu, along with two career politicians, former alderman Mary Ann Smith and former Cook County Assessor Jim Houlihan, who at least bring a modicum of experience to the table.

The mayor is a Cubs fan, so I suspect he'll get this analogy: this is the worst trade since the Cubs sent Lou Brock, a future Hall of Famer, to the St. Louis Cardinals, in 1964. In a single, boneheaded stroke, Emanuel has weakened the foundations of landmark preservation in Chicago.

The Commission on Chicago Landmarks often serves as the last line of defense between civilization and the sort of civic barbarity that, in the early 1970s, reduced Louis Sullivan and Dankmar Adler's great Chicago Stock Exchange Building to rubble.

The commission plays an equally important role in regulating changes to existing landmarks, as at the latest meeting, when its permit-review committee approved Target's aesthetically respectful proposal to put a new store inside Sullivan's masterful former Carson Pirie Scott building at 1 South State Street.

Accordingly, the standards for sitting on the nine-member commission are high. Or so goes the civics-textbook version of reality.

The city law governing the panel says its members "shall be selected from professionals in the disciplines of history, architecture, historic architecture, planning, archaeology, real estate, historic preservation, or related fields, or shall be persons who have demonstrated special interest, knowledge, or experience in architecture, history, neighborhood preservation, or related disciplines."

Yet if the City Council approves Emanuel's nominees, the panel will have no architects and no architectural historians for the first time in recent memory.

In the past, their presence brought crucial authority to often-contentious battles over city landmarks, like the time years ago when a developer pressed to attach balconies to the graceful facade of the century-old Montgomery Ward warehouse at 600 West Chicago Avenue.

Architects on the commission's permit-review committee, which passes judgment on changes to landmark buildings, sure-handedly explained why such a move would have mangled the building's beauty. The proposal was shelved.

"It is critical to have experienced voices at that table," said Jim Peters, president of the advocacy group Landmarks Illinois.

Real estate broker John Baird, a commission member for more than twenty-five years, agreed. "I'm particularly concerned that we don't have an architect to run the permit-review committee," he said.

Emanuel spokesman Tom Alexander said the administration would only discuss the nominees, who still must be ratified by the City Council, as a group. He declined to provide qualifications for Blanchard and Hu, neither of whom returned calls.

"The appointees strongly represent the broad scope of issues facing the commission, and the team that has been assembled brings outstanding professional experience, personal background and diversity to the commission," Alexander wrote in an email.

Granted, the commission will still include a landscape architect, Ernest Wong, and a historian, Christopher Reed. Smith and Houlihan, who helped develop Cook County's historic-preservation tax incentives, will bring something to the table. And the commission's excellent staff will be led by an architect, Eleanor Gorski.

Yet the absence of architectural expertise stands to weaken the commission at the very moment, with a decision nearing on whether to protect old Prentice Women's Hospital from demolition, when it will need that authority most.

While credentials aren't the sole measure of a candidate's fitness to serve on a landmarks board, there can be no substitute for experience and expertise.

The key is for cities to create an informed balance between the often-conflicting perspectives of laypeople and design professionals, real estate developers and architects, the fashions of the moment and the long view of history.

In Chicago, that balance could soon be lost.

Postscript: The landmarks commission's absence of architectural expertise was keenly felt in 2012 and again in 2013 when the panel twice

Evanston's Harley Clarke Mansion: some deemed it expendable, but the people prevailed. Photo by Blair Kamin.

rejected preservationists' attempts to prevent the destruction of old Prentice Women's Hospital. Emanuel did not reappoint Blanchard and Hu to the commission in 2015.

Evanston Plan to Demolish Historic Harley Clarke Mansion: Public Vision or Hidden Agenda?

JULY 14, 2018

With a lack of transparency that would be stunning even in Chicago, Evanston is about to move forward with a plan that would privately fund the demolition of a publicly owned building that's an official city landmark and part of a district listed on the National Register of Historic Places.

Flaunting six towering chimneys and a red-tile roof, the ninety-one-year-old Tudor Revival Harley Clarke Mansion at 2603 Sheridan Road is a powerful architectural presence. It also has some prominent neighbors.

Evanston mayor Stephen Hagerty, who recently said it was time to resolve the long-running debate over the building's future, owns a lakefront mansion on a secluded street just to the south. Nicole Kustok, one of the public faces of a group that would bankroll the demolition, lives almost across Sheridan Road. And Charles Lewis, a philanthropist who has acknowledged supporting the pro-demolition group, resides in another lakefront mansion a few blocks north.

The group, which calls itself Evanston Lighthouse Dunes, is selling its proposal as a public-spirited gesture, one that will take a long-festering problem off the hands of the financially strapped city by replacing the shuttered mansion with a swath of parkland, beaches, and dunes. But because the group isn't a registered nonprofit, it doesn't have to list its leaders and document fundraising activities.

That leaves critical questions unanswered: Who belongs to it? How much are they giving? What percentage of them live nearby? Would their property values rise if the Harley Clarke Mansion were converted to open space, ensuring that the site never could be developed? Or would their plan, as they claim, benefit the community as a whole?

These questions assume fresh urgency with Evanston's City Council about to consider an agreement with the Lighthouse Dunes group. The so-called "memorandum of understanding" could take the city a significant step farther down the path toward demolition.

While Lighthouse Dunes' leaders have committed to reveal who the donors are, they need to list both the funders and the amount of their donations *before* the council takes up the plan. Otherwise, the disclosure will be meaningless.

"I don't see any legitimate way that the council could vote to accept this without knowing who's paying for it," said Evanston alderman Thomas Suffredin, who opposes demolition.

For the record, my requests to the Lighthouse Dunes group for donor information went unanswered. Hagerty could not be reached for an interview. Kustok has said in past public meetings that demolition would not open views of Lake Michigan from her home.

Yet even assuming that the Lighthouse Dunes group passes the conflict-of-interest sniff test, its desire to dispatch with the mansion, which has been closed since the Evanston Art Center moved out in 2015, makes little sense.

The house, designed by architect Richard Powers for a utilities magnate, is structurally sound. And it's a rare architectural gem—potentially, a people's gem.

A successful reuse could bring much-needed social diversity to the city's nearby Lighthouse Landing Park, US Rep. Jan Schakowsky wrote in a recent letter to the mayor and council. Schakowsky, whose district includes Evanston, urged the city's leaders "to step back and take a time-out from advancing the irreversible decision to demolish the building." (A listing on the National Register typically does not protect a building from being torn down.)

The council's rejection of previous reuse proposals—one, from Jennifer Pritzker, would have converted the home into a boutique hotel, while another, from the Evanston Lakehouse & Gardens group, suggested an environmental-education center—should not automatically trigger the wrecking-ball option.

Smart cities mothball such treasures and play for time. Chicago did that with the once-decrepit Reliance Building, now a posh hotel. And private capital isn't the only way to save such buildings. The 1960s effort that saw architects and preservation-minded citizens join to save Henry Hobson Richardson's Glessner House, now a museum, attests to that.

Plans by the Lighthouse Dunes group to remake the Harley Clarke Mansion's landscape, which was designed by Jens Jensen, also deserve sharp scrutiny.

The group proposes to restore "key elements" of Jensen's garden. It will be interesting to see how it defines those elements—with integrity, or for maximum wiggle room that would enable it to preserve only parts of Jensen's landscape.

The group also pledges to provide $50,000 to $75,000 for landscaping in addition to a promised $447,000 for demolition.

Yet at least one experienced landscape architect characterizes that funding promise as insufficient to achieve the group's stated aim of "restoring the beach, park, and dunes to their natural states." About $150,000 to $250,000 "would be more realistic," said Mike Ciccarelli, an associate principal at Chicago's Hoerr Schaudt Landscape Architects, who has designed private landscapes in other North Shore towns.

Evanston taxpayers should not be subject to a bait and switch that forces them to cover unanticipated demolition and landscaping costs. Nor should they be left in the dark about the $64,000 question of this controversial plan: Is the Lighthouse Dunes group treating the city's lakefront as a public trust, or as a private fiefdom?

The view from here is that the landscape-restoration plan is a ruse to get rid of a building that should be saved.

Postscript: After the Evanston City Council approved the agreement with the Lighthouse Dunes group that sought to demolish the Harley Clarke Mansion, preservationists led by Suffredin forced the city to place an advisory referendum on the ballot in 2018. More than 80 percent of voters supported saving the house. In response, the City Council reversed itself and chose not to appeal the Evanston Preservation Commission's decision to deny a demolition permit for the mansion. In 2021, the city selected one of four reuse proposals for the mansion from a nonprofit group called Artists Book House. Headed by best-selling author and Evanston native Audrey Niffenegger, Artists Book House plans to transform the mansion into a book arts and literacy center. Plans call for the group to complete renovations and open the house to the public in 2026.

A Plaque on Emmett Till's House Is Just a First Step. Chicago Can Do a Better Job of Protecting Black History Sites

SEPTEMBER 4, 2020

The slipshod manner with which Chicago often treats its African American landmarks was visible for all to see the other day when the real estate developer who bought Emmett Till's house let drop that he had no idea the red-brick two-flat at 6427 South St. Lawrence Avenue was once home to a seminal figure in Black history.

The developer, Blake McCreight, was speaking to the Commission on Chicago Landmarks, whose members voted unanimously to grant preliminary landmark status to Till's house. The vote was good news, but sticking a plaque on the house, now a likely outcome, will be a meager victory.

Visitors who make a pilgrimage to see the home of the fourteen-year-old who was brutally murdered sixty-five years ago, helping to ig-

Emmett Till house: when a developer bought it, the home of the historic African American figure faced an uncertain future. Photo by Lee Bey.

nite the civil rights movement, surely will want to step inside and see the three-bedroom, second-floor apartment where Till lived with his mother, Mamie Till-Mobley.

They also might expect to look at photographs of the open casket Till's mother chose for his funeral to show mourners and the world the horror and violence her son endured after he was accused of harassing a white woman while visiting relatives in Money, Mississippi.

Things like that would furnish a house museum that would bring alive a significant chapter in the African American story and could even be part of a trail of Black history sites, including the planned Obama Presidential Center, on the South Side.

Maybe one of the two vacant lots north of the house could be part of the museum, giving visitors a quiet place to contemplate Till's story, which has taken on fresh resonance since the police killing of George Floyd.

Could such a transformation actually happen? It won't be easy. Dreams are often hard to achieve on the South Side, not for a shortage of vision but for a shortage of dollars.

McCreight, who told the commission he supports landmark status that would protect the building from significant changes or demolition, said in a subsequent interview that he bought the house last year to renovate and rent it out. The developer only learned of the property's connection to Till a few months ago, he said, from Mary Lu Seidel, the community-engagement director of the nonprofit advocacy group Preservation Chicago.

"The reality is we're taking a step back at this point in time and understanding what our options are and what's going to be best for the community," he said.

McCreight is in a pickle he never should have been in. It doesn't matter that he's a white developer in a Black neighborhood. A Black developer would have faced the same problem. Dimwitted procedures and policies don't discriminate.

If the city had a survey of African American and Latino historic sites—and it used that resource to let developers know what they were getting into—this little mess wouldn't have arisen.

Maurice Cox, the city's commissioner of planning and development and a member of the landmarks commission, made that very point at the commission's meeting. He urged the panel to direct his department to make a survey documenting Black and brown historic properties.

Such sites are often ordinary, everyday buildings, Cox correctly noted, more significant for their associations with important figures than for their architecture.

Doing such a survey would be in keeping with Mayor Lori Lightfoot's drive to make Chicago's monuments and memorials more diverse and equitable. Modest buildings can serve as monuments even though they're not monumental in scale. You don't need marble and massiveness to touch the heart.

The Till house is a monument hidden in plain sight.

So is the house of Chicago blues legend Muddy Waters at 4339 South Lake Park Avenue.

Waters owned and lived in the red-brick 1889 house from 1954 until he moved to suburban Westmont two decades later, according to published accounts and interviews. He and other musicians held jam sessions in the basement.

But the condition of the house is worthy of a blues ballad. Its battered, beaten-down appearance, including boarded-up windows, is especially galling because the block on which it sits has some handsomely restored Victorian homes, red-brick and graystone affairs that exude solidity and prosperity.

Yet there's hope. Plans to give the house new life got a boost recently when the National Trust for Historic Preservation announced grants for projects that preserve African American history. The trust awarded $50,000 to the Muddy Waters MOJO Museum, which is raising funds to turn the house into a museum and recording studio. But the grant, like previous efforts to draw attention to the house, can only go so far.

In front of Waters's house is an information-packed sign, a Chicago Tribute marker, funded by the Chicago Tribune Foundation and the Chicago Cultural Center Foundation. The foundations put up such signs to "articulate the connection between the city of today and the historic individuals and events that continue to shape our world."

The Waters house sign was dedicated in 1999. Now it's bent and rusting.

Plaques and signs are nice. Real restorations, the kind that make history come alive, are infinitely superior.

Postscript: The City Council approved landmark status for the Till home, officially known as the Emmett Till and Mamie Till-Mobley House, in 2021. Blacks in Green, a local nonprofit, purchased the house from McCreight before the council's vote and announced plans to turn it into a museum. Later in 2021, the council also designated the

Muddy Waters house an official city landmark. In addition, funding for an assessment of significant African American and Latino sites was included in the 2022 budget approved by the City Council. The landmarks commission staff is scheduled to provide a progress report on the survey by the end of 2022.

The Despised Pilsen Landmark District Is About to Get a Hearing. Here's How to Save the Treasured Neighborhood

DECEMBER 1, 2020

There's no doubt Chicago's Pilsen neighborhood has the stuff to become an official city landmark district. Yet a plan to do just that is widely despised in the community, viewed by the local alderman, activists, and many residents as an anything-but-benign move that would dramatically accelerate displacement and gentrification.

The proposal, which would create one of Chicago's largest historic districts and the city's first in a Latino area, is about to come before the City Council's Committee on Zoning, Landmarks, and Building Standards. How should the committee treat the plan, which the Commission on Chicago Landmarks previously recommended for approval?

Compromise.

By cutting the size of the proposed district roughly in half and limiting protected structures to Pilsen's commercial strips, the committee can safeguard an area of undisputed architectural and cultural distinction without imposing a financial burden on residential property owners. A significant share of the commercial building owners, it should be noted, are absentee landlords.

Though it contains significant individual structures, like the shuttered St. Adalbert Catholic Church, Pilsen is primarily distinguished by its urban fabric—continuous rows of "Bohemian Baroque" buildings, impressive Classical Revival structures, and the colorful murals that are the neighborhood's visual signature.

That fabric reveals the cultural footprint of nineteenth-century Eastern European immigrants, including the Czechs who gave Pilsen its name, and the Mexicans and Mexican Americans who moved there in the 1960s, many of them displaced by the construction of what is now the University of Illinois at Chicago.

Eighteenth Street in Pilsen: Chicago sought to make it the city's first Latino landmark district—residents said no. Photo by Lee Bey.

Recognizing this legacy, the federal government listed Pilsen on the National Register of Historic Places in 2006. The honor makes property owners eligible for historic-preservation tax credits, but typically does not prevent demolition. And the demolition threat is real, driven in part by Pilsen's proximity to downtown and UIC.

Since 2006, city officials say, developers have torn down ninety buildings in Pilsen, often replacing two-, three- and four-flats and their affordable apartments with expensive single-family homes. Without intervention from the city, more ugly modern structures could further rip apart Pilsen's urban fabric, a fate that has already befallen gentrifying neighborhoods on the North Side.

The risks are cultural as well as aesthetic. Since 2000, Pilsen's Latino population has dropped by about 14,000, city officials say. If unregulated development continues, more Latinos are likely to be pushed out.

Previously floated by the administration of Mayor Rahm Emanuel as part of a multipronged plan to preserve Pilsen and nearby Little Village, the historic district would cover roughly nine hundred buildings along the Eighteenth Street commercial strip and in a mostly residential extension to the south.

Yet the proposed district has gone over like a lead balloon, putting Mayor Lori Lightfoot's chief planner, Maurice Cox, on the defensive. Among other things, city officials have been forced to counter claims that the district would saddle property owners with exorbitant rehab costs prompted by the need to meet the landmarks commission's exacting standards.

The landmark plan, opponents claim, will save buildings, not people.

But the remedy suggested by the local alderman, Byron Sigcho-Lopez (Twenty-Fifth), promises to be a paper tiger. He's calling for a "demolition-free district" that would follow the same borders as the proposed landmark district. Within it, the city would be prohibited from issuing demolition permits or approvals for major projects until the alderman had a public meeting. Yet the city's planning department would still have the final say, potentially rendering the alderman's hearings meaningless.

Given the City Council's tradition of aldermanic prerogative, which gives aldermen near-total control over development in their wards, Sigcho-Lopez might prevail at the upcoming committee meeting. "We will generally tend to support the alderman" on development issues, the committee chair, Ald. Tom Tunney (Forty-Fourth), told me.

Here's a better idea: the committee should reduce the size of the proposed district to about 465 buildings, mostly commercial structures on Eighteenth Street and Blue Island Avenue. This alternative, suggested by planning-department officials during three October community meetings, would preserve Pilsen's architectural heart without affecting homeowners.

The alternative also would address the fact that a sizable share of property owners on Eighteenth—nearly 45 percent, according to a 2020 survey by the University of Illinois at Chicago's Great Cities Institute—live outside Pilsen. Absentee landlords typically act differently than longtime, local owners. They often treat their properties as investments, not cultural resources, opening the way for demolition.

Unlike the alderman's proposed "demolition-free district," a landmark district offers a proven legal tool to prevent both locals and outsiders from selling to developers who would swing the wrecking ball. City officials also are suggesting smart steps, like an express permit process for rehab projects affected by landmark designation, that would prevent a repeat of the travails faced by Marcos Carbajal, owner of the Carnitas Uruapan restaurant on Eighteenth Street. Carbajal was forced to hire a permit expediter just so he could put up an exterior sign that would meet stringent landmark requirements.

In this debate, the two sides appear so polarized that it's hard to know if any compromise is possible. Without one, a treasured Chicago neighborhood will be vulnerable to more waves of gentrification and demolition. That would be a tragedy for Pilsen's people and buildings, and all of Chicago.

Postscript: In keeping with the tradition of aldermanic prerogative, the City Council's zoning committee unanimously rejected the proposed Pilsen landmark district after Sigcho-Lopez spoke against it. But the committee also voted down the alderman's plan for a six-month moratorium on almost all demolitions within the boundaries of what would have been the landmark district. Pilsen's historic buildings were not left completely defenseless, however, because in 2021 the City Council approved an "anti-deconversion" ordinance designed to make it more difficult for developers to demolish old multifamily apartment buildings and replace them with expensive single-family homes.

THE STRUGGLE TO SAVE—AND BETTER UNDERSTAND— BUILDINGS OF THE RECENT PAST

In the cartoon-melodrama version of historic-preservation fights, profit-hungry developers wear the black hat. In reality, as the bitter Chicago battle over the Bertrand Goldberg–designed old Prentice Women's Hospital showed, nonprofit institutions are just as capable of swinging the wrecker's ball. The loss of the Brutalist hospital illustrated the challenges preservationists face when trying to save buildings less than fifty years old. Yet preservationists won a major, albeit partial, victory when the State of Illinois agreed to sell the once-threatened Helmut Jahn–designed James R. Thompson Center to a developer who pledged a gut rehab of the contention-producing postmodern structure. And the University of Chicago commissioned a sensitive yet forward-looking renovation of an oddball mid-century modernist building by the architect of Chicago's Aon Center, Edward Durell Stone. That project revealed there's a better way to treat the underappreciated architecture of the recent past than getting rid of it.

As Prentice Comes Down, Stakes Rise on Its Replacement

OCTOBER 12, 2013

The Twitterverse reacted swiftly when I posted photos and videos of a wrecking machine clawing away at old Prentice Women's Hospital.

"Sad failure of creative and civic imagination," wrote *New York Times* architecture critic Michael Kimmelman.

"Painful to see," added *Los Angeles Times* architecture critic Christopher Hawthorne.

"Sad day for Chicago and shame on Northwestern," tweeted Alan Brake, executive editor of the *Architect's Newspaper.*

"Wrecking ball +1; Architecture 0," wrote Ariella Cohen, executive editor of the online publication *Next City.*

The day had been coming for months, but the first visible evidence

Demolition of old Prentice Women's Hospital: Chicago unleashes its infamous savagery. Photo by Heather Charles / *Chicago Tribune* / TCA.

of demolition on the powerfully sculpted, structurally innovative Brutalist high-rise at 333 East Superior Street nonetheless felt like a punch in the gut. Here was fresh evidence that, despite the postindustrial sheen of Millennium Park, Chicago can still unleash its old and infamous savagery. The outcry from critics across the country attested to that.

No other American city is quite so proficient at building landmarks and destroying them. There is, accordingly, no better place to witness the bare-bones beauty of architecture, either as it is rising up or being torn down.

Stripped of the everyday clutter of people and furniture, architecture is reduced to its essence—columns, beams, cantilevers, arches. It is, at root, a structural art, as the late Richard Nickel showed so poignantly in his 1961 photograph of a bulldozer plowing away beneath the bare metal arches of Louis Sullivan's doomed Garrick Theater.

That photograph came to mind as I walked along Superior Street taking in Prentice's slow-motion disappearance. Its architect, Bertrand Goldberg, who died in 1997, is best known for the iconic corncob-shaped towers of Marina City. Prentice, completed in 1975, is widely considered one of his finest hospital designs.

From the sidewalk, I could see that the unremarkable metal-and-glass facade of Prentice's boxy podium was gone, revealing the steel beams and columns that supported it. Above, and still intact, was the building's glory: four bulging "shells" of concrete, punctuated by port-hole windows and rimmed at the bottom by remarkably thin arches.

Inside the pre-demolition cloverleaf-shaped tower were "quiet villages" of new mothers—semicircular clusters of patient rooms wrapped around a circular nurses' station at the building's core. With typical humanism, Goldberg set the bedrooms close to the station and a nursery where newborns were closely watched.

See it now—before it disappears.

The demolition will be finished by the end of next year, said Alan Cubbage, a spokesman for Northwestern University, which owns old Prentice. Northwestern, he added, is on schedule to start construction in early 2015 for a $370 million biomedical research tower that will replace Prentice.

Having persuaded Mayor Rahm Emanuel and Chicago's landmarks commission that Prentice should be sacrificed for jobs and other economic benefits, Northwestern now has a special burden: It can't just build a good building. It has to build a great one. But will it?

The three Chicago architectural firms competing for the project—Perkins & Will, Goettsch Partners, and Adrian Smith + Gordon Gill Architecture—are all highly respected and capable of top-notch work. But they lack the conceptual gravitas of the eight Pritzker Architecture Prize winners, including Frank Gehry, Italy's Renzo Piano, and Japan's Tadao Ando, who signed the petition urging that Prentice be saved. And it can hardly be a coincidence, as preservationists have pointed out, that top executives of the short-listed firms were conspicuously absent from the petition.

Whether or not Northwestern is guilty of playing architectural politics, the university deserves a chance to replace Goldberg's very good Prentice with something better. Such trade-ups have happened in Chicago. William Le Baron Jenney's Home Insurance Building of 1885, often celebrated as the first skyscraper, was torn down in 1931 to make way for the Field Building, a restrained Art Deco gem at 135 South La-Salle Street.

The stage is set, then, for "Prentice: The Sequel." Given the significance of old Prentice's widely mourned demolition, the stakes of this architectural drama could not be higher.

Postscript: In 2019, Northwestern opened the first phase of old Prentice's replacement, a thirteen-story building at 303 East Superior Street that will eventually stretch to thirty-one stories. Designed by Ralph Johnson of Perkins & Will and called the Simpson Querrey Biomedical Research Center, the building is highly functional, carefully detailed, and sensitive to its surroundings. But for now, at least, its stumpy proportions leave it far short of delivering the world-class architecture Northwestern had promised.

Spare Jahn's Thompson Center from Rauner's Death Sentence

OCTOBER 14, 2015

Not so fast, Gov. Rauner.

In announcing that he wants the state to sell the Helmut Jahn–designed James R. Thompson Center in Chicago's Loop, the private-equity-investor-turned-governor all but endorsed its demolition. The building, he opined, is "just not usable for much of anything."

But handing down a death sentence for Jahn's thirty-year-old postmodern glitter palace is both premature and ill-informed. By viewing the building's future through the prism of a spreadsheet, the governor is ignoring the vital role it plays in the life of the Loop—and how renovation could transform it into a far more appealing civic hub than it is today.

Renovation and repurposing, in short, should be considered before demolition.

Chicago is now the epicenter of the debate over how to handle troubled postmodern buildings. A recent panel discussion at the Chicago Architecture Biennial labeled postmodernism "preservation's new frontier." That discussion transcends the city's borders and offers alternatives to the governor's myopic vision.

The City Council of Portland, Oregon, is about to consider spend-

James R. Thompson Center: for years, the State of Illinois urged the demolition of Helmut Jahn's controversial postmodern design. Photo by Lee Bey.

ing up to $195 million to renovate one of America's first major post-modern buildings, the Michael Graves–designed Portland Building. The fifteen-story municipal office building opened in 1982, three years before the Thompson Center made its controversial debut as the State of Illinois Building.

With its stylized garlands, abstracted keystones, and a "Portlandia" statue, the Portland Building was in the vanguard of postmodernism. Ascendant in the 1980s, the style used bright colors, bold decoration, and irony-laced versions of classical details to assault the modernist austerity of the steel-and-glass box. Yet form did not always serve function, particularly when construction budgets were tight.

Like the Thompson Center, which infamously suffered from sauna-like heat spikes, a leaky roof, and noise and smells that wafted up from the food court at the bottom of its atrium, the Portland Building is widely viewed as an awful place to work. Its tiny, tinted windows are especially irksome to its roughly 1,300 occupants. Last year, the *Oregonian*, Portland's leading newspaper, called its interior "dark, leaky and claustrophobic."

After considering demolition, however, Portland officials are backing a proposal to gut and renovate the structure's interior. Aging mechanical, electrical, and plumbing systems would be replaced. The controversial exterior that won the building a spot on the National Register of Historic Places would be retained.

"It's the cheapest alternative," Fred Miller, Portland's chief administrative officer, told me by phone.

Besides being tens of millions of dollars less expensive than demolition and replacement, Miller said, the retrofit is expected to reduce energy bills and substantially increase the amount of natural light that filters into offices.

It's not hard to envision a comparable transformation of the seventeen-story Thompson Center, where Jahn fashioned a dramatic but flawed synthesis of the postmodern exuberance of the Portland Building and the high-tech aesthetic of Paris's 1977 Pompidou Center. But the benefits of a revamp would extend far beyond the building's workplaces.

The center's soaring, light-filled atrium, which was inspired by the domes of great public buildings and draws tourists and office workers by the thousands, is as vital a public space as Daley Plaza and the other outdoor piazzas of the Loop. In addition, more than 5.5 million passengers entered the center's Clark/Lake CTA station last year, making it the second-busiest station in the city.

To be sure, the cityscape would be better off if the center's tawdry

Thompson Center interior: despite its functional flaws, one of downtown's great public spaces. Photo by Lee Bey.

glass walls (robin's-egg blue and salmon—ugh!) were replaced with something that matched the built-for-the-ages dignity of neighboring government buildings, the City-County Building and the Daley Center. Yet the bigger question is whether a revamp makes economic sense.

In a statement, Jahn began to outline a response to Rauner's announcement. He called for upgrading the building's shops and food court, marketing its large office floors to high-tech companies, and adding a hotel, apartments, and condominiums. Architectural history "is full of examples where such repurposing has brought new life to structures like this," he said.

The commercial success of his Sony Center in Berlin—a tent-topped, triangle-shaped wedge of offices, apartments, condominiums, and entertainment attractions—lends credence to his vision. So does the assessment of Barbara Schenberg, an executive director with commercial real estate services firm Cushman & Wakefield.

Preserving the center would be "a challenge," Schenberg told the *Tribune*'s Kim Janssen, but developers "can be very inventive putting space to use."

Even though Jahn must share the blame for the center's woes—they're not solely due to deferred maintenance and repair, as he argues—I'd love to see him get another crack at the building. He's seventy-five now, an aging master rather than the brash wunderkind he was when former governor James Thompson commissioned him for the project.

Life and architecture rarely give us second chances to correct (and improve upon) our early errors. This could be one—but only if Rauner, Mayor Rahm Emanuel, and prospective buyers consider the merits of reinventing postmodernism's star-crossed Chicago poster child.

Postscript: In a stunning reversal from Rauner's position and his own bad-mouthing of the Thompson Center, Gov. J. B. Pritzker announced in late 2021 that the state would sell the center to the Prime Group, a Chicago developer that plans to modernize the building's office and retail space and possibly open a hotel on its upper floors. Prime Group's CEO, Michael Reschke, characterized the plan as a "gut reno-vation," saying it will include a new glass exterior wall that will dramat-ically cut solar heat gain and air-conditioning bills; new heating and air-conditioning systems; and new interior glass walls that will seal off the building's offices from the noise and smells emanating from the atrium. As part of the $70 million sale, the state will buy back a third of the renovated building's office space for about $148 million. Pritzker, who previously had opined that the center was a second-rate version of Jahn's work, said the Prime Group plan was a good deal for taxpayers because the state would not have to buy or lease another building for its downtown workforce.

While the Prime Group plan largely followed the gut-rehab template of the Portland Building, which reopened in 2020, preservationists and architecture critics noted a significant difference: unlike the Portland renovation, its Chicago counterpart will strip the Thompson Center of its distinctive postmodern colors. Yet as architectural historian Elizabeth Blasius, cofounder of the group Preservation Futures, wrote in a *Chicago Tribune* op-ed, the outcome was nonetheless a win on the fronts of public space, transit equity, and climate-change mitigation, the last because it will take less energy to renovate the center than to tear it down and build something else. Sadly, Jahn, who was killed in a bicycle accident in 2021, did not live to see this dramatic shift in the center's fortunes, but the Prime Group wisely hired his firm to handle the renovation.

The U of C's Architectural Oddball, by the Designer of the Aon Center, Gets a Vibrant, Energy-Saving Remake

MAY 10, 2019

Even for the brainiacs at the University of Chicago, it was a brain-teaser.

Here was this oddball building by Edward Durell Stone, architect of Chicago's Aon Center, that was a knockoff of Stone's much-admired US Embassy in New Delhi of 1959. The exotic, templelike structure at 1307 East Sixtieth Street was old, dirty, forlorn, and—because it sat atop a raised platform—anything but welcoming.

How could it ever be turned into the inviting, light-filled, modern hub of the university's Harris School of Public Policy?

"It was the least lovable ugly building on campus," Chicago architect Doug Farr told me before a recent tour. Like a "coffee drinker meets a smoker's teeth."

Newly rededicated, the Keller Center, as the building is now known, has been transformed into the vibrant headquarters of the U of C's Harris School, which teaches data-driven policy analysis to undergraduates, graduate students, and business people.

While the $80 million project has buffed up the building's once-decaying exterior, its interior is appropriately more of a reinvention than a restoration. It avoids slavish adherence to the past to forge a bold new identity for both the structure and the school it houses.

University of Chicago's Keller Center: a vibrant, energy-saving revival of quirky, mid-twentieth-century design. Photo by Lee Bey.

Working with Woodhouse Tinucci Architects of Chicago, Farr and his colleagues at Farr Associates have torn out floor slabs and inserted skylights to turn once-constricted spaces into expansive, informal places to study, meet, and exchange ideas. The most notable element, a light-washed four-story atrium, serves as a teeming indoor piazza.

Through example, the building's energy-saving features teach important lessons to future policymakers.

Looming above it all is the ghost of Stone, an Arkansas native who codesigned the sleek 1939 home of New York's Museum of Modern Art, then broke from modernist orthodoxy to embrace a style of architecture called New Formalism.

New Formalism's adherents reacted against lookalike, steel-and-glass buildings and embraced design elements that were anathema to modernists—strict symmetry, decoration, even references to local materials, climate, and culture. Stone's New Delhi embassy, a temple with concrete sunscreens as well as a reflecting pool that magnified its projection of American power, was one of the style's finest expressions.

A year after the embassy's debut, Stone designed the U of C's Center for Continuing Education, which initially served as a conference center and hotel for visiting scholars. The building, which opened in 1962 and later became a dorm for graduate students, was, as Farr puts it, India "air-dropped to Chicago."

Indeed, the center was an outlier on the U of C campus even though its exterior picked up on the limestone cladding and strong vertical lines of the university's collegiate Gothic buildings.

Decorative hexagon patterns incised into the building's thin concrete columns and the underside of its wafer-thin roof canopy were more Moorish than Gothic. The standoffish structure loomed above the Midway Plaisance to the north and turned its back on the Woodlawn neighborhood to the south. The high point of its interior, an ellipse-shaped two-story atrium, was artificially lit, typifying the technocratic mindset of an era that severed connections between architecture and nature.

Restoring such links has long been part of Farr's practice, an approach he demonstrated in the 2002 conversion of an old West Side factory into the Chicago Center for Green Technology. He's also been a forceful advocate of reinventing existing buildings, a skill he displayed in the 2009 transformation of an old Sears power plant on the West Side into a charter school called Power House High.

To Farr and other advocates of green architecture, saving energy and preserving the architectural past go hand in hand. The greenest building, they like to say, is the one that's already built.

Those ideas come together at the Keller Center, for which Farr also shares credit with two associate principals at his firm, Gabe Wilcox and Kelly Moynihan. (The building's new name recognizes a $20 million contribution from Dennis Keller, a U of C trustee and retired chairman of Adtalem Global Education, formerly the DeVry Education Group, and his wife Connie.)

The transformation begins before you enter. The building's platform has been made less forbidding, courtesy of a wheelchair-accessible ramp and a flight of stairs cut into its northwest corner. The restored exterior impresses with the layered spaces of its tall colonnades and the intricacy of its hexagon-shaped patterns. A fourth-floor glass addition, set back from the front of the facade, respects the building's original symmetry.

While this isn't Stone's best work, it joins with Eero Saarinen's neighboring Laird Bell Law Quadrangle at 1111 East Sixtieth Street and Ludwig Mies van der Rohe's School of Social Service Administration at 969 East Sixtieth Street to form a unique trio of buildings by mid-twentieth-century masters.

Farr and his colleagues have done their most creative work inside, contrasting the bones of Stone's twentieth-century steel-reinforced concrete structure with insertions that are clearly of the twenty-first century.

Entering from Sixtieth Street, you pass beneath an ultrawide, exposed-concrete beam, part of the original structure, that seems to press down on you. Then you're released into the atrium, a dazzling burst of open space that extends from the basement to new skylights.

Ringed by glass-walled classrooms and featuring a creative version of the amphitheater-style seating that is ubiquitous these days, the atrium buzzes with activity. It encourages serendipitous meetings that rarely occurred in the school's former home at 1155 East Sixtieth Street.

In the old building, said the school's dean, Katherine Baicker, "people scurried through little rat mazes" to their offices and classrooms.

Throughout the Keller Center, walls and other surfaces are covered in wood that introduces much-needed warmth to the interior's cool industrial palette. The wood, it turns out, comes from ash trees that Chicago officials cut down during the emerald ash borer beetle infestation that struck the city a few years ago. A mill set up by Chicago artist and U of C faculty member Theaster Gates turned the trees into lumber.

There are more chances for interaction, as well as exercise, on a handsomely detailed set of switchback stairs just off the atrium. Wrapped in a frame of blackened steel, the stairs encourage people to walk from floor to floor rather than taking the elevator.

As you would expect from Farr, the Keller Center is aiming for the highest level of energy-saving design—the US Green Building Council's Leadership in Energy and Environmental Design platinum certification. Rooftop solar panels generate 11 percent of the building's energy. Rainwater is routed from the rooftop through visible pipes to a 15,000-gallon tank in the basement that provides water for flushing toilets.

Sometimes, energy-saving architecture is merely a litany of such technical features, but that's not the case here. There's more delight than drudgery in this building, especially in its glass-walled fourth-floor addition, whose conference rooms and classrooms overlook the Midway and the university's collegiate Gothic towers to the north.

To be sure, the center is not faultless. Low ceilings that the architects inherited from Stone make faculty office corridors feel tightly constrained. And the impact of the building's new back entrance, which seeks to build a bridge to neighboring Woodlawn, is undercut by the presence of a surface-parking lot and cul-de-sacs that continue the regrettable separation of the university from Woodlawn.

Still, this is an exemplary work of architectural recycling. The key to its success is the way it respects, but loosens up, Stone's architectural temple, creating an academic center that is noble yet not stuffy. It is, in short, a less formal version of New Formalism, one that gives new life to the U of C's architectural oddball.

A Different View of the Masterful Farnsworth House—Hers

JULY 2, 2020

The Farnsworth House, Ludwig Mies van der Rohe's modernist masterpiece in Chicago's far southwest suburbs, needs no introduction. As graceful as a Greek temple and as serene as a Shinto shrine, the single-room house seems to float over a meadow alongside the

Farnsworth House exhibition: revealing a female client's role in the creation of Ludwig Mies van der Rohe's modernist masterpiece. Photo by William Zbaren.

Fox River—one of the purest and most poetic distillations of the International Style.

But what about Dr. Edith Farnsworth, who paid for the house, lived in it, and lost a bitter legal battle with Mies over cost overruns and architect's fees? Who, exactly, was she?

A daring and fascinating new exhibition, *Edith Farnsworth's Country House*, does more than flesh out the impressive résumé of this overlooked figure, who grew up on Chicago's Gold Coast and became a leading kidney doctor plus a translator of Italian poetry. The show restores her presence to the house that bears her name, but where for years she was all but absent.

The exhibition performs this trick by dispatching to the warehouse the home's coolly elegant, metal-framed Miesian furniture, including the architect's signature Barcelona, Brno, and MR chairs. In their place are replicas of pieces that Farnsworth herself chose, like a lovely wood-and-metal dining-room table by the American designer Florence

Knoll. Moroccan wool carpets are laid out on the travertine marble floor, along with potted plants.

We also see objects that represent Farnsworth, from a black leather doctor's bag to bathroom towels with her monogram "EBF" (the "B" stood for "Brooks") to a bottle of the sweet vermouth she sipped each afternoon.

For anyone who's been to the Farnsworth House before, this transformation is likely to elicit a pleasing shock: the interior seems warmer, more in tune with nature, and, above all, more livable—in sum, more influenced by the humane Scandinavian modernism of the Finnish architect Alvar Aalto than its hard-edged, German-American counterpart personified by Mies.

To frame matters in terms of gender rather than style, this is *her* house, not his—the closest we've ever come to seeing the Farnsworth House as its namesake lived in it, not as Mies would have furnished it.

There's a bigger issue here than Farnsworth and Mies. For as long as architects have wielded drafting tools, the designers of houses, almost always men, and their clients—in this case, an accomplished woman who was anything but a typical postwar housewife—have battled for control of the interior.

When Frank Lloyd Wright stayed overnight at houses he'd designed, he was known to rearrange furniture to his liking while his clients slept. Wright even designed dresses for female clients so their outfits would not clash with a home he conceived as a total work of art—a Gesamtkunstwerk, as the Germans call it.

Not surprisingly, this controlling impulse has generated blowback, as it did one day in the early 1950s when one of Mies's associates telephoned Farnsworth to inform her that the furniture the architect had chosen for her home, including two Barcelona chairs, was about to be delivered.

The essence of her reply: she hadn't ordered the furniture and had no intention of using it.

"The fact is that Mies has no taste and if you stop to think about it, that is not surprising," she said in an exchange with an English architect recounted in the well-told, deeply researched new book, *Broken Glass: Mies van der Rohe, Edith Farnsworth, and the Fight over a Modernist Masterpiece*, by Alex Beam.

"I would hate to be forced to break with him, but I would never consent to his ideas on furnishing," Farnsworth said. "One's house is almost as personal as one's skin. I don't see how he could seriously think that I would go with him beyond the erection of the house itself."

Beam's pro-Farnsworth sympathies pervade the exhibition, which was curated by Scott Mehaffey, the Farnsworth House's executive director, and opened late because of the coronavirus. During the delay, floodwaters once again threatened the house, which is located in Plano, about sixty miles southwest of the Loop. It emerged unscathed due to the stilt-like steel columns that lift it above the ground. (In the past, even the stilts could not prevent water from pouring in.)

Part of a larger reexamination of Farnsworth's role that is on display at the house and its visitors' complex, the exhibit also was shaped by veteran Chicago interior designer Robert Kleinschmidt and Nora Wendl, who teaches architecture at the University of New Mexico and is an expert on Edith Farnsworth. The National Trust for Historic Preservation, which has owned the home since 2003 and runs it as a house museum, deserves credit for cooperating with this provocative endeavor.

Granted, the show presents an idealized picture of what was, at first, a weekend retreat. Based on historic photographs and Farnsworth's writings, the exhibit re-creates the house as it looked in 1955, just four years after it opened—not in the 1960s, when Farnsworth was living in it regularly and the house became a cluttered mess.

There are no mounds of dirty dishes in the sink, no piles of magazines and newspapers, and no dog vomit from Farnsworth's poodle, all of which visitors recounted seeing. Also absent is the ungainly screen Farnsworth had installed on the house's upper terrace to keep away voracious mosquitoes. On the lower terrace, however, are smaller versions of the stone Chinese lion statues (the so-called foo dogs) that Farnsworth placed there in a comically bad departure from Mies's less-is-more abstraction.

Yet even if the reconstituted house is a little too precious, like a furniture showroom, it has the virtue of putting Farnsworth back into the picture.

She pretty much disappeared after she sold the house to British real estate developer (and now Baron) Peter Palumbo in 1972. Palumbo

Inside the Farnsworth House exhibition: how the house *really* looked when Edith Farnsworth lived there. Photo by William Zbaren.

and Mies's grandson, Chicago architect Dirk Lohan, lovingly and meticulously restored the house's exterior and turned its interior into a kind of Mies museum, complete with the decor the architect would have preferred. While that treatment was true to Mies's vision for the house, it perpetuated a false impression by erasing Farnsworth's presence, although introductory material in the visitor center always included her.

In the exhibit's telling, Farnsworth isn't the sad figure who, as the Mies crowd put it, thought the architect came with the house (for a time, the two were close friends and may have been romantically involved). She emerges as formidable rather than pitiful—first because she hired Mies to design the house, and then because she defied him in furnishing its interior.

As Beam's book recounts, Farnsworth had help from her friend Kitty Baldwin Weese, the wife of Chicago architect Harry Weese and the cofounder of the influential Baldwin Kingrey design store in Chicago. The store championed furniture and housewares designed by such renowned figures of postwar modernism as Knoll and Aalto.

Indeed, after visitors enter the house and are greeted by a replica of Farnsworth's seventeenth-century violin, they see a Knoll dining table to the left, and to the right, a small circular Aalto table, on top of which are binoculars and a guide to birdwatching by American ornithologist Roger Tory Peterson.

Throughout the exhibition, Farnsworth's presence is palpable. So is the underlying tension between architect and client, especially in the show's frank depiction of Farnsworth's revolt against Mies's allotment and placement of closet space.

Originally, Mehaffey told me, the architect gave Farnsworth a tiny closet in the house's galley kitchen. Yet she wanted more room and didn't want food smells to ruin her clothes. So she secretly got a Mies associate to design a tall wood wardrobe that was placed just off the house's living area. The wardrobe provided the needed storage space and created a room-like writing nook, which was furnished, as the exhibition shows, with a sleek modern desk and an Olivetti typewriter.

The wardrobe violated the openness of Mies's interior, a victory of function over form.

The exposure of such tensions is among the show's strengths. There would be no Farnsworth House without Mies's singular talents, of course, yet the house could not have come into existence without Farnsworth's probing mind and innovative spirit.

Great architecture is impossible without great clients, even when the relationship between architect and client devolves into bitterness, as it did here. It is fitting that this exhibition brings Farnsworth fully back into the house's story and, in the process, explores the always-fraught relationship between architect and client, art and habitation, transcendent idea and everyday reality.

Postscript: In 2021, the National Trust for Historic Preservation re-dedicated the house, changing its name to the Edith Farnsworth House. The shift recognized the client's essential role in the creation of the modernist masterwork and officially restored her to the house's narrative. It was part of the National Trust's "Where Women Made

History" campaign, which seeks to protect places where women made a lasting mark on American culture.

PRESERVING BUILDINGS OF THE DISTANT PAST: YESTERDAY'S DESIGNS, SOME VIEWED AS RADICAL, ARE TODAY'S CLASSICS

In contrast to the struggles Chicago preservationists faced in trying to save buildings of the recent past, they won several clear-cut victories in their quest to preserve older buildings in the city and its suburbs. Two pathbreaking designs by Frank Lloyd Wright—Unity Temple and the Robie House, both of which had been in terrible shape in the 1990s—reopened after superb restorations. Two white elephants seemingly beyond repair, Chicago's Art Moderne Old Post Office and the Beaux-Arts old Cook County Hospital, got new uses and new life. A multiyear revamp turned beloved, once-crumbling Wrigley Field into a modernized National Historic Landmark. And historic Union Station was saved from a blockheaded scheme that would have placed a graceless hotel on its roof.

These successes, particularly the restorations of Unity Temple and the Robie House, showed how crucial it is for once-radical, initially unloved buildings to survive demolition threats today so they might be seen through more enlightened eyes tomorrow. "History," as the Pritzker Prize–winning French architect Jean Nouvel once said, "is a succession of modernities."

Delayed Restoration of Unity Temple Was Well Worth the Wait

MAY 20, 2017

Frank Lloyd Wright was never one to fret about meeting deadlines, sticking to budgets, or patching leaking roofs. So there is something fitting about the delayed, but altogether triumphant, restoration of Wright's Unity Temple, the Oak Park landmark that is the finest public building of Wright's Chicago years and home to one of the most beautiful rooms in America.

Instead of finishing on schedule last fall, the $25 million project is wrapping up just in time for the 150th anniversary of Wright's birthday,

Unity Temple: a precise restoration brought back the original unity between its severe exterior and serene interior. Photo by Lee Bey.

June 8. It's as though Wright himself had willed the timing to demonstrate afresh his genius at the very moment when public attention will be riveted on his legacy.

For decades, scholars and critics have remarked upon the striking contrast between Unity Temple's exterior and interior: the former, made of exposed concrete, is monumental, monochromatic, and seemingly impenetrable. The latter, a skylit room with multiple seating tiers, is grand yet human-scaled, enlivened by a rich palette of earth-toned colors. It's as airy as the concrete cube is heavy.

The fine-tuned restoration breaks down this familiar dichotomy, revealing a strong aesthetic connection between the radically severe exterior and the warm, intimate interior—a new unity, if you will, for Unity Temple. The key step involves the return of robust interior finishes that once wove a thread of nature-inspired continuity between inside and outside. Without them, we now know, Unity Temple was simply not whole.

Practically minded readers also should be delighted to know that the restoration delivers creature comforts, like air conditioning, that will prevent the heavenly interior from turning hellishly hot come summer. The exterior is even said to be leak-free. We'll have to see about that, given Wright's infamous track record of leaky flat-roofed buildings that forced their occupants to haul out drip buckets for what they referred to as "one-bucket," "two-bucket," and "three-bucket" rains.

Success, it's often said, has many fathers, and so it is here: a team of consultants led by Chicago's Harboe Architects has lavished exacting care on every aspect of this project, from the restoration of jewel-like art glass to the recreation of textured plaster walls. This high level of quality was made possible by $10 million lead grant from Chicago's Alphawood Foundation, $1.75 million from the congregation, and the rest from private donors.

Yet there's a catch, as there always seems to be with Wright, who frequently lived beyond his means: the nonprofit that spearheaded the project, Unity Temple Restoration Foundation, still must raise roughly half the project's budget. For now, a bridge loan covers those costs. The superb restoration, it turns out, is also a superb advertisement, one that should encourage foundations and individuals to make up the balance.

From the first, financial constraints have shaped Unity Temple, which sits amid Oak Park's thriving downtown at 875 Lake Street. After the congregation's Gothic Revival church burned in 1905, its leaders asked Wright, who was born into a Unitarian family in 1867, to design a new building on a prominent site along Lake Street's noisy streetcar line. The budget, a mere $45,000, did not allow for expensive materials or elaborate ornament. So Wright, ever the innovator, fashioned his design from inexpensive poured-in-place concrete.

Victorians accustomed to embroidered surfaces must have been shocked by the monolithic abstraction of the completed 1908 building, a high-walled house of worship joined by a foyer to a social hall and classroom building called Unity House. The passages to, and through, the sanctuary were equally radical. A circuitous route—the classic Wright sequence known as the "path of discovery"—led from Lake Street to the entrance on a quiet side street. Inside, more turns took the worshipper from dark, tightly confined ground-floor spaces that Wright labeled "cloisters" on up and into the sanctuary's spectacular explosion of space and light.

It was—and still is—an extraordinary gathering place, in which space flows freely, liberated from the convention of the box. Yet there's a profound sense of order and repose, as if one had come upon a light-dappled glade. The intimacy is palpable, courtesy of tiered balconies that ensure no seat is more than forty-five feet from the pulpit. Sunlight filters down from a grid of skylights, creating an effect that Wright compared to a "happy cloudless day." Instead of turning their backs on the minister to exit, congregation members pass through doors cut into walls on either side of the pulpit. In theory, at least, one enters as an individual and leaves as a member of a community.

"Unity Temple is where you will find the first real expression of the idea that the space within the building is the reality of that building," Wright remarked in 1952, seven years before his death.

But like many Wright buildings, Unity Temple challenged the patience and finances of its occupants. Even after a 1973 renovation covered the failing original exterior with a layer of "shotcrete," a pneumatically applied concrete, cracks and chipping persisted. Naturally, the building's many roofs leaked. Seepage from internal drains, which were concealed in interior columns, weakened the structure's concrete bones. When a large chunk of the ceiling fell in the middle of the night nine years ago, "it was a wake-up call about the instability of the building," recalled the reverend Alan Taylor, Unity Temple's senior minister.

The restoration team has done meticulous work, beginning with

Inside Unity Temple: restoring the textures, color palette, and spatial drama of Frank Lloyd Wright's original. Photo by James Caulfield; courtesy of Unity Temple Restoration Foundation.

the exterior, where portions of the 1973 shotcrete have been removed and replaced with new swaths of the material. Along with new roofs, restored art glass, and enlarged internal drains, the new shotcrete is supposed to create that rarest of conditions in a Wright building—a structure that doesn't leak like a sieve.

"The system is good. It's been tested," said architect Gunny Harboe, who worked on the project with colleague Bob Score.

But replacing the shotcrete presented an aesthetic challenge. Unity Temple's exterior is not a simple flat gray but a richly textured aggregate of cement, sand, and pebbles that range in color from white to brown to flint. Getting the right blend was like finding the elusive mix for a perfect cocktail. Contractors had to do some spots two or three times before the work was pronounced satisfactory.

The outcome largely avoids the pitfalls of a patchwork, although close inspection reveals slight variations in color. Yet time, weathering, and the curing of the shotcrete should eventually blur those distinctions. And it will be no great sin if some of them remain. Unity Temple's exterior has always had a certain mottled look. One of Wright's prime tenets was to build "in the nature of materials," which meant respecting their inherent properties. New in-ground night lighting showcases the handsomely refurbished exterior and its decorative concrete columns.

The real revelations, though, are inside, where all interior surfaces have been returned to their 1908 appearance. That may not sound dramatic, but it's a major shift when you realize that multiple coats of paint, even modern latex paint, had been slathered onto the original walls. That rendered them flat and textureless, which was not what Wright intended.

Drawing on historic photographs and microscopic paint analysis, Harboe Architects and Philadelphia's Building Conservation Associates re-created three types of textured plaster walls (rough, semi-rough, and smooth) and Wright's earth-toned color palette (pale yellow, green, and brown). Contractors applied glazes over the plaster, giving them both their color and a luminous sheen appropriate to a sacred space. The outcome is subtle but striking, especially within the sanctuary.

From the skylight to the ground floor, the freshly remodeled interior walls have a new sense of texture and motion, restoring a lost layer of visual richness. Just as important, the interior now engages in a quiet but unmistakable dialogue with the building's textured-concrete exterior. Inside and outside are opposites yet part of the same whole, a yin-yang relationship that makes tangible Wright's elusive gospel of an "organic architecture."

"No one's seen it that way in a long time," Harboe said.

Throughout, the design team deftly addressed practical issues without aesthetic sacrifice. LEDs were installed beneath the sanctuary's skylights to give worshippers in the top seating tiers improved lighting as they read from prayer books. Mechanical systems were deftly inserted in the four hollow columns that support the building. Geothermal wells—nine of them, descending five hundred feet beneath the front lawn—will provide the air conditioning the building has long lacked. New theater lights will improve Unity Temple's ability to host performances.

Comparable formal and functional improvements are being made to Unity House.

What a change has transpired since 2000, when the Landmarks Preservation Council of Illinois (now Landmarks Illinois) placed the deteriorating Unity Temple on its annual list of the state's most endangered structures! Today, Unity Temple is a landmark renewed, an enduring statement of Wright's genius and a vivid reminder that his brilliance extended far beyond the Prairie Style houses for which he is best known. The revived house of worship presents an altogether fitting way to celebrate the 150th anniversary of Wright's birth.

The Robie House Is Again a Full-Fledged Architectural Symphony

MARCH 25, 2019

It's a masterpiece. The word, often overused, fits. Let's use it.

The artistry of Frank Lloyd Wright's Robie House is dazzling, from its sweeping horizontal planes to its delicate bands of art glass to its extraordinary manipulation of interior space. Completed in 1910 alongside the Gothic Revival towers of the University of Chicago, the house culminated the architectural revolution of Wright's Prairie Style and inspired a generation of European modernists. Here, the drive for architectural modernity crystallized into a design that still shapes how we live today.

For years, though, the Robie House limped along, a shadow of its former self. This sad state of affairs resulted from neglectful owners or well-meaning stewards who lacked the funds to put the landmark back in order. Visitors saw the outlines of Wright's vision rather than

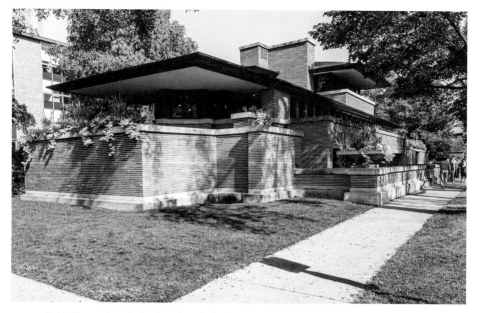

Robie House: the culmination of Frank Lloyd Wright's Prairie Style, superbly restored. Photo by Lee Bey.

the total work of art the architect intended. A restoration began in 2002, then stalled.

Now, though, the $11 million–plus revamp is finally complete, and it reminds us anew why the Robie House is one of Chicago's, and the world's, architectural treasures.

Building on previous phases of the restoration, which whipped the house's once-crumbling exterior into shape and installed modern mechanical systems, the new work has brought back the interior's autumnal color palette, restored oak ceiling trim and other woodwork, and rebuilt lost features like an art-glass front door that was smashed during 1960s student demonstrations.

In turn, the university's Smart Museum of Art has returned a star attraction of the house, a Wright-designed dining table, with six straight-lined high-back chairs and geometric lighting at the corners. The homecoming of the table, which remains in the museum's collection, symbolizes how the house has been returned to its full-fledged glory for the first time in decades.

Credit for this transformation goes to the Frank Lloyd Wright Trust, the Chicago-based nonprofit that conducts tours of the Robie House and other Wright sites: Unity Temple and the architect's home and studio, both in Oak Park; the Emil Bach House, at 7415 North Sheridan Road; and the light court of the Rookery building, 209 South LaSalle Street, where the Trust is headquartered. Chicago's Alphawood Foundation was the lead funder, providing grants of $3 million.

The Trust and its president, Celeste Adams, had both the wisdom and the wherewithal to put the interior job in the hands of Chicago's Harboe Architects, whose award-winning 2017 revamp of Unity Temple was as exacting as their work on the Robie House.

If Unity Temple, completed in 1908, is the finest public building of Wright's Chicago years, the Robie House is the greatest home of that period. It ended with a jolt in 1909, when Wright scandalized Oak Park by abandoning his young family and running off to Europe with the wife of one of his clients.

As with many of Wright's houses, the saga of the Robie House—located at 5757 South Woodlawn Avenue, kitty-corner from the U of C's Rockefeller Chapel—is almost as interesting as the house itself. The house's namesake, bicycle manufacturer Frederick C. Robie, had an inventive spirit that was a perfect match for the iconoclastic Wright. But Robie lived in the house for less than two years. With his marriage falling apart, he sold it in late 1911.

Fifteen years later, in 1926, the Chicago Theological Seminary bought the house from another owner and turned it into a dormitory. Prairie Style furnishings disappeared and the house's exterior was treated crudely. In 1957, when the seminary tried to tear down Robie to build new dorms, Wright, then nearly ninety years old, led a successful campaign to save it.

"It all goes to show the danger of entrusting anything spiritual to the clergy," he famously said of the seminary's demolition scheme.

Eventually, the building was transferred to the U of C, which in 1997 designated the Trust (then known as the Frank Lloyd Wright Home and Studio Foundation) as the house's operator. But the Trust had its hands full due to years of deferred maintenance. The long, narrow Roman bricks of the house's exterior were falling apart. Air conditioners were jammed into some of the delicate art-glass windows.

Today, thanks to a renewed appreciation of Wright sparked in part by the 150th anniversary of his birth, in 2017, it's a different story. With the Robie House back in fine form, we can again fully appreciate how it represents the crowning achievement of Wright's nearly decade-long push to break out of the box of the Victorian house.

Stand at the corner of Fifty-Eighth Street and Woodlawn Avenue, and you can see how Wright shattered every convention of domestic architecture—and how the restoration has brought his achievement back into sharp focus.

The first phase of the project restored the Roman bricks and deeply incised mortar joints that accentuate the house's prairie-inspired horizontal proportions. It also bolstered structural steel, not visible to the passerby, that makes possible Robie House's dramatic cantilevered roofs. As a result, the house looks magnificently sculptural—a dynamic, asymmetric composition that at once seems to hug the earth and fly into space.

The newly completed, final round of restoration—based on old black-and-white photographs, architectural drawings, and a scientific study of wall surfaces—gives credence to Wright's fuzzy-sounding contention that his architecture was "organic," interweaving inside and outside, space and structure.

The delightful details begin with a recreation of the house's hard-to-find front door, a stunning array of diamond-shaped art glass that features amber, green, and white pieces of glass set within thin zinc frames.

Throughout the house, existing plaster walls, which for years had been covered only by a dull primer coat, were carefully repainted to reintroduce Wright's original texture and colors. To fix the plaster, every strip of wood, including scores of oak ceiling bands, had to be removed from the house, restored, and then put back.

The project's exemplary attention to detail extends beyond such surfaces to spaces. In an area of the second floor just off the main staircase, for example, a re-created wood screen acts like a veil, partly concealing the visitor's view of a remade inglenook next to the living room's fireplace.

"It's a tease," said Gunny Harboe, principal of Harboe Architects, referring to Wright's ability to entice visitors from one space to another.

The culmination of this movement, the second floor, is a single expansive space, revolutionary for its time, that encompasses both the living and dining rooms. (It's subdivided by a portion of the house's chimney.) Lining the south side of those rooms are twenty-four art-glass windows, which continue the autumnal palette and diamond pattern of the front door. The space and its furnishings have a new luster because Harboe and his team have reestablished the room's serene, meditative mood with such re-created details as handblown globe lights.

Reanimated by such features, the restored Robie House is again a full-fledged architectural symphony of structure, space, art, and furnishings. It's a vivid display of the way Wright's architecture and design redirected the course of modern architecture. Everybody who loves architecture should see it. It's the latest reminder of why Chicago is the indispensable city of American architecture and why there is no better place in the world to sample Wright's genius.

Postscript: In 2019, eight Wright buildings, including the Robie House and Unity Temple, were named to the UNESCO World Heritage List. They were the first works of US modern architecture to be inscribed on the list, a catalog of the world's most significant natural and cultural sites.

Union Station Plan on the Wrong Track: All the Grandeur of a Holiday Inn

JUNE 25, 2018

Daniel Burnham's ghost and his much-quoted exhortation to "make no little plans" haunt the just-released, utterly underwhelming design for a vertical expansion of Chicago's Union Station.

To put things in Burnham-speak, these plans are little—very little. They bring minimal creativity to the dubious idea of stacking a chunky addition on the station's roof.

There's nothing wrong with putting a 330-room hotel *within* the upper floors of the station's historic main building, especially because the hotel would provide cross-country travelers and railroad buffs with a history-laden spot to stay. The trouble is a planned apartment addition that would plunk a squat modernist box *atop* the existing struc-

Proposed addition to Chicago's Union Station: how not to treat a landmark. Image credit: Solomon Cordwell Buenz.

ture's neoclassical pedestal. They go together as well as Rauner and Pritzker, the City Council and ethics reform.

The proposed seven-story addition and its 404 rental apartments would bring to the forlorn but grand train station all the grandeur of a Holiday Inn.

The plans, unveiled at a public meeting hosted by downtown alderman Brendan Reilly (Forty-Second), are by Chicago architects Solomon Cordwell Buenz for Riverside Investment & Development. Amtrak picked the Chicago developer last year to carry out a $1 billion–plus redevelopment of the station and property around it. Riverside's initial plans, from Chicago architects Goettsch Partners, offered few bold ideas. The new ones aren't much better, though they would make it easier for the public to move through the chronically claustrophobic station.

Such desultory prospects are a far cry from Burnham's 1909 Plan of Chicago, which envisioned Union Station as a magnificent gateway to the West Loop. The architect died in 1912, leaving his successors at the firm of Graham, Anderson, Probst & White to design the station, which was partially completed in 1925.

A planned office building atop the station was never built, though foundations were laid for it. The addition would have endowed the truncated station with handsome proportions and a sense of aesthetic completion. Such was its enduring power that, in 2002, Chicago architect Lucien Lagrange used the design as a takeoff point for a four-hundred-foot office, hotel, and residential tower that would have gone atop the station. But that plan, too, fell through.

Solomon Cordwell Buenz has tried a different approach: not a harmonious replication of the original design, as Lagrange attempted, or a wild, Soldier Field–style addition that offers a jarring juxtaposition of past and present. Instead, the firm's John Lahey and Steve Hubbard sought to make the addition compatible with, but differentiated from, the original building.

The addition tries to achieve this balance in several ways, beginning with a recessed base that would visually separate old from new. Articulated metal columns would continue the upward reach of the station's limestone piers. A rectangular floor plan, hollow in the middle, would allow sunlight to filter down to the skylight over the station's soaring Great Hall.

The addition's backers tout the fact that it would be only 235 feet tall (245 feet if you count elevator equipment)—far shorter than the approved height for the Lagrange plan. But that very shortness is a weakness.

The addition would be top-heavy, a ponderous presence, weighing on the original station rather than creating a lightweight counterpoint to it. Worse, the addition's exterior, a skeletal metal-and-glass grid, is at odds with the station's carefully composed classical aesthetic.

Despite the architects' best efforts, it's as though one era of architecture had been piled, willy-nilly, atop another. The design also happens to be wet-blanket banal, which Burnham's bold buildings never are.

True, there are good strokes. Union Station's exterior has always seemed a bit forbidding, a quality that Solomon Cordwell Buenz would remedy by creating a new entrance in the middle of the station's Clinton Street facade. These and comparable canopied entrances—one to the hotel along Adams Street, the other to the apartments along Jackson Boulevard—promise to make the exterior more inviting and to funnel more traffic through the moribund Great Hall.

But the 1.5 million square foot office building that would replace a neighboring Amtrak parking garage remains a major question mark. Riverside wants zoning approval for the high-rise as part of the same development package as the addition to the station. The design has yet to be unveiled.

The deeply flawed plan to add to Union Station does not inspire confidence. A building that's an essential part of the Burnham legacy deserves better, especially because it forms an iconic gateway to Chicago.

Postscript: Critics had a field day attacking the planned Union Station addition, comparing it to an ice cube for a colossal architectural headache, a self-inked address stamper, or a suburban office building lifted off its foundations by a tornado and dropped atop the station. A few months later, the developers dropped the addition from their plans. But the proposed fifty-story office building, designed by Goettsch Partners and later named the BMO Tower, was approved and is expected to be complete in 2022.

With Cubs' Commercial Excess Mostly in Check, Wrigley Field's Nearly Complete Multiyear Renovation Is a Hit

APRIL 18, 2019

There have been times during the long-running renovation of Wrigley Field when the Cubs seemed intent on blighting the very ballpark they had pledged to save.

Wrigley Field: bringing back the architectural beauty of a beloved old ballpark. Photo by Lee Bey.

In 2013, the team proposed putting an advertiser's name on the streamlined circular clock atop Wrigley's iconic center-field scoreboard. Fortunately, that money-grubbing scheme never materialized.

A year later, the Cubs won permission from Chicago's pliant landmarks commission to cram Wrigley's once-ad-free outfield with seven large signs. Wisely, albeit timidly, the National Park Service, which administers the federal tax breaks the Cubs seek for the renovation, cut the number to six. So far, only three have been built.

Left unchecked, such examples suggest the Cubs and their owners, the Ricketts family, might well have marred the major league's second-oldest ballpark even as they poured nearly $1 billion into remaking Wrigley and its environs. Yet now that the multiyear renovation of the historic ballpark is nearly complete, it's clear that such a calamity has not come to pass.

The renovation has simultaneously modernized Wrigley for the digital age and retained the ballpark's industrial-age grit. It also has fortified Wrigley's once-crumbling structure, positioning the 105-year-old sports mecca to deliver more joy (and the Cubs being the Cubs, more heartache) for decades to come.

To be sure, some excesses have slipped through and the bulked-up, slicked-up streets around Wrigley no longer possess the raffish authenticity that once flavored the pilgrimage to the baseball shrine.

But the renovation mostly strikes the right balance between Wrigley as a cathedral of sport and Wrigley as a revenue-generating cash machine that in 2016 helped the Cubs win their first World Series in more than a century.

Design credit for the latest round of changes goes to Populous, a Kansas City, Missouri–based firm that specializes in sports architecture. Previous phases, which began after the 2014 season, were chiefly handled by the Chicago office of Stantec, a large Edmonton, Alberta–based design firm.

Among other things, the new work has completed the restoration of the ballpark's facade, remade Wrigley's concourses, inserted three premium suites into and below the seating bowl, provided more wheelchair-accessible seating, and created a big underground locker room for the Cubs below Wrigley's plaza along Clark Street.

Once federal and state officials certify that the work meets national historic-preservation standards, the Rickettses can be expected to receive between $100 million and $125 million in tax credits, said team spokesman Julian Green. That's a sizable chunk of change for the owners. But the public is benefiting too.

The upgrades are first apparent on Wrigley's exterior, which used to be covered with ugly gray concrete panels that all but screamed "bad 1960s modernism."

Before the 2016 season, the panels were stripped off the ballpark's left-field side and replaced with picturesque decorative features that adorned Wrigley in the late 1920s—ornamental grillwork topped by elegant sunburst patterns and terra-cotta roofing on the street-level portion of the facade. Now, Populous has extended the treatment to cover the entire right-field side.

The restored facade is both a pleasure to behold and a reminder that Wrigley, which began its life in 1914 as a single-deck ballpark designed by Zachary Taylor Davis, displays a succession of styles (Chicago School, Arts and Crafts, and Art Deco), not a single aesthetic. Architects like Graham, Anderson, Probst & White and Holabird & Root skillfully layered those styles onto the structure without turning it into a pastiche.

The only blemishes on the otherwise handsomely restored exterior are a pair of boxy gray structures, which house elevators and restrooms, that bookend the outdoor terrace of one of the new premium suites, the Catalina Club. Another fault: the digital-advertising pylons that mar Wrigley's otherwise attractive plaza, now called Gallagher Way, along Clark.

Like the walls of a living room, the clean-lined, Stantec-designed buildings that previously opened as part of the redevelopment—a six-story Cubs office building north of the plaza and the seven-story Hotel Zachary (named for the architect) across Clark—effectively enclose the people-friendly outdoor space. It's open to ticket holders on game days and to the public at other times. That's quite an upgrade from the grungy surface-parking lots that used to occupy the site. Just ask the kids who play catch on the bright green turf.

Inside Wrigley, the pluses also outweigh the minuses. New steel and concrete have shored up the ballpark, where netting once had to be installed to prevent chunks of concrete from falling on fans.

Getting around is generally easier than before, courtesy of the well-lit, smartly designed concourses. From the grandstand, Wrigley's sight lines remain as intimate as ever. New outdoor decks, especially in the bleachers, give fans the option of standing and partying as they watch.

While there are too many small advertising signs on the outfield walls, these revenue generators at least share the ballpark's green-and-white palette and are displayed in an orderly manner.

Art Deco graphics and green and white colors also help the jumbo-sized left-field video board seem at home at Wrigley, but it still over-

Inside Wrigley Field: despite big videoboards and blaring music, it's still the Friendly Confines. Photo by Blair Kamin.

shadows the historic center-field scoreboard. And the advertising never stops. Must we know that this replay is brought to you by Vital Proteins, the official collagen of the Cubs?

Worse, as the *Tribune*'s Paul Sullivan has noted, the Cubs now pump ridiculously loud music through the public-address system. Wrigley may still *look* pastoral but it no longer *sounds* pastoral.

Even so, the fact that there are only three big outfield signs allows the rooftop perches along Waveland and Sheffield Avenues to retain their prized views into the field—and to remain a part of Wrigley's distinctive urban character. The ballpark enlivens the city around it, just as the city brings life to the ballpark.

All in all, the renovation is a hit—not quite perfect, but nonetheless a skillful and mostly sensitive reinvention of a national treasure. It has taken a cramped, outdated ballpark that was long on charm and short on modern conveniences and fortified, expanded, and modernized it.

Wrigley is still Wrigley—Paradise Changed, not Paradise Lost. Let's hope the Cubs don't screw it up.

Postscript: The US Department of the Interior in 2020 named Wrigley Field a National Historic Landmark, a listing the federal government reserves for "historic places that hold national significance." As anticipated, the designation made the Cubs' owners eligible for millions of dollars in historic-preservation tax credits. Meanwhile, new large-scale buildings outside the ballpark continued to gentrify Wrigleyville. Accentuating concerns about the neighborhood's shifting character, the Cubs in 2021 won city approval for a two-story addition to Wrigley that will house their betting facility, or sportsbook.

Chicago's Old Post Office, the Nation's Largest Reuse Project, Delivers the Goods

OCTOBER 17, 2019

It's early in the much-ballyhooed new life of Chicago's once-hulking, now-hip Old Post Office, and early assessments, truth be told, are dangerous. You never know how a building, especially one sized XXXL, is really going to work. This one, once the world's largest post office and now promoted as the US's largest reuse project, is so ginormous— a single floor can fit up to two thousand office workers—that I wonder if people there will feel like they're toiling away in an ant farm.

But given the physical prominence of the building, which straddles the Eisenhower Expressway, and the fact that the first tenants are about to move in, I took a look and came away hopeful that this massive structure, for years so visible but so isolated, is about to reconnect with its environs and revitalize them.

Still in the midst of an $800 million–plus redevelopment that's scheduled to be completed next year, the Old Post Office has been modernized (and, you might say, millennialized) without sacrificing its historic character.

The office floors, which once hummed with conveyor belts and all manner of heavy-duty equipment, still contain corkscrewing mail chutes and other relics, like vaults and scales, that help tell the building's story. The restored main lobby, nearly as long as a football

The Old Post Office: empty and isolated for years, an architectural sleeping giant finally awoke. Photo by Lee Bey.

field, is so elegant that it's fit for a wedding. Indeed, some are already scheduled.

The cityscape also gains. Motorists and pedestrians alike will note that the once-crumbling Art Moderne facade looks better than it has in decades.

In short, the Old Post Office—an architectural sleeping giant—has finally stirred after years of false hopes and cockamamie plans. And it's beginning to make what could be a seismic impact on downtown's southwest edge.

With two-thirds of its 2.5 million square feet already leased to such high-profile tenants as Uber and Walgreens, the building seems destined to become a new commercial hub, like a skyscraper turned on its side. It's a good bet that some people who work there will want to live within walking distance, which bodes well for investors in the residential high-rises that are popping up nearby, along the Chicago River's South Branch.

Such benefits help justify historic-preservation tax breaks that are expected to save the building's owners, New York–based 601W Companies, $100 million over the life of the project. Yet the owners still must make good on a planned riverfront plaza, which they expect to open next year. And Mayor Lori Lightfoot's urban planners will need to do everything in their power to ensure that the energy of the Old Post Office spills out into the now-sterile streets around it.

Even so, what has transpired so far at 433 West Van Buren Street is a near miracle, coming just eight years after the eccentric British multimillionaire Bill Davies floated a loony, $3.5 billion plan to transform the former post office and its environs into a sprawling urban mall and entertainment complex topped by five skyscrapers ranging in height from 40 to 120 stories.

Davies, who always seemed more interested in inflating the building's value than actually developing it, died five days before the sale to 601W. The company and its lead architects, the Chicago office of global firm Gensler, moved methodically to restore confidence in the battered landmark, removing asbestos and lead paint, installing new mechanical and electrical systems, stabilizing the facade and bringing back the main lobby's luster.

Gensler, whose efforts were led by principals Sheryl Schulze and Grant Uhlir, joined with a team of consultants to creatively confront the functional challenges posed by the enormous building—actually, three structures of varying heights (six to twelve floors)—erected in 1921 and the early 1930s.

Among those challenges: the Eisenhower cuts through an opening in the first floor that was left for a highway when the building was constructed. The opening necessitated a new set of escalators to move people to the second floor and a superlong corridor that serves as the building's "Main Street."

But there were opportunities hidden in plain sight. The Old Post Office is easily accessible, located within walking distance of three downtown train stations, a major CTA bus terminal, and the CTA's Blue Line. In addition, its sheer size—800 feet long by 340 feet wide—opened the way for vast expanses of floor space that could house scores of workers on a single floor.

Then there was the building itself, which began its life as a kind of Amazon fulfillment center, a post office shipping goods from Chicago-based Sears and Montgomery Ward, as well as letters, around the nation. It was a Depression-era sibling of the even-larger Merchandise Mart, whose 4 million square feet made it the world's largest building when it opened in 1930.

Chicago architects Graham, Anderson, Probst & White designed both structures, giving them prominent limestone piers, pronounced corner towers, and recognizable decoration (American eagles for the post office) that mitigated their massiveness and created a handsome, utilitarian beauty that was more austere than the elegant exuberance of Art Deco.

By the time 601W took ownership, however, the Old Post Office had been vacant and neglected for about twenty years; a new facility had replaced it in the 1990s. Windows were boarded up. Portions of the masonry facade were crumbling.

Now, as a result of painstaking work of Gensler and the Chicago office of Wiss, Janney, Elstner architects, the facade is no longer an eyesore.

More than 2,100 windows have been installed, according to the architects. They are both energy efficient and replicate the profile of the originals. Scores of limestone panels were repaired or replaced. A monumental north entrance along Van Buren also has gotten much-needed TLC. Its grandly scaled windows have been restored, its white marble portals have been repaired, and handsome new railings adorn the flight of stairs that last-minute tax filers used to rush up on April 15.

The entrance serves as a warm-up for the ball-gown-beautiful grandeur of the main lobby, a dazzling, soaring space outfitted with restored geometric lanterns, walls of fluted marble and gold mosaic tile, as well as decorative panels that illustrate the march of transportation advances (from pony express to airplane) that sped delivery of the mail. Open to the public, the lobby communicates a faith in government that seems lost today. Gensler and McGuire Igleski & Associates skillfully handled this portion of the restoration.

It's too early for a definitive assessment of the rest of the ground floor, which will contain a Walgreens and a food hall that open onto the planned riverfront plaza. But Gensler has dealt smartly with the second floor, where tenant-only territory begins. Among the features there are a chic bar with a bocce court and a big gym that's been jazzed up with a boxing ring. They are among the Old Post Office's 80,000 square feet of amenities, an ample amount that compensates for the dullness of the surrounding neighborhood.

Atop the building is another buzzworthy feature: an under-construction roof deck, which will include landscaped open space, paddle-tennis courts, basketball courts, and a quarter-mile walking and jogging trail. Occupying 3.5 acres, it's said to be the nation's largest private rooftop deck. That's smart. If you've got a big roof, why not take advantage of it?

The same goes for the building's office floors, which capitalize on the current preference for vast expanses of horizontal space that enable people to easily communicate with each other. I was skeptical of this arrangement, particularly because 601W, citing the need for flexibility, rejected the possibility of light wells that would have drawn in natural light but also interrupted the floors' openness.

Yet sixteen-foot-high windows and nineteen-foot-high ceilings allow in a surprising amount of natural light, even to the center of the floors. This effect is accentuated by the wide spacing of the building's columns and by the way Gensler took advantage of different floor levels in the three buildings, creating upward and downward views from one section of the Old Post Office to another.

It's going to be fascinating to see how office workers react to their giant new home. Will it be bustling or bureaucratic, expansive or anonymous? Will additional design features endow the giant with at least a measure of human scale?

What's already compelling is the revival of this building, which, as recently as a few years ago, was considered an irredeemable white elephant. Now that the project has reached the milestone of taking in its first tenants, it seems as meaningful to Chicago as the transformation of industrial-era transportation infrastructure like elevated freight lines, docks, and railroads into the green spaces of the 606, the downtown Riverwalk, and Millennium Park. Such reinventions of the past form a key with which Chicago and other cities can unlock a brighter future.

Postscript: Five months after this column appeared, the outbreak of the coronavirus in the US put landlords under intense pressure to retrofit, redesign, and reimagine densely packed, open-plan office spaces like those in the Old Post Office. The immediate response: a profusion of plexiglass shields at work stations and social-distancing circles stuck on floors. As the pandemic dragged on, interior architects experimented with innovative features like work-station clusters that can be reconfigured so people don't face each other, reducing chances for the virus to spread. Developers focused on improving ventilation systems for indoor spaces as well as providing access to outdoor spaces, like balconies and gardens, that enable workers to social distance. But with many offices remaining far below their usual levels of activity, experts speculated that the post-COVID-19 office would largely be used for meetings and other group endeavors, while "focused" individual tasks would continue to be done remotely. If that prediction proves accurate, it could be deadly for commercial real estate values, cities' property-tax revenues, and the vitality of central business districts.

Once Facing the Wrecking Ball, Old Cook County Hospital Reemerges, Handsomely Remade

MAY 22, 2020

The renovation and reinvention of the old Cook County Hospital is a triumph of historic preservation, one that should resonate far beyond the walls of the beloved Beaux-Arts landmark on Chicago's Near West Side.

Not only does it give new life to an ornate, more-is-more work of architecture that Cook County leaders, unconscionably, had in their demolition crosshairs seventeen years ago. It preserves a powerful

Old Cook County Hospital: a symbol of compassionate care for the poor escaped the wrecking ball and got new life. Photo by Lee Bey.

symbol of compassionate care for the poor, serendipitously coming amid a pandemic that has seen doctors, nurses, and other medical professionals battle heroically against the deadly coronavirus.

The project is the anchor of a much-needed, multiphase $1 billion redevelopment that promises to enliven Chicago's vast but dull Illinois Medical District with new housing, offices, and restaurants. The biggest chunks of the soon-to-open, $140 million hospital revamp are a Hyatt Place hotel and an extended-stay Hyatt House. The project also includes an eight-station food hall and Cook County medical offices.

A recent preview showcased the meticulous restoration of the old hospital's sumptuous classical exterior and the creative redesign of its once-crumbling interior, where mold, moss, ferns, and trees once grew and squatters covered the walls with graffiti.

For those of us who questioned the wisdom of tearing down the building at 1835 West Harrison Street without a vigorous public debate, as former *Tribune* reporter Patrick T. Reardon and I did in 2003, the project represents a remarkable turn of events.

In 2003, when then Cook County Board President John Stroger aimed to demolish the old hospital after a new one named for him opened to the south, it seemed like Chicago would repeat the civic barbarity it committed in the early 1970s when it allowed the destruction of Dankmar Adler and Louis Sullivan's Chicago Stock Exchange Building.

There was every reason to fight Stroger's plan, and not only because the old hospital had embedded itself in the public consciousness as the inspiration for the TV medical drama *ER* or because its illustrious medical history included the world's first blood bank.

Completed in 1916, largely to the design of Cook County Architect Paul Gerhardt, the old hospital stood out from the monolithic modernism of the medical buildings that later surrounded it.

Its proud but dilapidated Harrison Street facade, which featured pairs of three-story Ionic columns as well as faces of lions and cherubs, powerfully communicated the idea that the building represented a source of strength and succor to the poor and sick.

Such was the hospital's devotion to caring for indigent African Americans and Hispanics who had migrated to Chicago that it was called Chicago's "Ellis Island," even though it was not, strictly speaking, an immigration portal.

This spirit of inclusion was exemplified by the words affixed to a monument to the French medical researcher Louis Pasteur in a park across Harrison Street. "One doesn't ask of one who suffers: What is your country and what is your religion? One merely says, you suffer, this is enough for me, you belong to me and I shall help you."

We should be thankful that Cook County Commissioner Larry Suffredin and the advocacy group Landmarks Illinois mobilized a successful charge against Stroger's misguided plan and that County Board President Toni Preckwinkle backed the renovation of this treasure, which is both an official Chicago landmark and listed on the National Register of Historic Places.

The renovation was worth every cent of the $27 million in historic-preservation tax breaks the developers will receive. The consortium, called the Civic Health Development Group, is helmed by the Murphy Development Group and includes Walsh Investors, MB Real Estate, the Plenary Group and Granite Companies.

Skidmore, Owings & Merrill of Chicago, led by designer partner Brian Lee and managing partner Adam Semel, headed the architectural team. The Chicago firm KOO designed the hotel's interiors. Their combined work has the building's exterior, made of granite, brick, limestone, and terra-cotta, looking sharper and cleaner than it has in decades.

More than 4,500 pieces of terra-cotta have been replaced—roughly 2,800 more than anticipated. (The developers had enough in their contingency fund to pay for the extras.) Naturalistic details, including sculpted versions of grapes, emerge like we've never seen them before. Metal window frames match the profile of the wood originals.

A clunky blue-and-white entrance canopy is gone, replaced by a sliver-thin canopy of steel and glass that disappears, with appropriate modesty, as you look at the building head-on.

As strong as the restored exterior along Harrison is, the real revelations come inside, where, for the first time in years, we can see first-hand that the building's beauty is more than skin deep.

The main lobby, once chopped into a single-story entrance, has been restored to its original two-story height, complete with elegant classical details and a stylish staircase of gray Tennessee marble. Ultrawide, superlong corridors, no longer dark and dreary, retain their dimensions and handsome terrazzo tile floors.

In these and other interior spaces, KOO's Jackie Koo has successfully introduced playful contemporary light fixtures, wall coverings, and artwork to send the message that hotel guests are entering a freshened piece of history, not a stodgy museum or a sterile medical facility. No one is going to mistake this for an ordinary chain hotel.

The interior is brightened—literally—by the way Skidmore, Owings & Merrill took advantage of the old hospital's remarkably thin footprint. It measures 550 feet long by just 80 feet wide, the result of four original wings being demolished years ago. Removing walls that once blocked windows makes the old hospital seem far less cavernous.

KOO and the SOM team have carefully threaded 210 hotel rooms into the building's forest of structural columns. The rooms, some of which have quirky layouts, are outfitted with smart contemporary decor and easy-to-clean surfaces, a plus for a hotel that will open during a pandemic. Thick insulation blocks out the rush of vehicles barreling down the nearby Eisenhower Expressway.

My favorite interior spaces, on the eighth floor, are former skylit operating rooms with high, slanted ceilings and bands of windows that overlook the United Center, to the north, and the downtown skyline, to the east. Still to be renovated, but teeming with architectural possibility, are the even more impressive tiered operating theaters at the ends of the same floor. A use for them has yet to be determined.

Not everything is perfect. Metal panels on the building's rear, which cover the architectural scars left when the original wings were removed, respect the proportions and facade organization of the original design, but they're no prizewinners.

The panels eventually may be concealed by residential buildings, geared to medical workers, that the developers plan to construct behind the old hospital. They also plan high-rises on the flanks of the park across Harrison Street, which will leave the center of the park open, preserving the view of the old hospital's main facade.

The care that went into the project reflects the development team's awareness that they were working on a civic treasure, one that had personal meaning for John T. Murphy, who heads Murphy Development Group.

He's naming the food hall for his great-uncle, the renowned Chicago surgeon John B. Murphy, who is credited with numerous medical innovations and treated Theodore Roosevelt after the former president was shot by a would-be assassin, in 1912. In addition, Murphy's father and grandfather both did their residencies at the old hospital.

Ultimately, however, the meaning of this project is civic as well as personal. Its rebirth strikes a chord on many levels: architectural, historical, medical, and cultural. Chicago's great buildings, it reminds us, are found in the neighborhoods, not just in its downtown. And this is a great one—for the beauty of its design, the humane values it communicates, and the stirring stories it still tells.

Part Five

TWO MAYORS, TWO DIRECTIONS

WHO CAN MAKE THE CITY WORK FOR ALL?

As Rahm Emanuel exited the mayor's office, in 2019, it marked the end of thirty years of pragmatic, centrist leadership at City Hall— a way of governing that largely benefitted one part of Chicago far more than the other.

Like his predecessor, former mayor Richard M. Daley, Emanuel was intensely interested in the built environment, deploying architecture to simultaneously upgrade the public realm and advertise his ability to get things done. Yet sporadic improvements on the South and West Sides—a new CTA station here, a new public library there—did not add up to a comprehensive approach to rebuilding struggling business districts and residential neighborhoods. The battle over a proposed North Side megaproject, Lincoln Yards, crystallized the view that Emanuel was more attuned to the needs of the developers who financed his political war chest than to the plight of the city's poor and working class.

The election of Lori Lightfoot, the city's second Black mayor, opened the way for a significant leftward shift at City Hall: to planning policies focused on equity and the need to revive economically depressed areas of the South and West Sides. Building on his experience in Detroit, Lightfoot's planning commissioner, Maurice Cox, steered Chicago in that direction. Yet violent crime worsened during the pandemic,

Rahm Emanuel at the Chicago Public Library's Chinatown branch: a bright spot in a mixed legacy. Photo by Anthony Souffle / *Chicago Tribune* / TCA.

as it did in other American cities, overshadowing the redevelopment effort and leaving the impression that Chicago was careening out of control.

RAHM EMANUEL: RETROSPECTIVE AND CLIMACTIC BATTLE

Emanuel Thought and Built Big, but Progress Was Painfully Uneven

SEPTEMBER 6, 2018

When former mayor Richard M. Daley stunned Chicago in 2010 with the announcement that he wouldn't seek reelection after twenty-one years in office, this question was widely heard: Will Chicago still think big?

Rahm Emanuel, who just issued his own "I will not run again" shocker, answered that question strongly in the affirmative, though his many urban-planning accomplishments did not bring him widespread popularity.

Under Emanuel, Chicago completed the downtown Riverwalk that Daley began and reaped the economic benefits of a development boom that brought construction cranes back to the skyline after the hiatus forced by the Great Recession.

Also during his two terms, Chicago started revitalizing its creaking mass-transit system, installed miles of bike lanes, opened innovative neighborhood parks and libraries, and won the right to host the Obama Presidential Center.

But for all his achievements, Emanuel never could escape the shadow of the violence wracking the city's South and West Sides and the resulting drumbeat of bad news that fed the narrative that Chicago is a tale of two cities—one thriving, the other struggling.

For every construction crane and ribbon-cutting, there was another homicide and a steady exodus of African Americans, reversing the Great Migration that brought thousands of Southern Blacks to the city from 1915 to 1950.

Like Daley, who oversaw the construction of such grand projects as Millennium Park, the Museum Campus, and a revitalized Navy Pier, Emanuel was an exponent of the postindustrial city—a Chicago that could play as well as work, a city that retained its trademark grit but was alluring enough to draw tourists from abroad.

Yet unlike Daley, who doted on flowers, imitation-wrought-iron fences, and other beautification touches, Emanuel saw the city as a machine, a place where the trains literally needed to run on time.

It's no coincidence that some of his most notable public works— the Riverwalk, the 606, or the planned southern extension of the Chicago Transit Authority's Red Line—are linear in character. Or that the Riverwalk, which stands as his signature urban-planning achievement, combines the pleasure of open space with the necessity of getting around.

While his Washington experience helped Emanuel win funding for such projects, his high-handed manner—epitomized by his embrace of the massive Lucas Museum of Narrative Art for a lakefront site that would have been leased to the *Star Wars* creator for peanuts—won him enemies.

"You are not the king of this city," challenger Jesus "Chuy" Garcia told Emanuel during the 2014 election campaign.

A dance major at Sarah Lawrence College, Emanuel had a natural interest in the arts and what they could do for Chicago. That approach manifested itself in the way he threw himself behind the creation of the Chicago Architectural Biennial, the showcase for cutting-edge design that debuted in 2015.

The mayor wants "to have Chicago again on the international stage as not just a center where great buildings are built, but also as a place where architectural ideas are being considered," the biennial's then vice chair Jack Guthman said at the time.

At last year's biennial, the city expanded on that notion, asking architects to come up with new concepts for extending the Riverwalk along the Chicago River's South Branch. If those ideas ever take physical form and the river really does become the city's second great waterfront, Emanuel will get much of the credit, cementing his identity as the "River Mayor."

Even so, like Daley, he leaves a list of unfinished major initiatives, exemplified by the still-empty former US Steel plant on the Far South Side, where a developer's plans to build thousands of homes recently fizzled.

During an interview with me in 2015, Emanuel pushed back at the tale-of-two-cities narrative, pointing to a new Chinatown library, a boathouse in Ping Tom Memorial Park, and other public-works upgrades in Chinatown. They were demonstrations, he said, of his "essential building blocks" for thriving neighborhoods—a good public school, public safety, a park, a playground, a library, and access to transportation.

He furthered that agenda by establishing Chicago's Neighborhood Opportunity Fund, which charges developers more for the right to pack extra square footage into downtown buildings and uses that money for projects in economically depressed neighborhoods.

And yet, the exodus out of Chicago's violence-plagued neighborhoods continues.

"Rahm's done a great job building downtown and the near-in neighborhoods," a former city official who's now a developer wrote to me in an email. "What he hasn't done well is rebuild neighborhoods" beyond the city's affluent core.

"The development in [these] neighborhoods has been sporadic, like the Whole Foods in Englewood. . . . These have become one-off projects that were meant to spur additional investments and development, but have not been followed up with new housing or additional development. While downtown and near-in neighborhoods have added thousands of new housing units, there has been little if any new construction (particularly for-sale homes) in most South and West Side communities. There's no plan for re-densifying or repopulating these neighborhoods."

The big question for Emanuel's successor is not just whether he or she will continue to think big, but whether the next mayor can bring such thinking to a full-scale effort, an urban Marshall Plan, that spreads the benefits of boom times to each and every one of the city's fifty wards.

Postscript: The 2019 election of Lori Lightfoot, Chicago's second Black mayor, opened the way for such a plan. Before Emanuel left office, however, he would preside over an intense debate about a new round of Chicago megaprojects, which sharpened the issue of who benefits when developers build big.

An Incredible Transformation? Not Really.
The "Meh" Blocks West of Navy Pier Are a Cautionary Tale for Chicago's Next Round of Megaprojects

OCTOBER 18, 2018

Viewed from the air, it's a stunning transformation—in just thirty years, a gritty swath of cleared land and surface-parking lots has become a glistening new part of Chicago.

But people experience cities on the ground, not in the air. Put the sixty acres between Navy Pier and Michigan Avenue under a microscope and what you see is a cityscape of great expectations and half-kept promises.

The deal was simple: the city would let developers build tall at Cityfront Center, Chicago's largest real estate development of the 1980s. In exchange, there would be beautiful buildings, streets, parks, plazas, and a riverwalk.

Yet the architecture, with rare exceptions, is mediocre. The public

Cityfront Center, 1987 and 2010: a real estate success, a place-making flop. Photo by Lawrence Okrent; courtesy of Okrent Kisiel Associates, Inc.

spaces were supposed to be vibrant and interconnected. Instead, they are unfinished, underachieving, largely disjointed, and even, in one case, off-limits to the public.

Urban-planning flops like these loom large as city officials review new megaplans from developers who pretty up their visions of sky-scrapers with dazzling drawings of riverwalks, bike trails, and other amenities teeming with smiling, attractive people.

For the 54.5-acre Lincoln Yards on the North Side, developer Ster-ling Bay wants to construct 12 million square feet of buildings, includ-ing towers as tall as eight hundred feet. It's sweetening the deal by proposing amenities like an extension of the 606 bike-and-pedestrian trail east of the Kennedy Expressway.

At the 78, a sixty-two-acre Near South Side project whose name reflects its developer's aim to create Chicago's seventy-eighth com-munity area, that developer, Related Midwest, has laid out plans for 13 million square feet, including skyscrapers up to 950 feet tall. Its sweeteners include a hundred-foot-wide, half-mile-long riverwalk lined by restaurants and shops.

The planner of both projects, the Chicago office of Skidmore, Ow-ings & Merrill, codesigned Cityfront Center's master plan. But if City-front Center is any guide, some of the promised amenities will never materialize.

Real estate busts, changes in property ownership, and the absence of a firm timetable for improvements all share the blame. So does a lack of effective oversight by the city's Department of Planning and Development and the City Council's zoning committee, which were charged with monitoring Cityfront Center.

The district's shortcomings open a window onto a broader subject: whether public space serves the public or real estate developers— developers who promise more parks and plazas in order to win per-mission to build more profitable square footage.

Millennium Park has taught Chicagoans that great public spaces provide focal points of urban life and lead to millions of dollars of private investment around them. At their best, these parks and pla-zas act as a social glue, bringing together people of different back-grounds in a metropolitan area separated by the fault lines of race and class.

Clock sculpture at Ogden Plaza Park: a prime example of Cityfront Center's failure to create lively urban spaces. Photo by Lee Bey.

Bad public spaces do none of that, as revealed by a small piece of Cityfront Center—Ogden Plaza Park, a sloping one-acre parcel across Columbus Drive from the NBC Tower.

The plaza's pavement is cracked. In its center, the hands of a floor-clock sculpture by artist Vito Acconci are gone. Homeless men camp out behind the plaza's concrete walls, leading other people, like Kari Boyer, a claims specialist who works nearby, to remain on the park's edges.

Once, Boyer recalled, she saw human feces in the park, which was pretty unappetizing as she ate lunch. "So I sit out here a lot of the time," she said, referring to a bench along Columbus.

Three years ago, when developers floated plans for a new apartment tower next to the plaza, they dangled a $3.5 million proposal to redesign the park. Yet now that their forty-seven-story high-rise is finished and rent is pouring in, the park remains unkempt and unwelcoming.

"If it's space, not place, it dissipates energy," said Ethan Kent, senior vice president of a New York–based nonprofit, the Project for Public Spaces, who has walked through Cityfront Center.

High Aspirations, Harsh Realities

Bounded by Lake Michigan, Michigan Avenue, the Chicago River, and Grand Avenue, Cityfront Center is part of the Streeterville neighborhood, east of Michigan Avenue. It once was home to warehouses, factories, docks, and a canal-like channel of water called a "slip." The industrial facilities were built by the Chicago Dock and Canal Company, which was established in 1857 by Chicago's first mayor, William Ogden.

In the early 1980s, having reconstituted itself as a real estate investment trust, Chicago Dock joined with the real estate arm of the Equitable Life Assurance Society of the United States to redevelop its land into what became Cityfront Center.

Chicago, a city of big plans, had never seen anything quite like it. The project's cost was pegged at $3 billion, equivalent to more than $6 billion today. Some 13.5 million square feet of office space was planned—enough to fill 3½ Willis Towers. There would be hotels, apartments, and shops. And the design aspirations were high.

Reacting against sterile modernist complexes like Illinois Center, an island of steel and glass built in the 1970s, Skidmore, Owings & Merrill and New York's Cooper, Eckstut Associates drew up a master plan based on the traditional town-planning principles of the design movement called the New Urbanism.

The plan, whose aims were included in the 1985 ordinance that changed Cityfront Center's zoning, proposed extending Chicago's street grid through the district. It also called for masonry-clad buildings with setbacks and distinctive bottoms, middles, and tops. And it demanded public spaces that would be ample in size, not mere pocket parks.

"It's the spaces that endure over time in cities and that create the identity, the addresses, and the value," Alexander Cooper of Cooper, Eckstut observed back then. "The buildings will come and go." (Cooper declined to be interviewed for this story.)

The goal was a "progression of spaces which are intended to unify the entire mixed-use project," according to a 1987 document signed by then planning commissioner Elizabeth Hollander and Chicago Dock's president, Charles R. Gardner.

Thirty-one years later, no one disputes that Cityfront Center is a real estate success, even though it includes Chicago's most infamous hole in the ground—the foundation for the unbuilt Chicago Spire, the twisting, two-thousand-foot condominium tower that went bust in 2008.

The area, which turned out to be a better site for apartments than offices, is home to thousands of residents and generates tens of millions of dollars in annual property-tax revenue.

Its developers spent millions on street, park, plaza, and utility upgrades. They even kept a "view corridor" that preserves a vista of the Tribune Tower as you look west over the aforementioned slip, which is named for former mayor Ogden.

"We're proud of converting a former industrial park into a connected commercial and residential section of the city," Gardner said in a recent interview at his Cityfront Center apartment, which overlooks the Ogden Slip.

But the saga of a now-closed promenade at Gardner's residence—CityView Condominiums, a pair of twelve-story high-rises at 440 and 480 North McClurg Court—paints a more complex picture, one that hints at how private agendas have trumped public space at Cityfront Center.

When the buildings opened in 1991, there was an elevated public walkway between them, reachable by stairs from the street. The idea was noble: an aboveground path that would extend west to Ogden Plaza Park and its Acconci-designed floor clock. Yet residents complained about visitors hanging out along their private terraces, Gardner said. So the gates to the privately owned promenade were locked.

Instead of demanding a reinstatement of public access, city officials in 2012 granted the CityView Condominium Association's request to eliminate it.

The gates remain locked today.

Problem Promenades

The gating of that promenade is but one example of Cityfront Center's fragmented public spaces. The most prominent of them, a riverfront esplanade, gracefully lines the Chicago River's north bank east of Michigan Avenue before it comes to an abrupt end.

Chiefly designed by Chicago's Lohan Associates, which was hired to oversee implementation of Cityfront Center's master plan within the Chicago Dock portion of the complex, the esplanade is a handsome spot for strolling, lined by mature trees, obelisk-shaped light standards, and plantings.

But it doesn't continue all the way to Lake Shore Drive, as the master plan called for. Nor does it continue east to DuSable Park—the public space, east of the drive, that would honor Chicago's first permanent nonindigenous settler, Jean Baptiste Pointe du Sable.

There is no DuSable Park.

Instead, the esplanade runs smack into a shabby wood fence that lines the Chicago Spire's weed-strewn site.

"It'll be nice when it opens up," said Streeterville resident Betsy Peterson while she was walking her dog. "For tourists, it's terrible. We're stopped every day by tourists who don't know how to get to Navy Pier. They're lost and frustrated."

Related Midwest, the developer that now controls the 2.2-acre Spire site, has proposed finishing the esplanade and has promised $10 million for building DuSable Park as part of its plan for a two-tower residential and hotel complex on the property.

The developers also suggest an eastward extension of another Cityfront Center promenade, this one on the south side of Ogden Slip, to DuSable Park.

But who knows if all that will happen? The promenade along the slip could be vulnerable to NIMBY pressure, given the presence of adjoining town houses.

As the story of the gated plaza at CityView Condominiums suggests, not everybody wants strangers streaming past their front door.

Foundation hole of the unbuilt Chicago Spire: a drag on Cityfront Center's public realm. Photo by Lee Bey.

Dull Plazas and Weak Connections

Promenades are about moving; plazas are where you stop and take in the city. They are its living rooms. But Cityfront Center's plazas don't issue much of a welcome.

The problems begin at what's supposed to be the western gateway to the district—Pioneer Court, a large but underachieving expanse of pavement at 401 North Michigan Avenue, next to the new Apple store.

On the plaza's north side are rows of trellis-like pavilions, trees, and shrubbery. While those features provide much-needed places to sit, they block the view into the heart of Cityfront Center and partly obstruct the path to it. They even end in a cul-de-sac of fountains that forces pedestrians to retrace their steps.

Getting from one of Cityfront Center's plazas to the other, it turns out, is no walk in the park.

The portion of the project west of Columbus Drive is built on bi-level streets in sync with the double-decked stretch of Michigan Avenue; in contrast, the eastern zone is at ground level. Utilitarian outdoor staircases do their best to draw together these disparate realms. But they're no Spanish Steps.

To the east of Pioneer Court is Cityfront Plaza, which adorns an elevated roadway that links North Michigan and Columbus. A long rectangular space with sunken seating areas, it's hardly the bustling hub of activity envisioned by Chicago architect Adrian Smith, who helped craft the Cityfront Center master plan while at Skidmore, Owings & Merrill.

As he designed the handsome NBC Tower, one of Cityfront Center's few distinguished buildings, Smith conceived of the plaza as a front door for the buildings around it. They, in turn, would enclose the plaza and energize it when their inhabitants spilled out onto the streets.

Yet the plaza is still surrounded by surface-parking lots, including two that flank the NBC Tower. Metropolis Investment Holdings, which bought the properties in the 1990s, said in an email that it is "reviewing various options to build two beautiful buildings." But it declined to provide renderings or a timetable.

For now, then, Cityfront Plaza continues to feel like a nice little park that sits incongruously atop a road.

Things are worse at Ogden Plaza Park, which is also named for the former mayor and administered by the Chicago Park District. Modeled on an English garden, the plaza is a case study in good intentions gone wrong.

Take the concrete walls on the plaza's flanks, which shield it from the noisy traffic on Columbus. Unfortunately, the walls also provide a screen for the homeless men who sleep in the plaza. Put off by their presence, people walking their dogs typically stick to the plaza's fringes.

As the cracked pavement shows, the Park District is letting the plaza fall apart. And a previously announced effort to remake the public space, which would add stepped terraces and a dog-friendly area, doesn't seem to be going anywhere.

Hopes for such a remake rose in 2015 when Chicago developer Jupiter Realty floated its plan for the 465 North Park apartment tower. Ald. Brendan Reilly (Forty-Second), whose downtown ward includes Cityfront Center, said he would seek such a "public benefit" in determining whether to approve the developer's plan.

Yet now that the hypercurvy high-rise is open, no remade plaza accompanies it.

The public's been stiffed again.

Reilly did not return calls asking him to explain the situation.

Subpar Streets and Buildings

Seen from afar, Cityfront Center projects a sense of order. Its buildings along the Chicago River form a nearly continuous wall, much like the range of high-rises along North Lake Shore Drive. Lower buildings step down to the Ogden Slip.

But something's wrong when you walk the streets. They, too, are a kind of public space, but they do a poor job of accommodating the public.

Many are lined with blank-walled parking garages. Most lack interesting storefronts. They don't form the sort of coherent cityscapes— rows of carefully articulated buildings of brick and stone—that Cityfront Center's planners foresaw.

Why? For starters, developers and city officials failed to anticipate the impact of the 1995 reopening of Navy Pier, which turned the once-crumbling municipal dock into a popular entertainment hub that drew hordes of pedestrians.

The pier "was derelict at the time. There were those that thought it would wash into the lake," Gardner said.

Based on that incorrect prediction, Cityfront Center's big east–west streets, Illinois Street and Grand Avenue, were conceived as wide arterial roads that would move traffic to and from Lake Shore Drive and nearby expressways.

No matter how much you dress them up with trees and sidewalk plantings, they're so wide and busy with car traffic that they feel like drag strips.

Another reason for the bad pedestrian vibe: because Cityfront Center has no alleys, some of its streets, most notably New Street, must take on that utilitarian role, with entrances to loading docks and parking garages. They aren't alleys, but they're alley-like.

Ultimately, though, the blandness of Cityfront Center's streets can be attributed to the city's unwillingness to enforce its own design standards:

- One states that "the maximum effort shall be made to contain parking in belowground structures." The developers of 474 North Lake Shore Drive, a blunt sixty-one-story residential tower whose fifteen-story parking garage is covered with ugly louvers, apparently didn't get the memo.
- Another says that the first floor of all structures facing major roads like Illinois and Grand "shall maximize space with active uses such as retail, day care, restaurants, et cetera." Anyone who has walked past the visually intimidating base of the River East Center at 350 East Illinois knows that mandating human scale is easier said than done.
- Still another requirement, based on the idea that masonry walls are better at framing walkable streets than sleek glass ones, says, "Reflective glass shall not be allowed." Yet many of Cityfront Center's recent high-rises, like 500 Lake Shore Drive, have walls of, you guessed it, reflective glass.

Not all glass buildings are street-deadening, of course. But if you're going to have mandates, you need to stick to them. Or you need better mandates.

In retrospect, it was a mistake for Cityfront Center's planners to prescribe the use of certain types of materials and compositions. Styles and technologies invariably change over multidecade projects. So do owners and their tastes. It would be wiser to rethink the fundamentals of good urban design than mandate superficial features.

Real Change?

All this is not to say that Cityfront Center is beyond repair—or that its shortcomings portend failures at the 78, Lincoln Yards, or the proposed redevelopment of the 25.6-acre Tribune Media site at 777 West Chicago Avenue that the Chicago Plan Commission just approved.

The current development boom has put city officials in a stronger position to regulate public space—and deliver better results—than they occupied thirty years ago, said David Reifman, commissioner of the city's Department of Planning and Development.

He pointed to the success of Lakeshore East, a twenty-eight-acre cluster of mostly residential high-rises across Randolph Street from Millennium Park. Skidmore, Owings & Merrill planned the development.

Early in Lakeshore East's life—in 2005, when the first of the project's towers was completed—its developers opened a six-acre park with curving pathways, fountains, and swaths of grass. Today the park, designed by Houston-based landscape architects OJB, teems with activity. Reifman said it exemplifies the city's embrace of "place-led development," which views public space as a driver of commercial districts rather than a tacked-on amenity.

The commissioner also cited the rezoning ordinance for the Tribune Media site, which requires "un-gated and unobstructed public access" to proposed riverfront open space. And the ordinance mandates that successive chunks of the riverfront be completed before the city allows the first building in each phase of the multiphase project to be occupied.

"Today, we look at the idea of open spaces more carefully," Reifman said. "The thinking has evolved."

But Lakeshore East and the Tribune Media site are models of limited relevance for the 78 and Lincoln Yards. They're only about half the size of the megaprojects, and Lakeshore East's park is more of a hidden gem than a highly visible amenity.

While it's all to the good that city officials insist they're now taking a harder line on maintaining access to public space than they've done at Cityfront Center, little of a fundamental nature has changed since the district was planned more than thirty years ago.

The cash-poor city still relies on private developers to build and finance public space in exchange for zoning bonuses. It still links the required completion of public spaces to the completion of new construction.

As long as it continues to do so, delivery of the promised amenities will remain vulnerable to disruption from recessions and changes in property ownership.

Even when new high-rises that are supposed to produce better public spaces do open their doors, as the saga of Cityfront Center's Ogden Plaza Park reveals, city officials can't always be counted on to make good on their promises to produce a "public benefit."

Their assurances about the quality of future public space would be more credible if they had detailed plans for fixing existing parks and plazas.

Buzzwords like "place-led" development mean little without the sharpening of outdated standards for human-scaled streets and vibrant public spaces. All the dazzling renderings in the world are no guarantee that you'll be strolling along beautiful riverwalks.

There's a dramatic difference, Cityfront Center shows, between real estate success and building a great city.

Postscript: Prospects for Cityfront Center's public spaces brightened in 2020, when the Chicago City Council approved Related Midwest's plan for a two-tower project on the former site of the Chicago Spire, 400 North Lake Shore Drive. Chiefly designed by David Childs of Skidmore, Owings & Merrill's New York office, the plan calls for skyscrapers of 875 and 765 feet containing a total of 1,100 apartments, completion of the riverwalk along the Chicago River's north bank, and funding for the long-delayed DuSable Park. Yet in response to neighbors' concerns about unruly behavior by pedestrians in Streeterville, Related Midwest eliminated the previously planned walkway that would have created an east–west route along the Ogden Slip to DuSable Park. The developers hoped to begin construction on the $1 billion project in early 2021, but the coronavirus pandemic put their plans on hold.

Lincoln Yards site, looking north, 2017: a blank slate with vast potential, but who would benefit from redevelopment? Photo by Jason Jarrett; courtesy of Okrent Kisiel Associates, Inc.

Improvement or Invasion? Lincoln Yards Plan Is Too Tall and Out of Place. The Mayor and City Council Should Slow It Down, and Press Architects and Developers to Rethink and Redesign

DECEMBER 28, 2018

A great urban place is more than a motley collection of tall buildings and open spaces. It has lively streets, pulsing gathering spots, and buildings that talk to one another rather than sing the architectural equivalent of a shrill solo.

Daley Plaza, with its enigmatic Picasso sculpture and muscular county-courts high-rise, is a great urban place. So is the North Side's Armitage Avenue, lined with delightful Victorian storefronts.

The latest plan for the $5 billion–plus Lincoln Yards megadevelopment, which would transform 54.5 acres of former industrial land along the Chicago River into offices, apartments, shops, and entertainment venues, including a 20,000-seat soccer stadium, doesn't measure up.

It would be dramatically out of scale with its surroundings, piercing the delicate urban fabric of the city's North Side with a swath of downtown height and bulk. It also would be out of character with its environs, more Anytown than Our Town.

And that's what the debate over Lincoln Yards is really about—not just the zoning change the developers seek, which would reclassify their land from a manufacturing district to a mixed-use waterfront zone, but urban character.

What kind of city are we building? Who is it for? Does it have room for the small and the granular as well as the muscular and the monumental? The poor, working class, and middle class as well as the rich?

These questions have simmered as Chicago allows high-rises to expand far beyond the historic confines of the Loop. Lincoln Yards brings them to full boil.

To be sure, the Lincoln Yards plan is not without good strokes—most notably, proposed public spaces that draw inspiration from the area's hard-edged industrial past. But these are sweeteners. The core issue is density and what the public gets in return for allowing developers to build tall.

Two months ago, I examined a cautionary tale: Cityfront Center, a sixty-acre riverfront spread of office and residential high-rises between North Michigan Avenue and Navy Pier that was Chicago's biggest project of the 1980s.

Cityfront Center's developers got to erect more square footage than previous zoning allowed on land that once contained factories and warehouses. But more than thirty years later, the city is still stuck with its mediocre architecture and public spaces that are unfinished, underperforming, and largely disjointed.

Cityfront Center holds a lesson for Mayor Rahm Emanuel and his successor. Even the best-laid plans can go awry.

Yet Emanuel and his city planners appear intent upon rushing Lincoln Yards through to approval around the time city voters will elect the mayor's successor next spring.

Memo to the mayor: Slow down. Rethink. There's a chance to do

View of planned Lincoln Yards high-rises, facing south: a massive shift in scale. Image credit: North Branch Park and Nature Preserve.

that as your urban planners negotiate with Lincoln Yards' developers over further changes to the plan that are likely to be unveiled next year.

Memo to Ald. Brian Hopkins (Second), in whose ward Lincoln Yards would be built: Press for fundamental changes before giving this flawed proposal your blessing.

Looming Towers

In a crucial way, Lincoln Yards is an even more complex undertaking than Cityfront Center.

Its long row of high-rises, which the developers estimate would house more than twenty-four thousand workers and five thousand residential units, would be sandwiched between two historic low-rise neighborhoods, Lincoln Park, to the east, and Bucktown, to the west.

That proximity has bred contempt.

When Lincoln Yards' developer, Chicago-based Sterling Bay, unveiled the latest version of its plan at a recent community meeting, many neighbors were not impressed by the company's decision to give a meaningless haircut to the proposed high-rises.

The tallest of them would rise to 650 feet instead of the gasp-inducing 818 feet that the firm and its architects, the Chicago office of Skidmore, Owings & Merrill, proposed last summer.

The neighbors are right to be concerned. A 650-foot tower wouldn't just loom menacingly over the little shops of the Armitage retail strip. It even would be out of scale with Lincoln Park's tall buildings, which line the western edge of the park from which the neighborhood takes its name.

Lincoln Yards would have nine buildings in excess of four hundred feet. One of them, a 596-footer at the project's eastern edge, would be twelve feet taller than the twin corncobs of Marina City.

This isn't a gradual shift between Lincoln Yards and surrounding neighborhoods, as Skidmore, Owings & Merrill claims. It's an excessive leap in height.

Cities need to grow and change, but this is the sort of incongruous Dodge City growth you expect in Houston, a city infamous for its lack of zoning. And it could have lasting consequences, likely worsening the traffic congestion that already plagues streets like Clybourn and North Avenues.

Promised Public Spaces: Will They Materialize?

Flawed in the sky, Lincoln Yards is more promising at ground level, though there is cause for concern there too.

On the plus side, the plan calls for extending new roads, bridges, public transit, and public spaces, including an extension of the 606 bike-and-pedestrian trail, through the now-isolated site.

These steps, priced by city officials at $800 million, would be backed by controversial tax-increment financing (TIF). It would reimburse the developers, who would bear the upfront costs of the new infrastructure.

Critics call such financing a form of corporate welfare, because it would use the added property-tax revenue generated by Lincoln Yards to pay for the planned infrastructure rather than conveying those funds to taxing bodies, like the Chicago Public Schools, that desperately need the money.

But Planning and Development Commissioner David Reifman persuasively argues that by improving access to the site, the new infrastructure would unlock the economic potential of long-dormant land next to vibrant neighborhoods and near downtown.

Another positive: the open-space plan crafted by New York–based James Corner Field Operations, codesigners of Manhattan's High Line. The plan calls for more than twenty acres of parks and plazas, up from the previously promised thirteen acres, plus a mile-long riverwalk. Field Operations compellingly ties these elements together by treating the former industrial site as a kind of artifact, a "found object."

Russet-colored gateways would frame views and harmonize with the industrial-era bridges that span the river. A promenade would incorporate railroad spurs that once led to factories like the old A. Finkl & Sons steel plant. A "foundry playground" would allude to the industrial past with its tube-shaped slides.

Here, at least, Lincoln Yards looks authentic rather than imposed on its site. But it will take years, if not decades, for this tantalizing vision to materialize. Only a quarter-mile stretch of riverwalk would be built in Lincoln Yards' first phase, which calls for three office buildings along the river.

Having witnessed the failures of Cityfront Center, where the riverwalk remains unfinished, City Hall wants to create an accelerated schedule for the new parkland. When almost half the project's buildable area is completed, the city would require Sterling Bay to finish all the open space. But that still leaves the proposed public space vulnerable to real estate recessions.

Public-space advocates and some North Side aldermen also question whether Lincoln Yards will provide enough open space for families in the surrounding neighborhood. They back the creation of a twenty-four-acre North Branch Park and Nature Preserve, which would be built on the scruffy General Iron scrapyard site next to Lincoln Yards. It's a good idea. The park would prevent more high-rises from clogging the riverfront and begin to fill a nearly five-mile gap between publicly owned parks on the river's North Branch.

Last but hardly least on the list of ground-level issues is the need to fill Lincoln Yards with lively streets. With all the excitement over the downtown Riverwalk, it's easy to forget that such streets, framed by visually enticing storefronts and outfitted with pedestrian-friendly features like trees and benches, are the real building blocks of cities.

Yet the vagueness of the designers' language—the streets are supposed to be "safe and welcoming" and have an "active retail edge"—is troubling. The guidelines need to be fleshed out if Lincoln Yards is to avoid Cityfront Center's bland sidewalks and hulking facades. If Lincoln Yards doesn't have good streets, it will never become a great urban place.

Authentic or Generic?

The social and cultural architecture of Lincoln Yards is as important as its physical architecture. A vital district, after all, is inseparable from the activities that occur within it.

As is true in other cities, development in Chicago is often a relentless process of gentrification, with rising rents near new public works and high-rises near transit stations pushing out many longtime residents.

While the city requires developers of projects getting public monies or a zoning change to reserve 20 percent of their residential units for affordable housing, developers often get around the requirement by paying into a citywide affordable-housing fund.

In contrast, Reifman says at least a quarter of the affordable units the city will require Sterling Bay to build will go on-site, while at least another quarter could be built within two miles of the development. That would avoid the embarrassing irony of residences on former industrial land that working people could not afford.

How Chicago answers a related question also will affect Lincoln Yards' character: Will proposed entertainment venues backed by big corporate outfits like Live Nation be allowed to overpower beloved small music venues like the Hideout, in the 1300 block of West Wabansia Avenue?

Sterling Bay says it wants the Hideout to remain a neighbor, allowing Lincoln Yards to benefit from the venue's authenticity. Still, the risk is that the Hideout would drown in a sea of generic urbanism.

As *Tribune* music critic Greg Kot has written, "With each sell-out of its small but essential indie institutions, Chicago diminishes itself and blurs its essence not just as a metropolis made up of big buildings but a beehive of communities that make and share their creativity."

The Hideout: the authenticity of this small music venue made it the anti Lincoln Yards. Photo by Lee Bey.

Music and cities both benefit from a variety of voices, not the dull monotone of the safe and predictable. As the great urbanologist Jane Jacobs once wrote, "Cities have the capability of providing something for everybody, only because, and only when, they are created by everybody."

Does Sterling Bay get that?

The developer seeks an enormous power: a green light to shape an entire stretch of the Chicago's North Side.

Yet the zoning change it seeks is a privilege, not a right.

The company still has to earn that privilege by demonstrating it can deliver the great urban place that Chicago deserves.

Until then, City Hall's message to Sterling Bay should be simple and direct: "Do better."

Postscript: Stung by concerns that its proposal would further jam already congested North Side streets and stifle the authenticity of small-scale music venues like the Hideout, Sterling Bay dropped plans for the 20,000-seat soccer stadium and a cluster of corporate entertainment attractions. The stadium's elimination freed the southeast section of Lincoln Yards to become a district of freestanding low-rise buildings, containing shops, restaurants, and other uses, that could connect in scale and character with Lincoln Park. But Lincoln Yard's planned row of high-rises threatened to make significant parts of its open space an enclave for its affluent residents, like the Lakeshore East development near Millennium Park.

Ultimately, the political battle over Lincoln Yards centered on the proposed TIF district, which, critics said, would boost development in an already-prosperous area of Chicago at the expense of hard-hit neighborhoods on the South and West Sides. After her election in 2019, Lightfoot called for a delay on the vote to divert up to $1.3 billion in property-tax proceeds to Lincoln Yards and up to $700 million to the Near South Side megaproject, the 78. Yet in the end, the City Council approved TIFs for Lincoln Yards and the 78.

Delayed by the coronavirus, Sterling Bay did not hold a groundbreaking for Lincoln Yards' first phase, including an eight-story life-sciences building and a bridge over the Chicago River's North Branch that will improve access to the site, until late 2021. The developer planned to break ground on the next phase of Lincoln Yards in summer 2022. "In addition to a 19-story commercial building and a 15-story residential tower," the *Chicago Tribune* reported, "plans call for a 6½-acre park, riverwalk, seawall, a canoe/kayak launch, athletic fields, a children's play area and a dog run."

LORI LIGHTFOOT AND MAURICE COX: DETROIT PRELUDE AND CHICAGO BLUEPRINT

First in Detroit, then in Chicago, Mayor Lori Lightfoot's planning commissioner, Maurice Cox, made equity much more than a progressive buzzword. It became, instead, the basis for a systematic series of policies and plans, the most prominent of which was called Invest South/West, geared toward redirecting resources to areas of the city that had long lacked them. In addition, building on the Chicago tradition of public-private partnerships previously employed for such glittering downtown projects as Millennium Park, Cox enlisted developers to bring private capital to the gritty neighborhoods targeted for improvement. He also marshaled the talents of the city's architects to ensure that Invest South/West projects would be built to high design standards. The plans that developed and the amount of investment associated with them, about $1.4 billion, held out great long-term promise, but it remained unclear whether they could overcome the destabilizing impact of the city's gun violence.

Detroit's Downtown Revival Is Real, but the Road to Recovery Remains Long

APRIL 15, 2017

So you think Chicago is a tale of two cities? The gulf between its booming downtown and its violence-plagued neighborhoods is nothing compared to the gaps that a visitor witnesses in Detroit.

Along Woodward Avenue, Detroit's main drag, a new streetcar line will soon start running. Construction crews are turning old high-rises into microlofts and building a sports arena that will open next fall. On the site of the old Hudson's department store that was imploded in 1998, the Quicken Loans magnate and real estate developer Dan Gil-

Detroit's QLine streetcar and the GM Renaissance Center: Will the downtown revival spread to the city's beleaguered neighborhoods? Photo by Brian A. Mahany.

bert has proposed a skyscraper that would rise higher than the glass-sheathed Renaissance Center, currently the city's tallest building.

Yet outside the resurgent downtown core, it's another story. Elegant old neighborhoods like Indian Village, a national historic district, quickly give way to expanses of empty lots that bring to mind Chicago's impoverished Englewood area. Detroit has roughly twenty-five square miles of vacant land—enough to fill the entire island of Manhattan and then some. Thousands of blighted homes have been torn down.

As Chicagoans know from the innovations that followed the Great Fire of 1871, necessity (or is it desperation?) often serves as the mother of invention. Accordingly, Detroit is evolving new ideas for how to revive its stricken neighborhoods. Here's what they boil down to: Turn emptiness into opportunity. Make a new kind of city—still urban, but more spread out. And while you're at it, avoid the gentrification that typically goes hand in hand with redevelopment.

"What's going to distinguish Detroit's recovery from any other comeback city is its ability to be an equitable recovery," Maurice Cox, Detroit's planning director, told me.

Cox, who grew up in Brooklyn, brings a fascinating skill set to the task. He once was mayor of Charlottesville, Virginia, and later served as director of design for the National Endowment for the Arts. He also has academic chops, having been associate dean for community engagement at Tulane University's School of Architecture.

Since Detroit mayor Mike Duggan hired Cox, in 2015, the two have made Detroit a must-see laboratory for the reimagining and remaking of a shrinking city. Yet the hill they're climbing is incredibly steep.

Battered by plant closings, racial tensions, and the ongoing flight of residents both white and Black, Detroit's population plummeted from a peak of more than 1.8 million in 1950 to fewer than 680,000 in 2015. It is no longer one of the nation's twenty most populous cities. Nor is it the manufacturing hub it once was. The once-mighty Motor City is down to two vehicle-assembly plants, one operated by General Motors, the other by Chrysler. Photographs of Detroit's abandoned, decaying landmarks, like the once-grand Michigan Central Station, are known as "ruin porn."

With thousands of good-paying jobs gone, skeptics question whether the city will ever regain the economic wherewithal to ensure that its renaissance extends beyond the downtown core.

"It's problematic to imagine that, just because you've got an attractive neighborhood running up Woodward, it's going to serve the needs of a poor kid living five miles away, let alone five blocks away," said Northwestern University historian Kevin Boyle, who grew up in Detroit and has written extensively about the city.

Detroit is nevertheless making strides—not with big plans, but with small steps. In 2016, two years after the city emerged from its landmark bankruptcy, it finished a multiyear effort to install 65,000 streetlights and eliminate fear-inducing zones of darkness. "You can't ask people to plan, which is inherently aspirational and visionary, if you can't provide basic services," Cox said.

The city is also going back to basics downtown, embracing anew the idea that city streets should accommodate transit, not just cars.

Bright red, articulated QLine streetcars will start operations next month. The sleek QLine, which seems sure to be extended beyond its initial length of 3.3 miles, could not be more different from Detroit's People Mover, the elevated, automated light-rail system that opened in 1987 and is raised on expressway-like stilts.

Unlike the People Mover, which encircles downtown, the street-level QLine extends into neighborhoods, encouraging residents to leave their cars behind. "We are trying to establish the public's trust in transit that's something accessible to all, not just something for the poor," said Cox.

One of the neighborhoods along the QLine—Brush Park, which sits between downtown and Detroit's midtown business district—shows the impact such steps can make.

Once boasting nineteenth-century Victorian mansions, Brush Park succumbed to decline as its residents moved farther away from downtown and its grand houses were split into apartments and later demolished. Today, a large portion of the neighborhood is almost entirely vacant, its plots covered with grass even though downtown skyscrapers and stadiums, and the under-construction Little Caesars Arena, are close by.

Yet spurred in part by the QLine, Gilbert is moving ahead with an innovative 410-unit residential complex in the heart of Brush Park.

The complex, called City Modern, will incorporate four surviving Victorian mansions within a street-friendly cluster of contemporary houses and apartments. Chicago's Studio Dwell architects designed the townhouses, which promise to effectively mix modern design with traditional urbanism—a blend Cox encourages. City Modern is Detroit's largest new residential development.

"Detroit has switched from the city of demolition to the city of planning to the city of building," said Melissa Dittmer, an Illinois Institute of Technology graduate who is director of architecture and design at Bedrock Real Estate Services, the real estate and development company for Gilbert's Detroit properties.

Even more powerful evidence of Detroit's revival could emerge if Gilbert realizes his recently unveiled proposal for a skyscraper on the old Hudson's department store site. The store closed in 1983; ever since the building was imploded, in 1998, its empty downtown site has symbolized the city's steep decline.

A design by New York's SHoP Architects calls for a fifty-two-story residential tower atop a swoopy nine-story podium that would house shops and enable other uses. While the plan is not aesthetically persuasive—the podium is overcooked; the tower, undercooked—it nonetheless sends a strong message: downtown Detroit has reached the point where a showcase residential tower is not seen as a laughing-stock.

At 734 feet, this one would nudge a little higher than the 727-foot Renaissance Center, which is now home to General Motors' headquarters. It's time for Detroit to go "vertical," Gilbert has said.

Once you drive the freeways outside downtown, however, it's hard to maintain such optimism. One neighborhood I visited, Brightmoor, about thirteen miles northwest of downtown, had numerous blocks with more empty lots than houses. Many of the remaining houses had holes in their walls and roofs. Uprooted trees lay across yards. The sidewalks were empty. In such areas, the prospects for change seem as dim, or dimmer, than they do in the troubled neighborhoods on Chicago's South and West Sides.

Yet Cox and his staff—which includes his deputy, Janet Attarian, formerly with Chicago's Department of Planning and Development—see opportunity in the voids. So do other urban planners.

One nonprofit group, the Greening of Detroit, has produced a booklet of options for transforming vacant lots into uses like orchards, pocket parks, and cut-flower stands. In the Cody Rouge neighborhood, which lines the Rouge River on the city's west side, officials have partnered with other groups to turn empty lots into "bio-retention gardens" that capture stormwater. Parts of Cody Rouge were inundated by a 2014 flood.

In a particularly innovative move, Cox and his staff have discarded traditional neighborhood boundaries and are putting troubled areas and nearby stable neighborhoods within a single urban-planning framework. Vacant land in Brightmoor, for example, might be turned into new parkland that would serve the adjoining Rosedale neighborhood, which has an impressive stock of well-kept homes. Throughout the city, new houses could have broad side yards or sit alongside meadows.

"The next generation of urban living is a city that is land-rich," Cox told me, contrasting Detroit's ample spaces with the tight confines of other cities.

He also foresees a Detroit that remains affordable to people from a wide spectrum of incomes due to the price-moderating influence of its huge supply of land. That would be a very different outcome from gentrified Brooklyn and cities where rising prices have forced out middle- and working-class families.

Detroit "might be a more equitable Brooklyn or a more inclusive Brooklyn," Cox said.

There are signs such thinking is having an impact. A new plan for Detroit's eastern riverfront, prepared by Chicago architects Skidmore, Owings & Merrill, doesn't simply turn the waterfront into a public space for people living in expensive homes nearby. It includes greenways that would extend to the north, providing access for people living in less expensive areas.

But it will take much more than that to close Detroit's "tale of two cities" gap.

I ended my visit with a stop at the impressive Detroit Institute of Arts, where a photographic exhibit, *Detroit after Dark*, showed haunting images of brightly lit downtown skyscrapers juxtaposed with darkened abandoned buildings in the neighborhoods nearby.

"The night can emphasize the contrast between the city's decline and renewal—well-lit areas represent activity and development while unlit ones reflect vacancy and neglect," the wall text said.

Detroit has the lights on, to be sure. But it has miles to go before it can span the gulf between downtown redevelopment and neighborhood emptiness that remains painfully evident in broad daylight.

Postscript: Detroit's redevelopment efforts have since yielded more notable successes. Ford Motor Company purchased the iconic Michigan Central Station in 2018 and announced plans to convert it into a corporate campus in Detroit's Corktown neighborhood. Construction began on Gilbert's mixed-use tower, although it was scaled down to 680 feet. But the city's population continued to decline. The 2020 US Census showed it had dropped to just over 639,000, down 10.5 percent from 2010. Duggan disputed the results.

Maurice Cox on the roof of City Hall: the mayor's top planner sought to revitalize business districts on Chicago's South and West Sides without gentrification. Photo by Zbigniew Bzdak / *Chicago Tribune* / TCA.

Changing Course: Lightfoot's Top Planner Will Focus on the City's "Soul," Its Neighborhoods, not Just Its Downtown "Heart"

OCTOBER 25, 2019

Maurice Cox, the highly regarded, design-savvy urban planner whom Mayor Lori Lightfoot lured away from Detroit to spread the wealth to the city's South and West Sides, could be Chicago's most consequential urban planner in decades.

But, he admits, he's still learning the city's street names.

In his first in-depth Chicago interview, coming days after Lightfoot announced a $750 million plan to revitalize ten battered business districts on the South and West Sides, Cox expressed publicly what he's been telling audiences privately: he sees Chicago as having a heart (its booming downtown) and a soul (its motley collection of neighborhoods). And the soul will be his prime focus.

Cox will oversee downtown, but will delegate day-to-day responsibility to a deputy, allowing him to concentrate on the task of reversing the decades of discrimination, decay, and disinvestment that have plagued minority neighborhoods.

"I think we have to first stop the bleeding," Cox said, sitting in a conference room in the Department of Planning and Development's tenth-floor offices at City Hall. "We have to give residents a sense of where their neighborhood is going."

In the interview, Cox touched on a wide range of other development topics. Among them:

• The Obama Presidential Center offers a "once in a generation" chance to revitalize the South Side, he said, so he hopes Chicagoans can move past the debate over whether the center should be built in Jackson Park. "As far as I'm concerned, let's consider that decision done and look more at the benefits and how we can assure that it doesn't just sit as a building in a park, but that it has a catalytic role in reimagining an economic center for the South Side."

• Tax-increment financing that subsidizes the cost of roads and other infrastructure is well-suited for the planned redevelopment of the former Michael Reese Hospital site at Thirty-First Street and Lake Shore Drive, Cox said, because new housing and public spaces there would benefit the nearby Bronzeville neighborhood. In contrast, he indirectly criticized the $1.3 billion TIF deal for the massive Lincoln Yards project on the North Side, which the City Council approved and Lightfoot signed off on before she took office. "I would like to see TIF used to advance a more equitable distribution throughout the city," Cox said. "It's a very different model than 'let's cluster everything at the heart and then—the soul, we can forget about it.'"

The stakes associated with his efforts are enormous. Lightfoot campaigned on a platform that called for devoting more political and financial capital to the economically struggling, violence-plagued areas of the South and West Sides. If Cox can't deliver signs of progress, Lightfoot will likely get flak from residents and aldermen—and could be a one-term mayor.

Yet if anyone has a chance to marshal the forces of urban planning and architecture in favor of more equitable growth, Cox, sixty, is probably the guy.

During his four years as Detroit's planning chief, he planted seeds of revival in that city's devastated neighborhoods. Indeed, the Invest South/West plan that Lightfoot announced, with its emphasis on ten business districts, is straight out of Cox's Detroit playbook.

In Chicago, the ten areas targeted for revival are Auburn Gresham, North Lawndale, Austin, Englewood, Humboldt Park, New City, Roseland, South Chicago, South Shore, and an area that city officials identify as the Quad Communities, which includes North Kenwood, Oakland, and portions of Douglas and Grand Boulevard.

Why ten? And why these ten?

"Each one of these neighborhoods has unique assets, and they require a tailored strategy to leverage their assets," Cox said.

Some, he explained, have iconic historic buildings that might be converted into a theater or some other cultural use. Other have lots of publicly owned vacant land that present a chance for building apartments and shops. The ten will be a kind of laboratory that could offer lessons for as many as twenty-five more business districts on the South and West Sides. Cox calls such districts the "front door" of neighborhoods.

"My first thought," he said, "is how can people come in to the front door of their neighborhood and see revitalization playing out."

His vision of revitalization is very different from the modernist housing projects that tore through the urban fabric in the 1960s with isolated clusters of residential towers. It's more in keeping with the principles of New Urbanism, which stresses walkable streets and mixing uses like shops and housing to cut down on driving and save energy.

In line with such thinking, Cox is a proponent of "twenty-minute neighborhoods," in which everything residents need, from schools to shopping, is within a twenty-minute walk or bike ride. Such principles, he said, can contribute to public safety, creating the self-policing role that Jane Jacobs memorably labeled "eyes on the street."

"I think there's a direct correlation between the physical design of a community and the ability for it to be safe," Cox said when I pressed him on whether design solutions could overcome the gun violence that has wracked the city.

To help lure investors to shrinking neighborhoods, he plans to use forecasts that show that the number of residents will grow if the city allows developers to build new clusters of apartments. That technique worked in Detroit's east-riverfront district, he said, where a national grocery chain opened a store even though the planned housing had yet to be built.

The key, Cox said, was to "project what the future would look like."

One measure of the challenge he faces in Chicago came the day before our interview, when I visited the Englewood business district and came upon a barbecue place named Taylormade Que, at 6717 South Halsted Street. The owner, Channel Taylor, spoke to me from behind bulletproof glass. She said a pet project of former mayor Rahm Emanuel, the much-hyped Whole Foods Market at Sixty-Third and Halsted Streets, had made little impact on her business. Her observation didn't surprise Cox.

The Whole Foods, which sits behind a sea of parking lots, follows a suburban model that emphasizes getting around by car rather than on foot or by bike. The store is isolated from the sidewalks and pedestrian activity around it. Cox said he would not have recommended that the City Council approve the project in its current form had he been planning commissioner.

"My assumption is that people will come by car to shop, but they will also come by foot," he said. "And I think that the model you're describing assumed that no one was coming by foot."

He also criticized what he called a lack of coordination between city departments and related agencies, saying that public investments on the South and West Sides are not achieving their full "catalytic effect."

How long will it take before his vision starts to bear fruit? New and rehabbed buildings cannot appear instantly, of course.

Asked whether it will require a generation, rather than just one or two mayoral terms, to achieve his and Lightfoot's goals, Cox replied with a mix of realism and self-confidence.

"I think it is going to take a generation," he said, "but, quite frankly, we are the generation that will set it in motion."

Postscript: The recession brought on by the coronavirus pandemic and the looting that followed the police killing of George Floyd made Cox's challenges even more difficult. In addition to inflicting damage on

Conceptual proposal for Laramie State Bank and adjoining land: using overlooked historic architecture as an anchor for redevelopment. Image credit: Perkins & Will.

such high-profile downtown shopping strips as North Michigan Avenue and State Street, looters hit businesses in all ten Invest South/West districts, causing millions of dollars in property damage. Yet Cox insisted that the pandemic and the nation's racial reckoning made his job easier. "I think there's a greater sense of awareness of the need," he said. In 2022, however, Whole Foods announced it would close two Chicago stores, including the one in Englewood.

Time to Stop Planning and Start Building: It's Crunch Time for Lightfoot's Drive to Revive South, West Sides

AUGUST 26, 2020

Urban planning isn't for the faint of heart. You have to overcome naysayers and "not-in-my-backyard" types—the dreaded NIMBYs. And woe to the city planner who paints a rosy picture of a shining tomorrow but fails to deliver. He doesn't just flop—he breeds distrust among those who put faith in him.

That's the danger confronting Mayor Lori Lightfoot's top planner, Maurice Cox, commissioner of the city's Department of Planning and

Development, as he tries to keep her promise to uplift sections of the South and West Sides plagued by decades of disinvestment.

Is this much-ballyhooed effort the real deal, or a public-relations gesture?

We're about to find out.

As the *Tribune*'s Ryan Ori just reported, the city is requesting proposals from developers for three of the ten areas covered by Lightfoot's $750 million Invest South/West program (Auburn Gresham, Austin, and Englewood). Developers are to be selected by early next year and construction in the three areas is to be completed in late 2022, according to a timetable Cox showed at a recent public forum.

In a move sure to further raise expectations, the nonprofit Chicago Architecture Center will soon announce the winners of a juried competition designating design teams that developers could hire for Invest South/West projects. The jury winnowed a field of nearly two hundred architects down to thirty-two teams. The teams, which are 44 percent minority-owned, include architects responsible for such Chicago icons as the wavy Aqua Tower (Studio Gang) and the vibrant downtown Riverwalk (Ross Barney Architects).

What might such teams produce? Conceptual renderings done for the city by top architectural firms picture transformations that wisely do not indulge in Buck Rogers razzle-dazzle or wiping the slate clean, as did the failed urban-renewal projects of the 1960s. Rather, they suggest that developers retain and renovate beloved pieces of architecture and use them as anchors for rebuilding the areas around them.

One rendering, by Perkins & Will, shows a long-vacant and crumbling Art Deco gem, the Laramie State Bank at 5200 West Chicago Avenue, beautifully restored. Buildings fill vacant lots next to the bank, whose multicolored terra-cotta decoration includes representations of American eagles astride the globe. The new construction would add density to neighborhoods, but without the physical isolation and overwhelming scale of Chicago's notorious, now-destroyed high-rise public-housing projects.

The idea, Cox said during a recent forum hosted by the Federal Reserve Bank of Chicago, is to create vibrant centers of urban commerce and activity, like those in Chicago's pre-COVID-19 downtown.

Will it work? Why would some real estate developers risk their precious capital on crime-ridden, violence-plagued areas they've ne-

Laramie State Bank building: a crumbling Art Deco gem on Chicago's West Side awaited revitalization. Photo by Lee Bey.

glected in the past? Will big developers, like Sterling Bay, Related Midwest, and Magellan, join the smaller for-profit and nonprofit firms already working on the South and West Sides?

There are reasons for guarded optimism. For starters, the city will take steps to minimize developers' economic risk. It will subsidize the projects, using tax-increment-financing funds, its Neighborhood Opportunity Fund, and federal tax breaks within what the US deems "opportunity zones."

In addition, Invest South/West may lead some developers to look anew at neighborhoods they'd written off, particularly if they want to curry favor with a mayor who has made redevelopment of such areas a top priority.

"There are so many commercial developers that just don't know their way around these neighborhoods," said Richard Sciortino, founding principal of Northbrook-based Brinshore, which has developed a wide range of housing, including affordable units, in Chicago and the suburbs.

"I've always been a big believer in getting all these commercial developers just engaged in these neighborhoods. They can be an investor. They can be a mentor . . . They don't have to jump in with both feet. Just get a toe in the water," Sciortino said.

A recent example: Brinshore codeveloped 4400 Grove, a four-story, two-building, mixed-income apartment and retail project in Chicago's Bronzeville neighborhood. A mix of public and private funding backed the development, anticipating the financial engines expected to power Invest South/West.

The design was tailored to neighborhood needs. Several ground-floor retail spaces were intentionally left small to accommodate tenants who might not be able to afford bigger shops that typically go to chain stores. Future tenants include a pizzeria, a wine bar, a healing salon, and a Negro Leagues baseball store.

If Invest South/West can replicate such success stories at large scale and at rapid speed while still maintaining design quality—never an easy balance to strike—it may yet turn out to be something greater and more enduring than a City Hall public-relations gesture.

Postscript: There was more reason for guarded optimism, on both economic and urban-design fronts, when the City of Chicago completed its selection of developer-architect teams for Invest South/West in late 2021. Developers planned to invest more than $300 million in the ten targeted commercial corridors. Corporations and philanthropies committed more than $525 million. The city promised another $525 million, bringing the total to about $1.4 billion, according to the Department of Planning and Development. Just as significantly, the designs hewed to the city's carefully conceived planning guidelines.

Several teams proposed to renovate existing buildings and build new ones containing a mix of affordable apartments and street-activating, ground-floor shops. The Heartland Alliance and Oak Park Regional Housing Center, for example, called for spending $37.5 million to renovate the twenty-thousand-square-foot former Laramie State Bank building and fill it with a blues museum, bank branch, café, and business incubator. The plans also envisioned construction of a multistory apartment building with affordable units on adjacent land.

While there were bumps in the road—residents of Auburn Gresham protested a winning team's plan to put more affordable housing in their neighborhood—the Invest South/West program demonstrated three essential things: (1) the City of Chicago could use public dollars and assets to leverage private and philanthropic investment in neighborhoods long plagued by disinvestment; (2) some of these neighborhoods, often written off as wastelands, contained historic buildings that could serve as cornerstones of redevelopment; (3) architects and developers could successfully mix uses, as well as aged and modern buildings, to form compelling alternatives to the block-busting, single-use public-housing projects of the mid-twentieth century. Cox and the City of Chicago deserved credit for taking major steps forward during the pandemic, making it a pivot point, not just a pause, in the drive to build a more equitable city. The effort could be one of the Lightfoot administration's finest achievements and a national model if it helps reverse the lack of economic opportunity that is considered one of the underlying causes of the city's gun violence; provides Black and Latino residents a chance to build intergenerational wealth by establishing new businesses; and endows neighborhoods with stores and services they've long lacked. The first groundbreakings were scheduled to occur in 2022.

As encouraging as the plans were, however, they hardly guaranteed success. It was unclear if Invest South/West would achieve broad enough impact—"scale," in developer-speak—to make a meaningful difference. And the initiative proceeded within a toxic overall environment as Chicago struggled to contain waves of carjackings, expressway shootings, and looting on top of persistent gun violence. Without a semblance of order, was progress possible? Or would progress help restore order as well as vitality? In the short term, the turmoil eclipsed the Lightfoot-Cox vision of equitable growth. In the long term, it threatened to undermine attempts to realize that vision. Buffeted by such forces, what could architecture and urban design realistically hope to achieve? How effective could they be as the city seemed to teeter on the brink of chaos? On Chicago's South and West Sides, the design fields faced the ultimate test of their ability to help solve some of the most vexing urban problems of our time.

EPILOGUE

THE END OF A JOURNALISTIC ERA—
AND WHAT COMES NEXT?

When newspapers like the *Chicago Tribune* were rich and powerful, they possessed the resources and energy to make consequential contributions to the field of architecture. They erected iconic headquarters buildings that represented the civic role played by the fourth estate. And they hired architecture critics who gave unique dimension to that civic role by serving as watchdogs of the built environment.

On both these fronts, the *Tribune* was a leader. In 1922, it held one of history's great architecture competitions, leading to the construction of the landmark Tribune Tower. And in 1974, it named Paul Gapp its architecture critic; five years later, Gapp won journalism's highest honor, the Pulitzer Prize, for his distinguished criticism.

But by the second decade of the twenty-first century, the economic model that supported such noble endeavors was badly broken. While national publications like the *New York Times* nimbly transformed themselves to thrive in the digital universe, metropolitan newspapers like the *Tribune* struggled to adapt, their traditional revenue sources, like lucrative classified advertising and display ads, having dried up. The consequences were significant for Tribune Tower, for architecture criticism at the *Tribune*, and for a citizenry that depended on a vigilant press to keep it informed and hold public officials accountable.

A Farewell to Tribune Tower and a Shout-Out to Its Architects

JUNE 6, 2018

Deadlines focus the eye as well as the mind.

As *Chicago Tribune* journalists prepare to leave Tribune Tower, I find my eyes roaming over the tower's flamboyant neo-Gothic silhouette and its innumerable alluring details, like a sculpture of a wise old owl who clutches a camera and symbolizes the powers of careful observation. These last looks are both pleasurable and painful. I love this building, love it more deeply because we're about to leave it. Yet the anticipation of being kicked out is like waiting for a Band-Aid to get stripped off. As I've heard many of my newsroom colleagues say, "Let's get it over with!"

The responsibility for this complex set of emotions rests with two people: the architects of Tribune Tower, John Mead Howells and Raymond M. Hood.

Without their singular creativity, the *Tribune*'s move would be just another story in the litany of economically battered legacy newspapers forced to leave their historic homes by the migration of readers and advertisers to the web. But the tower's architecture elevates our coming exit into something more: the severing of a diminished but still-formidable newspaper from the skyscraper that has long represented its aspirations and, some would say, its arrogance. Other newspapers built grand headquarters, yet none was grander—or made a more vivid statement in support of traditional values—than the *Tribune*'s.

"The presbytery of Midwestern conservatism," Richard Norton Smith called the tower in his biography of longtime *Tribune* editor Robert R. McCormick, aptly distilling both the skyscraper and the political views that emanated from it.

The move marks the end of an era, though not, happily, the end of the building, which since 1989 has been a protected city landmark. Once the journalists decamp, the interiors of the tower and three shorter connected buildings, including spaces where *Front Page*–era reporters pecked away at manual typewriters and city editors screamed "copy!" will be turned into high-priced condos. We, in turn, will move to One Prudential Plaza, a prominent but architecturally

Tribune Tower: the fate of the neo-Gothic skyscraper and its namesake newspaper were intricately intertwined. Photo by Lee Bey.

undistinguished mid-twentieth-century high-rise just north of Millennium Park.

On the bright side, it could be worse; other newspapers, like the *Los Angeles Times*, are departing their historic downtown headquarters for the suburbs, far from public transit and the newsmakers they cover.

But honestly—there's no glory in being a tenant in somebody else's stolid modernist high-rise, especially when you're leaving such an architecturally distinguished building. One Prudential Plaza could be the box Tribune Tower came in.

Previously working separately, Howells and Hood joined forces in 1922, when the *Tribune* invited architects to participate in a design contest that immodestly aimed to produce "the most beautiful and distinctive office building in the world." The prize money—a total of $100,000, the equivalent of nearly $1.5 million in today's dollars—reflected the then-booming state of the newspaper business as well as the soaring ambition of *Tribune* coeditors McCormick and Joseph M. Patterson, who immodestly billed their sheet as "the World's Greatest Newspaper."

Howells was the more established of the pair; Hood, thirteen years younger, a relative unknown. Their design, which emerged from a field of 263 entries from twenty-three countries, shrewdly played to the *Tribune*'s conservative tastes. Many critics, including the great Chicago architect Louis Sullivan, preferred the trim vertical look of the second-prize design by the Finnish architect Eliel Saarinen. In Sullivan's view, the Saarinen entry was "a priceless pearl," while the winner represented "dying ideas."

Yet all these years later, it is hard to fault the *Tribune*'s choice. Howells and Hood successfully transformed the visual precedents of medieval Gothic church towers into a modern American office building that simultaneously expressed spiritual connotations (journalism as a higher calling, business as a civic enterprise) even as it served as a piece of self-advertising. With its steel frame clad in Indiana limestone, the tower was a study in uninterrupted vertical lines, its piers culminating in flying buttresses and pinnacles that created a spectacular crown and distinguished the building from the Loop's flat-topped high-rises.

Granted, as critics correctly noted, the buttresses don't actually support anything. But the tower worked in concert with the eclectic, clock-tower-topped Wrigley Building across the street to turn its once-dismal environs (a stinking soap factory sat to the south) into the glittering gateway of what eventually became the North Michigan Avenue shopping district. And the architects leavened the high-toned design with playful ornament. A monumental stone screen beneath the tower's arched entrance features characters from Aesop's fables and figures that represented the architects—Howells symbolized by a howling dog, Hood by a likeness of Robin Hood.

It is fitting that a skyscraper built by a communications company communicates so well to the man and woman on the street.

Launched by the competition, Hood went on to become one of the greatest skyscraper architects of all time. He and Howells teamed up again on New York's Daily News Building, a streamlined Art Deco high-rise designed for Patterson, the founder of the tabloid. Hood also led the team of architects that shaped New York's Rockefeller Center, perhaps the greatest urban ensemble of the twentieth century, and its iconic 30 Rockefeller Plaza skyscraper. He died young—at age fifty-three, in 1934, after suffering rheumatoid arthritis. Howells died at ninety-one, in 1959.

Today, on the verge of losing its namesake newspaper, Howells and Hood's creation has assumed new stature, its original distinctiveness enhanced by the telling contrast between its decorated exterior of stone and the bland mirror-glass high-rises that have grown around it.

Like many of my colleagues, I'm not going to miss the prosaic environs of the newsroom in which we work—a cubicle farm that might as well as be in Omaha—but I will miss the visual poetry of the tower and its hushed, church-like Michigan Avenue lobby. We, the journalists, are leaving, but our watchdog role will live on in our new quarters. And the architects' "signature" at the tower will remain.

It's right there, their names inscribed in English Gothic lettering, in the block of stone to the right of the skyscraper's entrance. I think of that block as a cornerstone of creativity.

Postscript: Tribune Tower reopened in 2021 as Tribune Tower Residences, with condominium price listings ranging from $700,000 to more than $7 million. Inside were the usual bells and whistles for luxury residential projects, like a golf simulator, as well as an amenity floor with more distinctive features, such as the fireplace from McCormick's office. In the same year, completing its architectural comedown, the *Chicago Tribune* moved its newsroom from One Prudential Plaza to its utilitarian Freedom Center printing plant. And that was not the only architectural farewell of 2021.

Reflections on Twenty-Eight Years of Reviewing Chicago's Architectural Wonders and Blunders— and Why Such Coverage Should Continue

JANUARY 13, 2021

When I became the *Tribune*'s architecture critic, in 1992, there was no Millennium Park, no Museum Campus, and no downtown Riverwalk. The massive public-housing high-rises of Cabrini-Green and the Robert Taylor Homes still stood. Sears Tower was still Sears Tower and the world's tallest building.

Since then, in more than 2,500 stories that have taken me to seven countries, throughout the US, and to every corner of Chicago, I have critiqued objects ranging in size from the Illinois license plate (at six by twelve inches, a cluttered mess) to the latest world's tallest building, Dubai's Burj Khalifa (at 2,717 feet, a surprisingly beautiful behemoth).

I have covered the gamut of human emotion, from the horror of 9/11 to the joy of Millennium Park; reviewed buildings by prodigious talents, from Frank Gehry to Jeanne Gang; and been smeared on the *Today* show by a soon-to-be-former president after I called out the huge, self-aggrandizing sign he slapped on his Chicago skyscraper.

Now, as I prepare to leave one of the great jobs in journalism, I want to thank you, the readers, who have accompanied me on this journey.

Whether or not you agreed with what I wrote was never the point. My aim was to open your eyes to, and raise your expectations for, the inescapable art of architecture, which does more than any other art to shape how we live.

So I treated buildings not simply as architectural objects or technological marvels but also as vessels of human possibility. Above all, my role was to serve as a watchdog, unafraid to bark—and, if necessary, bite—when developers and architects schemed to wreak havoc on the cityscape.

My columns sought to be a conversation between you and me, the readers and the critic, and I was often inspired by how you responded.

You engaged me to talk architecture at spots ranging from the Art Institute to the Belmont Avenue "L" station to O'Hare International Airport's security gates. Many wrote letters and emails to express how much you appreciate that the *Tribune* remains one of the few American newspapers that still covers architecture on a regular basis. Yet how could it not do so?

In this town, architecture was, is, and always will be newsworthy—and worthy of sharp scrutiny. Even the most cursory review of my years in the critic's chair proves the point.

New towers rose along the Chicago River as it changed from an open sewer to a recreational amenity, but some of them, particularly Donald Trump's, had to be subjected to searing criticism before they could hold their own on the skyline.

Pitched battles were fought to keep the lakefront free and clear of massive buildings that would have needlessly cluttered the great public space. In some cases, like the giant lump that was the proposed Lucas Museum of Narrative Art, the right side won. Not so on the renovated Soldier Field, a stadium once deemed forward-looking that now seems utterly out of date.

Scheming aldermen had to be watched like a hawk lest they strip nearly thirty sites, including buildings by Frank Lloyd Wright, Louis Sullivan, and Ludwig Mies van der Rohe, of protected status and gut the city's landmarks law. They failed on both counts, and the landmarks law—and financial incentives for making the past a part of the future—wound up dramatically strengthened.

Now, nearly ten months into the COVID-19 pandemic, as legions of people continue working from makeshift home offices, the very factor that once powered the growth of downtown Chicago—the need to bring dense clusters of people together to facilitate commerce—seems at risk.

Why am I leaving at this crucial time? There is never a good time to go, but after decades of stressful deadlines, I'm ready for fewer midnights rewriting paragraphs in my head as I try and fail to fall asleep.

Last year, I decided to stay on the job so I could review the culminating structures of the post–Great Recession building boom, like Gang's stirring St. Regis Chicago (the former Vista Tower). With that last leg of the race run, I'm ready to take an extended breather before embarking on my next journey, whatever it turns out to be.

Journalism, like architecture, is a team enterprise. So my sincere thanks go out to the immensely talented *Tribune* colleagues—editors, reporters, critics, photographers, and graphic designers—with whom I've been fortunate to work. The *Tribune*, to its credit, has never asked me to pull punches. And it has not shied from publishing provocative work that had a significant impact, like my 1998 series of articles on the problems and promise of Chicago's greatest public space, its lakefront.

Thanks, finally, to my wife, the author and former *Tribune* writer Barbara Mahany, and our sons Will and Teddy, for their unconditional love and encouragement.

It's been an honor to appear in these pages and to carry on this architectural conversation with you. The conversation must continue.

Imagine Chicago without a full-time skyline watchdog. Schlock developers and hack architects would welcome the lack of scrutiny.

Postscript: Following my departure, the *Chicago Tribune* did not name a new architecture critic. For the first time in almost fifty years, Chicago, which prides itself on being a global design capital, was without a full-time, on-staff architecture critic at one of the city's newspapers. Then, in 2022, the *Chicago Sun-Times* announced that Lee Bey, who had been the newspaper's architecture critic from 1996 to 2001 and had rejoined the paper as an editorial writer in 2019, would write a monthly column on architecture and urban design. The move marked a significant first step in filling the void created when I left the *Tribune*, and it had national importance, reversing the trend of shrinking architecture coverage at major daily newspapers. Still, given the enormity of the challenges facing Chicago, more frequent coverage is absolutely necessary. I continue to urge Chicago's design-oriented foundations, the Graham Foundation and the Driehaus Foundation, to join with other institutions to underwrite a new chapter in the history of the city's architectural criticism, one that encourages a lively, even fractious, diversity of voices and perspectives. What matters, in the end, is not whether architecture criticism is delivered in the pages of a newspaper or on its website. What matters is that it is delivered at all—regularly, intelligently, fearlessly, with the critic's eye always trained on the art of architecture and how it shapes human experience.

ACKNOWLEDGMENTS

Like architecture itself, a book that collects the columns of an architecture critic is the work of many hands, not one.

My first set of thanks goes to my former colleagues at the *Chicago Tribune*, where these columns were originally published. Several editors at the newspaper guided my efforts and sharpened my prose, most notably Mark Jacob, Mary Ellen Podmolik, and Trevor Jensen. Other editors who framed story ideas and ushered my observations into print included Kerry Luft, Alex Rodriguez, Kim Quillen, and Jocelyn Allison. I am also thankful for the unflagging support of the paper's top editors in the years covered by this book: Gerould Kern, R. Bruce Dold, Colin McMahon, Jane Hirt, Peter Kendall, and Christine Taylor.

Others at the *Tribune* and its business affiliates were instrumental in arranging for stories and photographs that appeared in the newspaper to be converted into book form. They are Par Ridder, general manager; Elaine Varvatos, senior manager for editorial administration; Amy Carr, now editor of *Chicago* magazine, and Rick DeChantal, sales director at Tribune Content Agency.

Photography forms a major part of any architecture book, setting its tone and illustrating its subject matter. Here, I want to express gratitude to my collaborator, Lee Bey. When Lee was the *Chicago Sun-Times'* architecture critic from 1996 to 2001, he and I competed in the old-school tradition of Chicago journalism, each spurring the other on to do ambitious, impactful work. Lee's talents span multiple fronts, encompassing photography as well as writing, so it's a pleasure to see his carefully composed photographs grace these pages. I extend heartfelt thanks to the Richard H. Driehaus Foundation and its executive director, Anne Lazar, for providing a grant that allowed Lee's photography to appear in the book.

I also am deeply grateful to the Graham Foundation for Advanced Studies in the Fine Arts and its director, Sarah Herda, for a grant that allowed the work of several *Tribune* photographers—John J. Kim, Brian Cassella, Chris Walker, Zbigniew Bzdak, Heather Charles, and Anthony Soufflé—to be published here. The foundation's grant will also support a public program, based on the book, at the Chicago Architecture Center. Thanks to the center's former president and CEO, Lynn Osmond, and her staff for backing the program.

My columns have been informed by the reporting and writing of numerous former *Tribune* colleagues, most notably Ryan Ori, Mary Wisniewski, Lolly Bowean, and Mary Schmich. Special thanks go to my great friends and former *Tribune* investigative reporters Gary Marx and Joel Kaplan, the latter now associate dean at Syracuse University's Newhouse School of Public Communications. And I thank former *Tribune* editor Ann Marie Lipinski, curator of the Nieman Foundation for Journalism at Harvard University, for granting me a Nieman fellowship during the 2012–13 academic year. The Nieman experience gave me a jolt of energy and provided the intellectual underpinning for many of the columns gathered here.

At the University of Chicago Press, I have been especially fortunate to work with executive editor Mary Laur. Mary has had a hand in each of my three books with the press; her insight and impact have grown with each one. She has been instrumental in the transformation of these columns, originally published as discrete pieces, into a whole that strives to be greater than the sum of its individual parts. Senior editorial associate Mollie McFee deserves credit for being an effective, detail-oriented organizer of the book's material. Thanks, too, to Stephen Twilley for his meticulous, gently probing copyediting; to Matt Avery for his captivating book design; and to senior promotions manager Tyler McGaughey for bringing the book to the public's attention.

Last but hardly least, I want to thank members of my family, especially Barbara Mahany, my wife and my passionate, compassionate partner for more than thirty years. I lean heavily on Barbara, an acclaimed author and former *Tribune* writer, for both professional and personal support. Her unflagging encouragement, gentle wisdom, and radiant spirit have delivered me through many a dark moment and have given me the courage and conviction to overcome seemingly insurmountable obstacles. Our sons Will and Teddy, whom we refer to as our "double bylines," are the joy of our lives. Thanks to them for putting up with their father's obsessive architectural behavior, including the dangerous habit of ogling high-rises while driving at high speed.

My appreciation goes out, as well, to my sister Brooke Kamin Rapaport, deputy director and chief curator of the Madison Square Park Conservancy in New York City, and my brother-in-law Brian A. Mahany, who did out-of-town photography duty for the book. If it takes a village to raise a child, it takes a family—and the support of treasured friends and talented colleagues—to write a book.

INDEX